The Fiqh of Islam:

A Contemporary Explanation of Principles of Worship

Volume 1

The Fiqh of Islam:
A Contemporary Explanation of Principles of Worship

Volume 1

Shaykh Muhammad Hisham Kabbani

Published by the
Institute for Spiritual & Cultural Advancement

Published and Distributed by:

Institute for Spiritual and Cultural Advancement (ISCA)
17195 Silver Parkway, #201
Fenton, MI 48430 USA
Tel: (888) 278-6624
Fax: (810) 815-0518
Email: staff@naqshbandiNaqshbandī.org
Web: http://www.naqshbandiNaqshbandī.org

First Edition: July 2014
The Fiqh of Islam: A Contemporary Explanation of Principles of Worship, Volume 1
ISBN: 978-1-938058-24-0

Library of Congress Cataloging-in-Publication Data

Kabbani, Muhammad Hisham.
  The fiqh of Islam : a contemporary explanation of principles of worship/ Shaykh Muhammad Hisham Kabbani.
      volumes cm
  Projected to be complete in 2 volumes--ECIP data.
  Includes bibliographical references.
  ISBN 978-1-938058-24-0 (alk. paper)
  1. Islamic law. I. Title.
  KBP144.K33 2014
  340.5'9--dc23
                        2014019237

PRINTED IN THE UNITED STATES OF AMERICA
15 14 13 12 11 05 06 07 08 09

The author receiving guidance from the founder of the Naqshbandiyya Nazimiyya Sufi Order, his spiritual guide, Sayyidi Shaykh Muhammad Nazim Adil al-Qabrusi (1921-2014).

The author giving a *suḥbah* (discourse) in the pre-dawn hours of the holy month Ramadan at the Michigan *zawiya* dedicated by Sayyidi Shaykh Nazim in 1993.

Contents

About the Author

World-renowned religious scholar Shaykh Muḥammad Hisham Kabbani is featured in the ground-breaking book published by Georgetown University, *The 500 Most Influential Muslims* in *the World*. For decades, he has promoted traditional Islamic principles of peace, tolerance, love, compassion and brotherhood, while rigorously opposing extremism in all its forms. He hails from a respected family of traditional Islamic scholars, which includes the former head of the Association of Muslim Scholars of Lebanon and the present grand mufti (highest Islamic religious authority) of Lebanon.

Shaykh Kabbani is highly trained, both as a western scientist and as an Islamic scholar. He received a Bachelor's degree in Chemistry and later studied medicine. Under the instruction of Shaykh 'AbdAllāh ad-Dāghestānī of Damascus, he holds a degree in Islamic Divine Law. Shaykh Muḥammad Nazim Adil, founder of the Naqshbandīyya-Nazimīyya Sufi Order, authorized him to teach and counsel students in Sufism.

In his long-standing effort to promote a better understanding of traditional Islam, in February 2010, Shaykh Kabbani hosted HRH Charles, the Prince of Wales at a cultural event at the revered Old Trafford Stadium in Manchester, U.K. The shaykh hosted two international conferences in the U.S., and regional conferences on a host of contemporary issues that attracted moderate Muslim scholars from Asia, the Far East, Middle East, Africa, U.K. and Eastern Europe. His counsel is sought by media outlets, academics, policymakers and government leaders.

For thirty years, Shaykh Kabbani has consistently promoted peaceful cooperation among people of all beliefs. Since the early 1990s, he launched numerous endeavors to bring moderate Muslims into the mainstream. Often at great personal risk, he has been instrumental in awakening Muslim social consciousness regarding the religious duty to stand firm against extremism and terrorism, for the benefit of all. His bright, hopeful outlook, with a goal to honor and serve all humanity, has helped millions understand the difference between moderate mainstream Muslims and minority extremist sects.

In the United States, Shaykh Kabbani serves as Chairman, Islamic Supreme Council of America; Founder, Naqshbandī Sufi Order of America; Advisor, World Organization for Resource Development and Education; Chairman, *As-Sunnah* Foundation of America; Founder, *The Muslim*

Magazine. In the United Kingdom, Shaykh Kabbani is an advisor to Sufi Muslim Council, which consults to the British government on public policy and social and religious issues.

Other titles by Shaykh Kabbani include: *The Illuminations Series* (5 volumes on Islamic spirituality & law) (2014), *The Benefits of Bismillāhi 'r-Raḥmāni 'r-Rahīm & Surat al-Faṭihah* (2013), *The Importance of Prophet Muhammad in Our Daily Life* (2013), *The Dome of Provisions* (2013), *The Hierarchy of Saints* (2013, also in French), *Healing Verses in the Holy Qur'an and Sunnah* (2013), *Salawāt of Tremendous Blessings* (2012, also in Turkish/Spanish), *The Heavenly Power of Divine Obedience and Gratitude* (2012), *The Sufilive Series* (2010-2012), *The Prohibition of Domestic Violence in Islam* (2011, also in French, Spanish), *At the Feet of My Master* (2010), *The Nine-fold Ascent* (2009), *Banquet for the Soul* (2008), *Illuminations* (2007), *Universe Rising* (2007), *Symphony of Remembrance* (2007), *A Spiritual Commentary on the Chapter of Sincerity* (2006), *The Sufi Science of Self-Realization* (Fons Vitae, 2005), *Keys to the Divine Kingdom* (2005), *Classical Islam and the Naqshbandi Sufi Order* (2004), *The Naqshbandi Sufi Tradition Guidebook* (2004), *The Approach of Armageddon? An Islamic Perspective* (2003), *Encyclopedia of Muḥammad's Women Companions and the Traditions They Related* (1998, with Dr. Laleh Bakhtiar), *Encyclopedia of Islamic Doctrine* (7 vols. 1998), *Angels Unveiled* (1996), *The Naqshbandi Sufi Way* (1995), and *Remembrance of God Liturgy of the Sufi Naqshbandi Masters* (1994).

Preface

The Fiqh of Islam: A Contemporary Explanation of Principles of Worship, is a compilation of talks addressing the essential practices of Islam based on its legal code, *Sharī'ah*, broadened through historical rulings of the jurists. Often a dry, rule-based domain, *Fiqh*[1] is the application of the Divine orders and prohibitions revealed to Prophet Muhammad[2] in the Holy Qur'ān over 23 years, expounded by him during his life and further elucidated by preeminent Muslim scholars throughout history.

Compiled by a globally recognized Muslim scholar and teacher of Islam's spiritual side, Sufism (*Taṣawwuf*), this prestigious series is written for those who seek a better understanding of Islamic tenets of worship. It comprises the *suḥbahs*, spiritual discourses, of the beloved Ramadan Series (2013), an annual event hosted by the author to honor the ancient tradition of his Sufi Masters.

The Fiqh of Islam: A Contemporary Explanation of Principles of Worship examines the essential practices of Islam based on its legal code, the Sharī'ah, broadened through historical rulings of the jurists. Differing from the commonplace methodology of primarily listing rules and regulations, Shaykh Kabbani presents his findings in much the same manner as Prophet Muhammad, peace be upon him, by giving practical applications in everyday situations and explaining the spiritual benefits supporting many detailed practices Muslims observe. In doing so, he has successfully integrated jurists' explanations with further elucidation from venerable Sufi teachings, underscoring the wisdom in combining legal and spiritual principles to reach the best possible outcome.

This volume defines the sources and value of heavenly knowledge, and the importance of finding genuine spiritual guides from whom to acquire such knowledge as a means to live a fulfilling and peaceful life. Much emphasis is placed on the value of superior manners and how good character increases knowledge, as exemplified by Prophet Muhammad, peace be upon him. The Islamic rights and overwhelming benefits of prayers and charity are examined, as are the bounties that reach Mankind in

---

[1] An in-depth examination of Islamic holy texts, legal rulings, jurists' opinions and religious principles.

[2] May the peace and blessing of God be upon him.

the holy month of Ramadan. Instructions in combatting evil entities and influences are also provided.

For fifty years, the author has sought to promote these ancient teachings for the good of all, a spirit we hope is reflected in this book. These universal lessons will make a fine addition to any study of Islam, Islamic law, Prophet Muhammad, Sufism, Islamic mysticism, spirituality and New Age teachings.

Publisher's Notes

This series is directed to those familiar with the Sufi Way; however, to accommodate lay readers unfamiliar with Sufi terminology and practices, we have provided English translations of Arabic texts and a brief glossary. Where Arabic terms are crucial to the discussion, we have included transliteration and explanations. For readers familiar with Arabic and Islamic teachings, for further clarity please consult cited sources.

The original material is based on transcripts of a series of holy gatherings known as *ṣuḥbah*, a divinely inspired talk given by the "shaykh," a highly trained spiritual guide. To present the authentic flavor of such rare teachings, great care was taken to preserve the speaking styles of both the author and the illustrious shaykhs upon whose notes this book is based.

Translations from Arabic to English pose unique challenges that we have tried our best to make understandable to Western readers. Please note our application of the common Arabic oral tradition of omitting definite articles such as "~~the~~ Prophet" and "~~the~~ Holy Qur'an," as practiced by Muslims around the world as intimate references.

We apply contemporary American English publishing standards and italicize foreign proper nouns (*Fātiḥah, Quṭb az-Zamān, Rasūlullāh, Sūratu 'n-Naml*), but not commonly known foreign-language nouns (jihād, Qur'an, shaykh) unless they appear in transliterations.

Quotes from the Holy Qur'an and Holy Traditions of Prophet Muḥammad are offset, italicized and cited.

The pronoun "they" is frequently used by Sufi guides to reference heavenly beings and holy souls who support them and give them orders, a usage that appears throughout this book. Where gender-specific pronouns such as "he" and "him" are applied in a general sense, no discrimination is intended towards women, upon whom The Almighty bestowed great honor.

Islamic teachings are primarily based on four sources, in this order:

- Holy Qur'an: the Islamic holy book of divine revelation (God's Word) granted to Prophet Muḥammad. Reference to Holy Qur'an appears as "4:12," which indicates "Chapter 4, Verse 12."

- *Sunnah*: holy traditions of Prophet Muḥammad ﷺ; the systematic recording of his words and actions that comprise the *ḥadīth*. For fifteen centuries, Islam has applied a strict, highly technical standard, rating each narration in terms of its authenticity and categorizing its "transmission." As this book is not highly technical, we simplified the reporting of *ḥadīth*, but included the narrator and source texts to support the discussion at hand.

⁂ *Ijmaʿ*: The adherence, or agreement of the experts of independent reasoning *(āhl al-ijtihād)* to the conclusions of a given ruling pertaining to what is permitted and what is forbidden after the passing of the Prophet, Peace be upon him, as well as the agreement of the Community of Muslims concerning what is obligatorily known of the religion with its decisive proofs. Perhaps a clearer statement of this principle is, "We do not separate (in belief and practice) from the largest group of the Muslims."

⁂ Legal Rulings: highly trained Islamic scholars form legal rulings from their interpretation of the Qur'an and the *Sunnah*, known as *ijtihād*. Such rulings are intended to provide Muslims an Islamic context regarding contemporary social norms. In theological terms, scholars who form legal opinions have completed many years of rigorous training and possess degrees similar to a doctorate in divinity in Islamic knowledge, or in legal terms, hold the status of a high court or supreme court judge, or higher.

The following universally recognized symbols have been respectfully included in this work and are deeply appreciated by a vast majority of our readers.

﷾ *Subḥānahu wa Taʿalā* (may His Glory be Exalted), recited after the name "Allāh" and any of the Islamic names of God.

ﷺ *ṢallAllāhu ʿalayhi wa sallam* (God's blessings and greetings of peace be upon him), recited after the holy name of Prophet Muḥammad.

۞ *ʿAlayhi ʾs-salām* (peace be upon him/her), recited after holy names of other prophets, names of Prophet Muḥammad's relatives, the pure and virtuous women in Islam, and angels.

﷛/﷝ *RaḍīAllāhu ʿanh(um)* (may God be pleased with him/her), recited after the holy names of Companions of Prophet Muḥammad; plural: *raḍīAllāhu ʿanhum*.

ق *QaddasAllāhu sirrah* (may God sanctify his secret), recited after names of saints.

Transliteration

Transliteration from Arabic to English poses challenges. To show respect, Muslims often capitalize nouns which, in English, appear in lowercase. To facilitate authentic pronunciation of names, places and terms, use the following key:

Symbol	Transliteration	Symbol	Transliteration	Vowels: Long	
ء	ʾ	ط	ṭ	آ ى	ā
ب	b	ظ	ẓ	و	ū
ت	t	ع	ʿ	ي	ī
ث	th	غ	gh	Short	
ج	j	ف	f	´	a
ح	ḥ	ق	q	ُ	u
خ	kh	ك	k	ِ	i
د	d	ل	l		
ذ	dh	م	m		
ر	r	ن	n		
ز	z	ه	h		
س	s	و	w		
ش	sh	ي	y		
ص	ṣ	ة	ah; at		
ض	ḍ	ال	al-/'l-		

Masters of the
Naqshbandī Golden Chain

May Allāh  preserve their secrets.

1. Prophet Muḥammad ibn ʿAbdAllāh ﷺ

2. Abū Bakr aṣ-Ṣiddīq ق
3. Salmān al-Fārsī ق
4. Qāsim bin Muḥammad bin AbūBakr ق
5. Jaʿfar aṣ-Ṣādiq ق
6. Ṭayfūr Abū Yazīd al-Bistāmī ق
7. Abūl-Ḥassan ʿAlī al-Kharqānī ق
8. Abū ʿAlī al-Farmadī ق
9. Abū Yaʿqūb Yūsuf al-Ḥamadānī ق
10. Abūl-ʿAbbās, al-Khiḍr ﷺ
11. ʿAbdul-Khāliq al-Ghujdawānī ق
12. ʿArif ar-Riwakrī ق
13. Khwāja Maḥmūd al-Anjīr al-Faghnawī ق
14. ʿAlī ar-Ramitānī ق
15. Muḥammad Bābā as-Samāsī ق
16. As-Sayyid Amīr Kulāl ق
17. Muḥammad Bahāuddīn Shāh Naqshband ق
18. ʿAlāuddīn al-Bukhārī al-ʿAṭṭār ق
19. Yaʿqūb al-Charkhī ق
20. ʿUbaydullāh al-Ahrār ق
21. Muḥammad az-Zāhid ق
22. Darwish Muḥammad ق
23. Muḥammad Khwāja al-Amkanakī ق
24. Muḥammad al-Bāqī billāh ق
25. Aḥmad al-Farūqī as-Sirhindī ق
26. Muḥammad al-Maʿṣūm ق
27. Muḥammad Sayfuddīn al-Fārūqī al-Mujaddidī ق
28. As-Sayyid Nūr Muḥammad al-Badawānī ق
29. Shamsuddīn Ḥabīb Allāh ق
30. ʿAbdAllāh ad-Dahlawī ق
31. Khālid al-Baghdādī ق
32. Ismāʿīl Muḥammad ash-Shirwānī ق
33. Khāṣ Muḥammad Shirwānī ق
34. Muḥammad Effendī al-Yarāghī ق
35. Jamāluddīn al-Ghumūqī al-Ḥusaynī ق
36. Abū Aḥmad aṣ-Ṣughūrī ق
37. Abū Muḥammad al-Madanī ق
38. Sharafuddīn ad-Dāghestānī ق
39. ʿAbdAllāh al-Fāʿiz ad-Dāghestānī ق
40. Muḥammad Nāẓim ʿAdil ق

Recitation before Every Association

A'ūdhu billāhi min ash-Shayṭān ir-rajīm.
Bismillāhi' r-Raḥmāni 'r-Raḥīm.
Nawaytu 'l-arbā'īn, nawaytu 'l-'itikāf,
nawaytu'l-khalwah, nawaytu 'l-'uzlah,
nawaytu 'r-riyāḍa, nawaytu 's-sulūk,
lillāhi Ta'alā fī hādhā 'l-masjid.

Ati'ūllāha wa ati' ūr-Rasūla
wa ūli 'l-amri minkum.

I seek refuge in Allāh from Satan, the rejected.
In the Name of Allāh, the Merciful,
the Compassionate.
I intend the forty (days of seclusion);
I intend seclusion in the mosque,
I intend seclusion, I intend isolation,
I intend discipline (of the ego); I intend to travel
in God's Path for the sake of God,
in this mosque.

Obey Allāh, obey the Prophet,
and obey those in authority among you.
Sūratu 'n-Nisā
(The Women), 4:59

You Were the Best of Nations Brought Forth to Humanity

A'ūdhu billāhi min ash-Shayṭāni 'r-rajīm. Bismillāhi' r-Raḥmāni 'r-Raḥīm.
Nawaytu 'l-arbā'īn, nawaytu 'l-'itikāf, nawaytu 'l-khalwah, nawaytu 'l-'uzlah,
nawaytu 'r-riyāḍa, nawaytu 's-sulūk, lillāhi Ta'alā fi hādha 'l-masjid.
Atī'ullāha wa atī'ū 'r-Rasūla wa ūli 'l-amri minkum. (4:59)

Alḥamdulillāh, Allāh ﷻ has honored us to be from *Ummat an-Nabī* ﷺ and this *ummah* has been given a description from Allāh ﷻ:

كُنتُمْ خَيْرَ أُمَّةٍ أُخْرِجَتْ لِلنَّاسِ تَأْمُرُونَ بِالْمَعْرُوفِ وَتَنْهَوْنَ عَنِ الْمُنكَرِ وَتُؤْمِنُونَ بِاللَّهِ

You are the best of nations evolved for Mankind, enjoining what is right,
forbidding what is wrong and believing in Allāh.[3]

"You are the best *ummah* that has been sent of humanity, *tāmurūna bi 'l-ma'rūfi wa tanhawna 'ani 'l-munkari*, calling for good and prohibiting what is bad." So when He said, "Calling for good," first of all, *kuntum khayra ummatin ukhrijat li 'n-nās*, "You were the best *ummah* that has been sent to humanity," it means your behavior, your characters, your moral excellence, the way you behave with people must be the best. When Allāh says, "*kuntum* you <u>were</u> of the best *ummah*," it means <u>all these perfect manners</u> Allāh has dressed on this *ummah*. That is why the intention of *al-bi'that al-Muḥammadiyya*, the Muḥammadan Mission to humanity through his *Ṣaḥābah* ﷺ to all people is to show that Muslims must have good manners. So first, they must establish *Tawḥīd* and then they must be good and then further they must be very good, loyal to Allāh ﷻ and His Prophet ﷺ and they must be generous in everything they have.

Allāh ﷻ has mentioned to us how much He loved this *ummah* and accepted the *du'ā* of Sayyīdinā Ibrāhīm ؑ, the grandfather of the Prophet ﷺ, who has established this *ummah* as its grandfather and the one who built *Baytullāh, al-Ka'bah*. So Allāh accepted Sayyīdinā Ibrāhīm's *du'ā* when he asked:

---

[3] Sūrat Āli-'Imrān, 3:110.

$$\text{رَبَّنَا وَابْعَثْ فِيهِمْ رَسُولاً مِّنْهُمْ يَتْلُو عَلَيْهِمْ آيَاتِكَ وَيُعَلِّمُهُمُ الْكِتَابَ وَالْحِكْمَة}$$

$$\text{وَيُزَكِّيهِمْ إِنَّكَ أَنتَ الْعَزِيزُ الْحَكِيمُ}$$

Our Lord! And send among them a messenger from themselves who will recite to them Your verses and teach them the Book and wisdom and purify them. Indeed, You are the Exalted in Might, the Wise.[4]

In this series, you might see somewhat of a shift in the kind of advice or lecture we are giving, because many people are asking this Ramaḍān to touch on issues of obligations people must do and further, how to behave according to the *aḥadīth* of the Prophet ﷺ and from a *Fiqh* point of view. So this Ramaḍān, we will begin describing different conditions and principles that we as Muslims have to carry and to learn. If we don't build the *Fiqh* structure, we cannot build the spiritual structure. Let us build the foundation, then it will be strong base on which to build the spiritual teaching which will be the walls and roof.

So in that verse of Holy Qur'ān, Sayyīdina Ibrāhīm ﷺ is saying "O Allāh, *wab'ath fihim rasūlan minhum yatlū 'alayhim āyātika,* send a messenger to teach them and to educate them in what You want from them, first to show them Your Way, O Allāh, and to teach them, *wa yu'allimuhumu 'l-kitāb,* and to teach them Holy Qur'ān and the Wisdom and purify them and raise them from the worldly matters to *Ākhirah* matters."

And so in this verse, Sayyīdina Ibrāhīm ﷺ is trying, as Allāh said in Holy Qur'ān:

$$\text{ادْعُونِي أَسْتَجِبْ لَكُمْ}$$

Call on Me, I will answer you.[5]

So Allāh wants Sayyīdina Ibrāhīm ﷺ to fulfill the requirements of *du'ā,* invocation, which we mentioned about two months ago, giving different types of *du'ās* as related in Ibn Qayyim al-Jawzīyya's book *ad-Dawā 'ish-Shāfi.* So Sayyīdina Ibrāhīm ﷺ wants to make that *du'ā* for *Ummat an-Nabī* ﷺ, "Yā Rabbī! Send them a messenger as my people are lost, my people are lost!" And Allāh sent a messenger from where? That was the *ḥikmah,* wisdom, behind giving Ismā'īl ﷺ to Sayyīdina Ibrāhīm ﷺ because the

---

[4] Sūrat al-Baqarah, 2:129.

[5] Surah Ghāfir, 40:60.

messenger, Sayyidinā Muḥammad ﷺ, came from the children of Sayyidinā Ismāʿīl. So when Sayyidinā Ibrāhīm ﷺ made that *duʿā*, Allāh accepted it and gave him Ismāʿīl to carry the light of Sayyidinā Muḥammad ﷺ, from one generation to another and that light was moving from one generation to another until it reached his father, Sayyidinā ʿAbdAllāh ﷺ, and then to the womb of his mother, Sayyida Āminā bint Wahab ﷺ.

And what is the *duʿā* asking? "Send them a messenger revealing Your verses of Holy Qurʾān, to teach them the Holy Book, teaching them wisdom and to purify them." It means that Allāh ﷻ has made a condition for every Muslim and *Muslimah* to learn the Holy Qurʾān—at least to learn how to read the Holy Qurʾān—and when you read the Holy Qurʾān Allāh ﷻ will dress you. So not only reading the Holy Qurʾān, but when reading the Qurʾān we are getting special satisfaction from Allāh ﷻ that He is dressing us with rewards that are beyond what we can ever understand. After we start reading the Holy Qurʾān and understanding the Holy Qurʾān, we need wisdom, so then Sayyidinā Ibrāhīm ﷺ asked Allāh, "teach them the Qurʾān, and teach them *ḥikmah*, wisdom."

That is why Sayyidinā ʿAlī ﷺ said:

راس الحكمة مخافة الله

The head of wisdom is fear of Allāh.

If we don't fear, you are not going to fulfill all the requirements that Allāh ﷻ wants from us, so Allāh put fear of Himself in hearts of people, not because Allāh ﷻ is necessarily going to punish humanity. That is why He said in Holy Qurʾān:

وَمَا نُرْسِلُ بِالآيَاتِ إِلاَّ تَخْوِيفًا

And never did We send those Verses for any other purpose
than to convey a warning.[6]

"We don't send verses except to warn people and to make them afraid." But Allāh's mercy is big, Allāh ﷻ will forgive with *shafaʿah* of the Prophet ﷺ but 'to fear Him' means we have to abide by the teaching of Holy Qurʾān and we have to abide with the wisdom of good people. And when we reach the level of *ḥikmah* that Sayyidinā ʿAlī said, "*Rās al-ḥikmata*

---

[6] Sūrat al-Isrāʾ, 17:59.

makhāfatullāh, the head of wisdom is fear of Allāh ﷻ," then at that time you will not do something that Allāh does not like and you begin to purify yourself.

And as Allāh ﷻ said:

فَأَلْهَمَهَا فُجُورَهَا وَتَقْوَاهَا

He inspired the self of its bad and it's good.[7]

That is a description of the self that Allāh has fixed and balanced, Allāh inspired it with what is good and what is bad. So you know you can balance the *nafs*, the self and you are inspired to balance what is good and what is not.

So Allāh accepted the *duʿā* of Sayyīdinā Ibrāhīm ﷺ and gave this *ummah*, as it is mentioned, "You are the best of nations that have been sent, *tāmurūna bi 'l-maʿrūf*, calling for the good—calling for good first to yourself, then calling others—and prohibiting what is bad." So this *āyah* shows the beginning of the favor that Allāh has given to Sayyīdinā Ibrāhīm ﷺ by accepting his *duʿā*. This favor, that "you were the best *ummah*", is going from one century to another and from one generation to another giving an ongoing increase in understanding and an ongoing improvement in lifestyle. We begin with a Stone Age and now we are in the Age of High Technology, and after some time you might see higher than all the technology that you see today.

And the Prophet ﷺ said:

إِنَّ فِي أَصْلَابِ أَصْلَابِ أَصْلَابِ رِجَالٍ مِنْ أَصْحَابِي رِجَالًا وَنِسَاءً مِنْ أُمَّتِي يَدْخُلُونَ الْجَنَّةَ بِغَيْرِ حِسَابٍ ثُمَّ قَرَأَ : وَآخَرِينَ مِنْهُمْ لَمَّا يَلْحَقُوا بِهِمْ .

Verily in the loins of the loin of the loins of men from my Companions are men and women of my nation who will enter Paradise with no accounting, then he recited "And they rejoice in the glad tiding given to those [of their brethren] who have been left behind and have not yet joined them."[8]

When Allāh gave him ﷺ these *āyāt* of Holy Qur'ān, he said Allāh gave him in the core, "in the womb of the womb of the womb," which means He wants to show so much that inside the *ummah* there are 'men,' *aṣlāb aṣlāb*

---

[7] Sūrat ash-Shams, 91:8.

[8] Sūrat Āli-ʿImrān, 3:170.

aṣlāb rijālan, "the 'cream of men', from my Companions," he said. "Verily there are among the *ummah,* in the core of the core of the core of the *ummah,* the cream of the *ummah* men from my Companions." Then he ﷺ said, *rijālan wa nisā'an* and when he said 'men' it means men and women, *yadkhulūna al-jannata bi ghayri ḥisāb,* entering Paradise with no question. Why? Because they are of good manners, they abide by the law that Allāh ﷻ has ordered us to follow and the way that we have to understand things with what Allāh gave us as wisdom in our minds. This will take us to be as described by this verse:

أَلَمْ تَرَ كَيْفَ ضَرَبَ اللهُ مَثَلاً كَلِمَة طَيِّبَة كَشَجَرَةٍ طَيِّبَةٍ أَصْلُهَا ثَابِتٌ وَفَرْعُهَا فِي السَّمَاء تُؤْتِي أُكُلَهَا كُلَّ حِينٍ بِإِذْنِ رَبِّهَا وَيَضْرِبُ اللهُ الأَمْثَالَ لِلنَّاسِ لَعَلَّهُمْ يَتَذَكَّرُونَ

Have you not considered how Allāh presents an example,
(making) a good word like a good tree, whose root is firmly fixed
and its branches (high) in the sky? It produces its fruit all the time,
by permission of its Lord. And Allāh presents examples
for the people that perhaps they will be reminded.[9]

He is describing, "You are like a good, nice tree, *ṭayyibah, mubārakah,* with *baraka* in it, tasty. *Aṣluhā thābit,* its trunk is strong and cannot shake; you will be like a tree that cannot shake and its branches are in Heavens, *aṣluhā thābit,* the root is fixed strong where it is, and *far'uhā fi 's-samā,* its branches are in Heavens and *tū'tī ukulahā kulla ḥīnin,* every moment it has fruit for you *bi idhni rabbihā,* by Allāh's order! So if Allāh is happy with us, every moment Allāh ﷻ will give us fruit from that tree, meaning that you, yourself become a fruitful tree. A tree symbolizes a person who is always peaceful, always in tranquility, not making a headache to others, not backbiting, not spreading bad rumors, but always his thinking is how to be better. If we better ourselves, that is what Allāh likes.

Allāh Guides to His Nūr Who He Wants

That is why from century to century Allāh is giving us more and more and more. Before we didn't have carpets like these carpets and fluorescent lights like these, we had kerosene or oil lamps and you had to work hard to put them together in order to produce light in the lamp. Now you simply push a

---

[9] Sūrat Ibrāhīm, 14:24-25.

button and you have light. Also, in the Islamic understanding, as long as you progress you become light upon light, *nūrun ʿalā nūr*.

وَاللَّهُ يَهْدِي مَن يَشَاء

And Allāh guides whom He pleases.[10]

What is *nūr*? What do you think when I say "*nūr*"? Light is one expression, intelligence is second, knowledge, wisdom, power, guidance; all these meanings come from one word. If you go and zoom inside the meaning of the word you begin to see it is a huge understanding and knowledge in one word, because *Nūr* is one of Allāh's Beautiful Names and Attributes, "*an-Nūr*."

قَدْ جَاءكُم مِّنَ اللّهِ نُورٌ وَكِتَابٌ مُّبِينٌ

*Indeed, there has come to you from Allāh a Light
(Prophet Muḥammad) and a plain Book (this Qurʾān).*[11]

Alif-Lām added to *Nūr*, that is "*al*" *at-taʿrīf*, the definite article. It signifies there is no one that carries that name, which is why Allāh Alone is "*an-Nūr*." When we say, "*Nūr*" it can be the name of someone, but "*al-Nūr*" is the only One, whereas *Nūr* can be many. That is why Allāh's Beautiful Names and Attributes are always with *Alif-Lām* at the beginning; no one is "*ar-Raḥmān*" but Allāh, no one is *ar-Raḥīm* except Allāh. Similarly He is "*al-Quddūs*," "*as-Salām*," "*al-Muhaymin*," "*al-ʿAzīz*," "*al-Jabbār*," "*al-Mutakabbir*" all begin with the definite article "*al*."

So Allāh said in Holy Qurʾān "*Qad jāʾakum min Allāhi nūran*," He didn't say "*al-Nūr*," that is for Him Alone. So He is saying to you, "O Muslims, Allāh has given to you, He is sending to you someone," from where is He sending him? "*Qad jāʾakum min Allāhi nūran*," that means Allāh is sending to you someone with Light, in the past, from the past when there was no time. "I am sending," sending what? What came from Allāh? *Nūrun*. He was able to say, "*Kitābun munīr wa nūr*," but He made the *Nūr* before *kitābun munīr* because that *Nūr* is who? That means Muḥammad ﷺ *wa kitābun mubīn*, I sent you Muḥammad and the Clear Book. He brought *Nūr* first, but he brought *kitāb* after. That *Nūr* is the one to whom Allāh taught Holy Qurʾān, taught

---

[10] Sūrat an-Nūr, 24:46.

[11] Sūrat al-Māʾidah, 5:15.

6

through His *Nūr* as Allāh opened for His Prophet to see everything; to see Holy Qur'ān, to see the meaning of the Holy Qur'ān, and to know the *āyāt* of the Holy Qur'ān and to know everything about the Holy Qur'ān! *Qad jā'akum min Allāhi nūran wa kitābun mubīn*, so *Nūr* came and Holy Qur'ān came with him.

So now we see *nūr* contains intelligence, knowledge, perception, guidance, light. What else? Prophet ﷺ brought to you too many things and everything that he brought is by itself an ocean of knowledge. When He says, "*Nūr*," in some *āyāt* it refers to guidance.

يَهْدِي اللَّهُ لِنُورِهِ مَن يَشَاء

Allāh guides to His Light whom He wills.[12]

By that *Nūr*, He will guide to His *Nūr* whom He wants. So what is the Light Allāh is speaking about when He guides someone to that Light and what does that Light consist of?

Every one of Allāh's Beautiful Names and Attributes contains immense knowledge. When you begin to enter that knowledge you become *shajaratun ṭayyiba*, as a tree *mubāraka*, with *baraka* on it, with the manifestation of Allāh's Beautiful Names and Attributes upon it, *aṣluhā thābit*, its roots are fixed meaning nothing can shake you; *shayāṭīn* cannot change you, and worldly desires cannot change you, you possess a strong, firm belief. And, *far'uhā fi 's-samā*, its branches are in the sky. When you look at a tree from a small plant it becomes a tall tree, why is it standing? Did you see any tree growing crooked, in a curvy way? Rather all are *shāmikhāt* "standing," and their top is always growing up, up, up? So that is why He said, "Its main branch is going up, always standing, never going down," even if wind comes it is still standing.

Tū'tī ukulahā kulla ḥīnin and every moment whenever Allāh wants He gives you fruit from it, but to achieve that, you must first be guided and follow the Light of the Prophet ﷺ. If you don't follow that *Nūr* you will fall down. So from century to century, from generation to generation, that *ni'mat*, favor, that Allāh gave is going forward increasing and increasing, given by Allāh ﷻ as a gift to humanity. That is why Allāh said in Holy Qur'ān:

---

[12] Sūrat an-Nūr, 24:35.

وَهُوَ الَّذِي بَعَثَ فِي الْأُمِّيِّينَ رَسُولًا مِّنْهُمْ يَتْلُو عَلَيْهِمْ آيَاتِهِ وَيُزَكِّيهِمْ وَيُعَلِّمُهُمُ الْكِتَابَ وَالْحِكْمَةَ وَإِن كَانُوا مِن قَبْلُ لَفِي ضَلَالٍ مُّبِينٍ

It is He who has sent among the unlettered a Messenger from themselves reciting to them His verses and purifying them and teaching them the Book and the Wisdom, although they were before in clear error.[13]

He is The One that sent to those who don't read and write, "a messenger from within themselves." It means you are *ummīyy*, you are illiterate; we cannot say that about the Prophet ﷺ, but if you are illiterate, it means your tribe is illiterate, they don't know how to write. Allāh sent someone illiterate to you but dresses him with all kinds of knowledge. That is a miracle. Describing the Prophet ﷺ as someone who doesn't know how to read and write is for us to understand, because Allāh knows we want to see a something miraculous. He said, "I am sending someone who did not read a book and am giving him a Book that is full of miracles and secrets." *'Aẓamatu 'n-Nabī*, the greatness of the Prophet ﷺ is that he is not reading or writing and yet in knowledge he is the highest person, the highest human being, higher than all angels, as he possesses *'Ulūm al-Awwalīn wa 'l-Ākhirīn*[14], given to him ﷺ by Allāh.

The Four Principles: Tilāwah, Taʿlīm al-Qurʾān, Ḥikmah, Tazkīyya

He said, "Do you want more? Know that I have sent a messenger from among, and from within those who do not know how to read and write, *yatlū ʿalayhim āyātihi* mentioning His signs, His *āyāt*, His verses of Holy Qurʾān. *Wa yuzakkīhim*, and he purifies them *wa yuʿallimuhumu 'l-kitāba*, and teaches them The Book, and teaches them Wisdom. *Wa-in kānū min qablu lafī ḍalālin mubīn*, and even though before they were in huge darkness, *ḍalāl*, they were deviant from reality, they were not straightforward."

So what was the first command in Islam then? There were four 'principles' according to that *āyah*, that every Muslim and *Muslimah* must understand. First is *at-tilāwah*, how to recite Holy Qurʾān, to teach them recitation of the Holy Qurʾān, its verses. And second to teach them *taʿlīm al-Qurʾān*, to teach them the knowledge of Holy Qurʾān. So first is how to read,

---

[13] Sūrat al-Jumuʿah, 62:2.

[14] Knowledge of all that is Before and Knowledge of all that is After.

tilāwah, in Arabic; Allāh is saying to Prophet ﷺ, "To teach them recitation and reading," as through reading you learn.

That is why he ﷺ said:

اطلبوا العلم ولو في الصين

Seek knowledge even unto China.[15]

"Seek knowledge even if it is far, run to it!" The first word of Holy Qur'ān is *iqrā*, "Read!" So first you have to learn how to read and recite. Second is to teach the meaning of the Holy Qur'ān, its principles and conditions. When you learn about Holy Qur'ān everything opens to you, you are reaching levels of wisdom.

وَعَلَّمْنَاهُ مِن لَّدُنَّا عِلْمًا

And whom We had taught knowledge from Our Own Presence.[16]

"We have taught him from Our heavenly knowledge" and heavenly knowledge is full of wisdom. So the third level is wisdom. After this is the fourth level: when you have wisdom you know what is good and what is bad, at that time then you reach "Purification of the Self," *Tazkīyyatu 'n-Nafs*, you know how to purify yourself. These are the first principles that the Prophet ﷺ has brought to the *ummah* when he was sent as a messenger, *bi'thah*, to teach these four: *tilāwah*, *ta'līm al-Qur'ān*, *ḥikmah* and *tazkīyya*, these are the four principles for *da'wah*. So anyone who wants to do *da'wah*, these are four principles and the basis of *Fiqh*, of religion, its main structure. And this is the meaning of:

وَإِنَّكَ لَعَلَى خُلُقٍ عَظِيمٍ

You are of the most exalted character.[17]

It means when you begin with *tilāwah* and teaching Holy Qur'ān, then you open to teach wisdom, and then you open further to purify the self, *Maqām al-Iḥsān*, so you go through all these stages. That is how the Prophet ﷺ introduced himself and introduced Islam to the *Ṣaḥābah* ﷺ at the beginning. After that, we began to have a constitution, and it began to have

---

[15] Bayhaqī.

[16] Sūrat al-Kahf, 18:65.

[17] Sūrat al-Qalam, 68:4.

9

different branches of the judiciary and *aḥkām*, rulings, and all these follow on these four issues.

That is why he said, "*Tahdhīb al-akhlāq*, to polish your manners and character and to purify your self, *tashghul makānan kabīran fī dā'irat hādhihi da'wat an-nabawiyya*, "good manners takes a huge place in the Prophetic call." So he ﷺ was building his *Ṣaḥābah* ؇ on this principle first, to build good manners and characters, then he began to give them *Fiqh* and *tashrī'a* and *aḥkām*. At the beginning, the main stress was on how to read the Holy Qur'ān and to attain wisdom, and to purify the self. *Inshā'Allāh* next time we will continue on that and before that, we say these are the ways, "the principles" of the Message of the Prophet ﷺ in Holy Qur'ān. So Islam calls for *akhlāq* and *akhlāq* is most important in Islamic principles and it is most important in the understanding of wisdom, because in Holy Qur'ān the understanding of the word "wisdom" has been associated with the word "*akhlāq*" respect in different areas and different places. And in one place it is:

لاَ تَعْبُدُونَ إِلاَّ اللَّهَ وَبِالْوَالِدَيْنِ إِحْسَانَاً

Worship none but Allāh and treat your parents with kindness.[18]

Allāh wanted from you two things: to worship Him and not to worship anyone else, and to be good with your parents, which means to be good as well with society, community, with school, with the children, with the hospital, with your work and not to cheat and do anything wrong. We will continue later *inshā'Allāh*. May Allāh forgive us.

This is the basis of what we are going to speak about in upcoming Ramaḍān *inshā'Allāh* this time and these are basics on which to raise up the building of different principles of Islam. So the first chapter will be on *Tawḥīd*, *inshā'Allāh* and then it goes with the proof of *Tawḥīd*, then sincerity in worshipness, what we have to do to be sincere in our worship and then to keep always living according to the Holy Qur'ān and the *sunnah* of the Prophet ﷺ. That is followed by the chapter of Love of Allāh ﷻ and His Prophet ﷺ and the love of the Family of the Prophet ﷺ, and followed by other essential topics, and we will try to go through it all.

Because many people are asking why we don't do sessions on *Fiqh* and you find an explanation of *Fiqh* in different chapters; however, we must

---

[18] Sūrat al-Baqarah, 2:83.

know that Islam stresses good manners and behaviors. For that reason *Maqām al-Iḥsān* is the highest level, but it has to be taught as the first level. So the highest level is "to worship Allāh as if you are seeing Him," which is the third level of Islam's fundamentals, "and know that if you are not seeing Him, He is seeing you." The first level you see is the Five Pillars, but consider, if you don't have these good manners, which are the third level, how are these Five Pillars going to work? If you don't have the Level of *Iḥsān*, Moral Excellence, in your prayers, in your fasting, in your *ṣadaqah* and in your *Ḥajj*, you are going to blend them all as a soup, all these Five Pillars mixed up with your bad manners. So *awlīyāullāh* say *Fiqh* issues are easy to learn from a book or from a teacher, but *Tazkīyyatu 'n-Nafs*, Purification of the Self, you cannot learn by yourself, you must have a *murabbī*, someone who will raise you up through different experiences that he puts you through, in order to understand how to polish your ego and yourself. Then your prayers improve, your fasting becomes better, then your *Ḥajj* becomes better, your charity becomes better, and your *Tawḥīd* becomes better.

That is why we emphasize *Taṣawwuf*, not as something that is innovated in Islam or deviant. Why do they say it is deviant? They pray, and like them we pray; it is the same prayer, it doesn't change. They say, "*Lā ilāha illa-Llāh,*" we say "*Ash-hadu an lā ilāha illa-Llāh wa ash-hadu anna Muḥammadu 'r-Rasūlullāh.*" Is it not good to have good characteristics and good qualifications? They don't like that? They want us to have bad qualifications and bad character, to be accepted by them? Is it not good to respect the elders? In the Sub-continent how do you show respect to elders in Pakistan, in India and Bangladesh? With what? You stand up from respect and kiss their hands in the morning. Is it not? Ask the Pakistanis and Bengalis. They come to you today and say, "Don't do that." Why won't you do that? You take the *riḍā*, satisfaction of your parents and go to work. That is *adab*. No, they say, "Don't, be rude." So that is why when they say you are doing your five obligations, Five Pillars and you bring the *Iḥsān*, Moral Excellence with it, then your prayer might be accepted.

But who can guarantee their Five Pillars are going to be accepted? Who can guarantee that? But if you have a good character and Moral Excellence, you try to work it out in order to make things work. Like for example, you have a watch, it has needles (to point at the numbers) but no battery, so what's the benefit? No benefit. It has needles but no battery, it is not moving. And vice versa, if you have the battery but no needles what is the benefit? So if you have Moral Excellence, you have good character, you have purified your self but you don't keep prayers? Some people say, "No need to pray, just do spirituality," but what's the benefit? It is like a watch with no needles! You have the battery, the charger is there but the needles are not there, so what is the benefit? Nothing. Now if you have *Fiqh*, you know how to pray and how to fast and so on, it means you have the needles but then you don't have good manners, so again what is benefit? When you blend them together as Imām Mālik said:

من تفقه ولم يتصوف فقد تفسق، ومن تصوف ولم يتفقه فقد تزندق
ومن جمع بينهما فقد تحقق

Man taṣawwafa wa tafaqqaha faqad taḥaqqaqa, "Whoever has balanced and brought these two together, the Five Pillars of Islam and the Moral Excellence, Purification of the Self, has proven himself true," as in the verse:

وَإِنَّكَ لَعَلَى خُلُقٍ عَظِيمٍ

Verily, you are of the highest level of conduct.[19]

And this is also what the Prophet ﷺ said:

أَدَّبَنِي رَبِّي فَأَحْسَنَ تَأْدِيبِي

My Lord perfected my good manners and conduct.

When you put these two together the watch is working, the battery is working and the needles are working, so then you know the time. And so may Allāh ﷻ teach us how to be good, although it is not easy, but we ask, we request, we beg.

One group of Muslims in Singapore, in order to stop us from giving lectures in different places, posted a *fatwā* showing a girl kissing my hand and on the other side a girl kissing my hand and I am kissing her head, this is what they said in the second picture. The first picture is my daughter kissing my hand. What did they say? "Deviant Naqshbandīs who allow women to kiss their hands." And on the other side, the other picture was Shaykh Nurjan and they put my name instead, and in it he is kissing his daughter's head. So they put both pictures as me; one she is kissing my hand and one I am kissing her head. Look, and they were distributing that everywhere, but: *al-Ḥaqqu yaʿlū wa la yuʿlā ʿalayh*, truth is always above everything.

---

[19] Sūrat al-Qalam, 68:4.

وَقُلْ جَاءَ الْحَقُّ وَزَهَقَ الْبَاطِلُ إِنَّ الْبَاطِلَ كَانَ زَهُوقًا

Say (O Muḥammad), "Ḥaqq (truth) has come and
bāṭil (falsehood) has perished."[20]

What do you want to say to them? Jealousy is everywhere and not only that people don't see these things as they don't travel, they don't go abroad, they are not exposed to where there are a majority of Muslims to see how is the reaction towards you. So I say when you want to pray in your house, put a turban and *jubbah*, not in public, as now Mawlānā Shaykh Nazim is saying to people don't dress in turban and don't dress in *jubbah*, be normal, because too many problems are coming.

May Allāh forgive us and may Allāh bless us.

Wa min Allāhi 't-tawfīq, bi ḥurmati 'l-ḥabīb, bi ḥurmati 'l-Fātiḥah.
And with Allāh is success. For the sake of the Beloved, for his sake we recite the opening chapter of Holy Qur'ān.

---

[20] Sūrat al-'Isrā, 17:81.

Fiqh and Good Manners

A'ūdhu billāhi min ash-Shayṭāni 'r-rajīm. Bismillāhi' r-Raḥmāni 'r-Raḥīm.
Nawaytu 'l-arbā'īn, nawaytu 'l-'itikāf, nawaytu 'l-khalwah, nawaytu 'l-'uzlah,
nawaytu 'r-riyāḍa, nawaytu 's-sulūk, lillāhi Ta'alā fī hādha 'l-masjid.
Atī'ūllāha wa atī'ū 'r-Rasūla wa ūli 'l-amri minkum. (4:59)

This is a continuation of the previous session, regarding Allāh ﷻ showing us the importance of wisdom in understanding things that are around us. And we have explained that it is very important when we read the Holy Qur'ān or read *ḥadīth*, understand the different meanings they contain. That is why the first message that Allāh has sent with Prophet ﷺ is to begin with *tilāwat* (recitation), to learn how to read the Holy Qur'ān. And it is like an order to every *mu'min* and Muslim to do *tilāwat al-Qur'ān*, recitation of the Holy Qur'ān. As the Prophet ﷺ related to his *Ṣaḥābah*, verse after verse, we have to read that, and that is what is called *tilāwat*.

Allāh said to Muslims in Holy Qur'ān:

هُوَ الَّذِي بَعَثَ فِي الْأُمِّيِّينَ رَسُولًا مِّنْهُمْ يَتْلُو عَلَيْهِمْ آيَاتِهِ وَيُزَكِّيهِمْ وَيُعَلِّمُهُمُ الْكِتَابَ وَالْحِكْمَةَ وَإِن كَانُوا مِن قَبْلُ لَفِي ضَلَالٍ مُّبِينٍ وَآخَرِينَ مِنْهُمْ لَمَّا يَلْحَقُوا بِهِمْ وَهُوَ الْعَزِيزُ الْحَكِيمُ ذَٰلِكَ فَضْلُ اللَّهِ يُؤْتِيهِ مَن يَشَاءُ وَاللَّهُ ذُو الْفَضْلِ الْعَظِيمِ

It is He who has sent among the unlettered a Messenger from themselves reciting to them His verses and purifying them and teaching them the Book and wisdom, although they were before in clear error. And (to) others of them who have not yet joined them. And He is the Exalted in Might, the Wise. That is the bounty of Allāh, which He gives to whom He wills, and Allāh is the Possessor of Great Bounty. [21]

"He is the one who sent from among illiterate people," and that is a miracle, that He sent from within illiterate people miraculous words and verses. "He recited to them miraculous verses to learn," and then Allāh gave him the authority to purify these Muslims. And the Prophet ﷺ was doing it, saying *"Yā Rabbī,* by Your order I am purifying them." Purifying here means on Judgment Day there will not be one Muslim who will not be purified by the Prophet ﷺ (through his *shafa'ah*).

---

[21] Sūrat al-Jumu'ah, 62:2-4.

That is mentioned in Holy Qur'ān: Allāh first mentions sending the *ayāts* of Holy Qur'ān and then he purifies them, then teaches them the Holy Qur'ān. When Allāh says *yuʿallimahumu 'l-kitāb*, "teaching them the Book," the Prophet ﷺ takes it on himself, as he is the one whom all prophets come to on Judgment Day to take *shafaʿah*. As Allāh taught Holy Qur'ān to the Prophet ﷺ with all its secrets, the Prophet ﷺ will teach the whole Ummah the Holy Qur'ān with all its secrets.

الرَّحْمَنُ عَلَّمَ الْقُرْآنَ خَلَقَ الْإِنسَانَ

(Allāh) Most Gracious! It is He Who has taught the Qur'ān.
He has created Man.[22]

To whom did Allāh teach the Quran? To the Prophet ﷺ. And then as Allāh ordered the Prophet ﷺ he taught the Ummah the Holy Qur'ān, not piece-by-piece rather he taught everything that Allāh gave to him, giving to the Ummah. He doesn't leave anything out as he wants to bequeath that knowledge to the Ummah. The Prophet ﷺ took the responsibility to teach the Ummah the Holy Qur'ān. So on Judgment Day we will be standing on full knowledge of the Holy Qur'ān, although we don't know the full knowledge of Holy Qur'ān by yourselves, but with the responsibility that the Prophet ﷺ took on his shoulders we will know it all. Then he taught them wisdom.

Sayyīdinā ʿAlī ؓ said:

راس الحكمة مخاة الله

The head of wisdom is fear of Allāh ﷻ.

The head of wisdom is fear of Allāh. That is not just to fear Allāh's punishment, but to fear being away from Allāh. On that day you will see your relatives closer to Allāh and imagine the effect on you and that Day you will say, "Why didn't I do more?"

So when Allāh says that He sent the Prophet ﷺ to "teach wisdom," that is wisdom you cannot imagine in your mind. I mention the *ḥadīth* that is evidence for this, that what we understand is not enough and is incomplete; what we understand is not up to the meaning of *ḥikmat*, wisdom.

---

[22] Sūrat ar-Raḥmān, 55:1-3.

To whom you give *ṣadaqah*? You give it to the poor people. If you give *ṣadaqah* to someone who is not poor, is it accepted to give him a donation, $100 or whatever? Normally you say no. Do you give *ṣadaqah* to someone who does not deserve it? Do you give *ṣadaqah* to a person who is stealing people's money? Do you give *ṣadaqah* to a lady who does *zinā*, a prostitute, or to a man who is, I am sorry to say, a pimp? No, you would not do that, but see this *ḥadīth*, which is going to flip everything we know, as if we know nothing. Everything we know in front of that *ḥadīth* is zero. As we said, we don't give *ṣadaqah* to a rich man, a thief or an adulterer, but this is going to change everything.

وعن أبي هريرة رضي الله عنه أن رسول الله صلى الله عليه وسلم قال: " قال رجل لأتصدقن بصدقة، فخرج بصدقته، فوضعها في يد سارق، فأصبحوا يتحدثون: تصدق على سارق! فقال: اللهم لك الحمد لأتصدقن بصدقة، فخرج بصدقته، فوضعها في يد زانية؟! فأصبحوا يتحدثون: تصدق على زانية فقال: اللهم لك الحمد على زانية، لأتصدقن بصدقة، فخرج بصدقته، فوضعها في يد غني, فأصبحوا يتحدثون! تصدق الليلة على غني, فقال: اللهم لك الحمد على سارق ، وعلى زانية، وعلى غني! فأتى فقيل له: أما صدقتك على سارق، فلعله أن يستعف عن سرقته، وأما الزانية فلعلها تستعف عن زناها، وأما الغني فلعله أن يعتبر ، فينفق مما آتاه الله"

(رواه البخاري بلفظه، ومسلم بمعناه).

Abū Hurayrah ﷺ related that the Messenger of Allāh ﷺ said:
A man said, "I am going to find someone in need and give him charity."

That man went out to give his charity to someone in need. He went out of his house and he saw someone, a thief, and put the money in his hand. Look, he went out from his house and put the donation in the hand of a thief. His intention when he went out was to put *ṣadaqah* in the hand of someone who deserves it and needs it. Then he puts it in the hand of a thief. Does the thief need it? No he does not.

So he said, Allāhumma laka 'l-ḥamd 'alā sāriq, "O Allāh! Praise be
to You. I have given charity to a thief."

It means, "It is not me, but it is Your Will, *Irāda*, that made me to put *ṣadaqah* in the hand of that thief."

Then he said a second time after many days, "I am going to give
from the ḥalāl money I made a ṣadaqah."

So he went out with his donation and put it in the hand of a prostitute; it might be he thought she deserves it. He gave it to her and the whole city began to speak about before he gave to a thief and now he gave to a prostitute, and they said how bad is that man.

And he said, Allāhumma laka 'l-ḥamdu ʿalā az-zānīyya.
"O Allāh! Praise be to You. I have given ṣadaqah to a prostitute."

It means, "I didn't want, but Your Will made me to put that charity in the hand of a prostitute."

Then he said, "Now I am going to put the money in the hand
of someone who deserves it and inshā'Allāh I will not make a mistake."
And he went out looking and looking and found a person he thought
is poor and he gave him money and it was a large amount of money.

If it had not been a lot, he would not have accepted. For example, a prostitute will not take 10 cents, she will throw it in your face. So the people of the city began to speak about him: he is giving his money to a thief, to a prostitute and to a rich person.

And he said, Allāhumma fa-laka 'l-ḥamdu ʿalā sāriqun wa ʿala zānīyyatin
wa ʿalā ghanīyy, "O Allāh! Praise be to You (for helping me) give charity
to a thief, a prostitute and a rich man."

He thanked Allāh that it was His Will that he gave to these. *Fa ūtīyya,* so it means either he heard or saw a vision or heard an angel saying, "your ṣadaqah to a thief might be the cause for Allāh to drop his being a thief and become a good person. It might be it makes him look bad to himself, and therefore, he stops stealing from people."

That means "With your ṣadaqah to a thief, Allāh will turn that bad person to a good person due to the good money you put in his hand. And as for the prostitute, Allāh might make her drop all her bad work due to the ṣadaqah you gave her. That means his ṣadaqah was accepted by Allāh ﷻ and by the Prophet ﷺ. As for the rich man, giving him charity might cause him to take an example that a poor man is giving him ṣadaqah while he doesn't give ṣadaqah to anyone, and that might inspire him to find the poor and give him ṣadaqah.

This *ḥadīth* is mentioned by none other than Bukhārī and so they cannot say it is weak, but from Imām Bukhārī, this *ḥadīth* shows that if your intention is good and your intention is to give ṣadaqah to someone in great need, not in need of money to spend, but in need of ṣadaqah to save him from the bad situation he is in, to know he is bad and while you don't deserve it, it gives you a moral lesson to stop doing the wrong you are doing. Similarly, it might be the cause for the rich person to begin to giving *ṣadaqah* to those who deserve it.

So not everything is just what we read literally, but the reality is behind the meanings, the secret of the wisdom. If we take this *ḥadīth* literally, the Prophet ﷺ explained what the man did to give a thief, a prostitute and to a rich person, and we see it turned these people back to a good life. Not everything you have to read literally as there are meanings behind them. Allāh wants us to have wisdom.

When we have wisdom then we can clearly give explanation of what we are reading; not reading like parrot with no understanding. Where the mission of the Prophet ﷺ is, as he said:

انما بعثت لاتمم مكارم الاخلاق

I have been sent to perfect the best of conduct (your behavior and character).[23]

Not to be loud and to be involved in *dunyā*. Now people have nothing but drugs, and hard rock and soft rock and rap music. What is going to take you where? That takes you to *dunyā*. It does not take you to *Ākhirah*. what takes you to *Ākhirah*? *Tahdhīb al-akhlāq* which means to fix, clean and purify your character.

The Prophet ﷺ said, "I was sent to perfect human beings character."

When we purify ourselves, when the self is purified then Allāh will inspire the heart.

فَأَلْهَمَهَا فُجُورَهَا وَتَقْوَاهَا

He inspired the self of its bad and its good.[24]

When Allāh inspires the self, you will be inspired with what is good and what is bad. It is like having two hands. Why do we have two hands? In order to balance. The Prophet ﷺ gave us a balance, by saying:

---

[23] Bazzār.

[24] Sūrat ash-Shams, 91:8.

إنما الأعمال بالنيات

Verily actions are by intentions.[25]

Verily if your intention is to do good, you will be given the reward of one doing good.

They asked Grandshaykh, "Why don't you teach *Fiqh*?" He is an *ʿAlīm* in Shafiʿī *Fiqh*. Once I asked Grandshaykh a question about the meaning of a verse. they say *samiʿnā wa atʿanā*, "we listen and obey," or "we hear and we obey." So when I asked Grandshaykh the meaning of one *āyah*, he said, "Oh my son. There is a *mufti* down in the city. Go ask him. Here (in this place) is the polishing of the self and how to implement good manners and good character."

Not everyone touches on this subject, where the Holy Qurʾān mentioned the highest level, *Maqām al-Iḥsān* in the verse:

وَإِنَّكَ لَعَلى خُلُقٍ عَظِيمٍ

Verily you are on the best of conduct. [26]

"Here," Grandshaykh said, "is only 'we listen and obey'. There are many teachers of *Fiqh*. I am not teaching *Fiqh* here, you can learn there."

Good Manners and Discipline Increase Wisdom

It is a very delicate balance we have here. *Akhlāq* is important. That is why you can learn *Fiqh*, but you might be *faqīh* and you have no discipline. That is what the Prophet ﷺ said in his *ḥadīth*:

نعوذ بالله من منافق عليم اللسان جهول القلب

As narrated by Umm Salamah ؇, Prophet ﷺ said: I seek refuge in Allāh from a hypocrite who has an eloquent tongue but an ignorant heart.[27]

It means "the thing I fear most for my *ummah* is a scholar who is ignorant in his heart." It is in the same category of *ḥadīth*, *akhwaf mā akhāfu ʿalā ummatī, ʿalīmun ʿalīmu 'l-lisān jahūl al-qalb*. He is very well spoken, but he

---

[25] Bukhārī and Muslim.

[26] Sūrat al-Qalam, 68:4.

[27] Muslim.

20

is ignorant in his heart. So Purification of the Self allows us to differentiate between what is good and what is bad. Grandshaykh said that Allāh gave everyone a mind and intelligence to differentiate what is good and what is bad. He said, "I am not teaching *Fiqh* here, but anything you want to do weigh it through the scale of good and evil. If your mind says to you 'This is good decision,' follow it and if it says, 'This is bad,' stop."

Allāh gave you mind to know what is good and what is bad. For example, you say to yourself, "I need to go to the movie theatre." If you say it is good, no, you are wrong; I say it is bad, as it takes time from your *dhikrullāh*. If you say, "I am making *dhikrullāh* and doing my prayers, so is it okay to go see a movie?" it is okay, if there is nothing bad in it. If you see good do it and if you see bad, stop and don't do it.

إنما الأعمال بالنيات

Verily actions are by intentions.

Allāh has sent in *Sūrat al-Isrā* verses 23-38 all that we need in our life. First, in understanding Islam is not to make *shirk* (associating partners with God), then to be good to parents, to be humble in front of them, to give the rights of relatives and those who are poor, to try not to waste wealth, to try to speak nicely, to make people happy, to not make adultery nor kill people, and to help the orphan. All of this is mentioned in *Sūrat al-Isrā*:

وَقَضَى رَبُّكَ أَلاَّ تَعْبُدُواْ إِلاَّ إِيَّاهُ وَبِالْوَالِدَيْنِ إِحْسَانًا إِمَّا يَبْلُغَنَّ عِندَكَ الْكِبَرَ أَحَدُهُمَا أَوْ كِلاَهُمَا فَلاَ تَقُل لَّهُمَآ أُفٍّ وَلاَ تَنْهَرْهُمَا وَقُل لَّهُمَا قَوْلاً كَرِيمًا وَاخْفِضْ لَهُمَا جَنَاحَ الذُّلِّ مِنَ الرَّحْمَةِ وَقُل رَّبِّ ارْحَمْهُمَا كَمَا رَبَّيَانِي صَغِيرًا

رَّبُّكُمْ أَعْلَمُ بِمَا فِي نُفُوسِكُمْ إِن تَكُونُواْ صَالِحِينَ فَإِنَّهُ كَانَ لِلأَوَّابِينَ غَفُورًا وَآتِ ذَا الْقُرْبَى حَقَّهُ وَالْمِسْكِينَ وَابْنَ السَّبِيلِ وَلاَ تُبَذِّرْ تَبْذِيرًا. إِنَّ الْمُبَذِّرِينَ كَانُواْ إِخْوَانَ الشَّيَاطِينِ وَكَانَ الشَّيْطَانُ لِرَبِّهِ كَفُورًا وَإِمَّا تُعْرِضَنَّ عَنْهُمُ ابْتِغَاء رَحْمَةٍ مِّن رَّبِّكَ تَرْجُوهَا فَقُل لَّهُمْ قَوْلاً مَّيْسُورًا وَلاَ تَجْعَلْ يَدَكَ مَغْلُولَةً إِلَى عُنُقِكَ وَلاَ تَبْسُطْهَا كُلَّ الْبَسْطِ فَتَقْعُدَ مَلُومًا مَّحْسُورًا إِنَّ رَبَّكَ يَبْسُطُ الرِّزْقَ لِمَن يَشَاء وَيَقْدِرُ إِنَّهُ كَانَ بِعِبَادِهِ خَبِيرًا بَصِيرًا وَلاَ تَقْتُلُواْ أَوْلادَكُمْ خَشْيَةَ إِمْلاقٍ نَّحْنُ نَرْزُقُهُمْ وَإِيَّاكُم إنَّ قَتْلَهُمْ كَانَ خِطْءًا كَبِيرًا وَلاَ تَقْرَبُواْ الزِّنَى إِنَّهُ كَانَ فَاحِشَةً وَسَاء سَبِيلاً وَلاَ تَقْتُلُواْ النَّفْسَ الَّتِي حَرَّمَ اللَّهُ إِلاَّ بِالحَقِّ وَمَن قُتِلَ مَظْلُومًا فَقَدْ جَعَلْنَا لِوَلِيِّهِ سُلْطَانًا فَلاَ يُسْرِف فِّي الْقَتْلِ إِنَّهُ كَانَ مَنْصُورًا وَلاَ تَقْرَبُواْ مَالَ الْيَتِيمِ إِلاَّ بِالَّتِي هِيَ أَحْسَنُ حَتَّى يَبْلُغَ أَشُدَّهُ وَأَوْفُواْ بِالْعَهْدِ إِنَّ الْعَهْدَ كَانَ مَسْؤُولاً وَأَوْفُوا الْكَيْلَ إِذَا كِلْتُمْ وَزِنُواْ بِالقِسْطَاسِ الْمُسْتَقِيمِ ذَلِكَ خَيْرٌ وَأَحْسَنُ تَأْوِيلاً وَلاَ تَقْفُ مَا لَيْسَ لَكَ بِهِ عِلْمٌ إِنَّ السَّمْعَ وَالْبَصَرَ وَالْفُؤَادَ كُلُّ أُولـئِكَ كَانَ عَنْهُ مَسْؤُولاً

And your Lord has decreed that you not worship except Him, and to parents, good treatment. Whether one or both of them reach old age (while) with you, say not to them (so much as), "uff," and do not repel them but speak to them a noble word. And lower to them the wing of humility out of mercy and say, "My Lord, have mercy upon them as they brought me up (when I was) small." Your Lord is most knowing of what is within yourselves. If you should be righteous (in intention), then indeed He is ever, to the often returning (to Him), Forgiving.

And your Lord has decreed that you not worship except Him, and to parents, good treatment. Whether one or both of them reach old age (while) with you, say not to them (so much as), "uff," and do not repel them but speak to them a noble word. And lower to them the wing of humility out of mercy and say, "My Lord, have mercy upon them as they brought me up (when I was) small." Your Lord is most knowing of what is within yourselves. If you should be righteous (in intention), then indeed He is ever, to the often returning (to Him), Forgiving.

And give the relative his right, and (also) the poor and the traveler, and do not spend wastefully. Indeed, the wasteful are brothers of the devils, and ever has Satan been to his Lord ungrateful. And if you (must) turn away from the needy awaiting mercy from your Lord which you expect, then speak to them a gentle word.

And do not make your hand ﷺ chained to your neck or extend it completely and (thereby) become blamed and insolvent. Indeed, your Lord extends provision for whom He wills and restricts (it). Indeed, He is ever, concerning His servants, Acquainted and Seeing. And do not kill your children for fear of poverty. We provide for them and for you. Indeed, their killing is ever a great sin. And do not approach unlawful sexual intercourse. Indeed, it is ever an immorality and is evil as a way.

And do not kill the soul which Allāh has forbidden, except by right. And whoever is killed unjustly, We have given his heir authority, but let him not exceed limits in (the matter of) taking life. Indeed, he has been supported (by the law). And do not approach the property of an orphan, except in the way that is best, until he reaches maturity. And fulfill (every) commitment. Indeed, the commitment is ever (that about which one will be) questioned.

And give full measure when you measure, and weigh with an even balance. That is the best (way) and best in result. And do not pursue that of which you have no knowledge. Indeed, the hearing, the sight and the heart—about all those (one) will be questioned. And do not walk upon the Earth exultantly. Indeed, you will never *tear the Earth (apart), and you will never reach the mountains in height. All that, its evil is ever, in the sight of your Lord, detested.*[28]

This shows the immensity of our duty to our Lord as well as to people on Earth with whom we live together. In it are 15 *ayāts*, including the prohibition of *shirk*, to order and command good manners and to leave bad manners, to leave forbiddens and observe the orders. And *awlīyāullāh* have counted 500 *mā'mūrāt*, orders by Allāh to follow and 800 forbiddens we are asked to drop from our life. We ask Allāh to forgive us and to purify us. We are all falling into the category of *shirk*, associating partners with the Lord, when we make our egos our lord. We are trying to make ourselves righteous, by claiming "Oh, we are good people!" No, we are not good people as long as we are listening to Shayṭān and making sins.

So we must always tell the bad ego we are bad, not good and then purify ourselves, as Allāh said in Holy Qur'ān:

فَلَا تُزَكُّوا أَنفُسَكُمْ

Don't praise yourself.[29]

Don't praise your ego, but be humble. '*Lā*' means never, never make yourself above others; try to be under everyone. Don't criticize anyone except yourself. Don't criticize others; they might be better than you. I will read it again now in Arabic.

That *ḥadīth* changes all the measures that we understand about *ṣadaqah* or even about Islam completely.

After he gave *ṣadaqah* to a thief, a prostitute and a rich person, and the people criticized him for this, he said, "It is your will *yā Rabb*, I intended to give *ṣadaqah*." *Fa ūtīya*, it came to him in dream as a vision or he heard a voice, "your *ṣadaqah* to that thief might cause him to repent, and as for the prostitute it might be a cause for her to repent and as for the rich one that one will understand that he is rich and he is giving only 'crumbs' and it will inspire him to give with full hands."

Not everything we read can be understood by purely the literal meaning. These fifteen verses describe what Allāh wants from every Muslim. That is literally and interpretation-wise, it is even more!

---

[28] Sūrat al-Isrā, 17:23-38.

[29] Sūrat an-Najm, 53:32.

May Allāh forgive us and may Allāh bless us.

Wa min Allāhi 't-tawfiq, bi ḥurmati 'l-ḥabīb, bi ḥurmati 'l-Fātiḥah.
And with Allāh is success. For the sake of the Beloved, for his sake we recite
the opening chapter of Holy Qur'ān.

Tawḥīd and Shirk

Allāhumma salli ʿalā Sayyīdinā Muḥammadin wa ʿala āli Sayyīdinā Muḥammad.
Aʿūdhu billāhi min ash-Shayṭāni 'r-rajīm. Bismillāhi' r-Raḥmāni 'r-Raḥīm.
Kalimatān khafīfatān ʿala'l-lisān thaqīlatān fi'l-mīzān ḥabībatān li'r-rahmān: SubḥānAllāh
wa bi-ḥamdihi subḥānAllāhi 'l-ʿĀẓīm.
Nawaytu 'l-arbāʿīn, nawaytu 'l-ʿitikāf, nawaytu 'l-khalwah, nawaytu 'l-ʿuzlah,
nawaytu 'r-riyāḍa, nawaytu 's-sulūk, lillāhi Taʿalā fī hādha 'l-masjid.
Atīʿullāha wa atīʿū 'r-Rasūla wa ūli 'l-amri minkum. (4:59)

O Believers around the world, may Allāh bless you! The first of *Ramaḍān* for the year 1434 is coming soon. *InshāʾAllāh* in a few more days we will be welcoming the month of *Ramaḍān*, the month of fasting. We must prepare ourselves in order to be in *riḍāullāh*, the happiness of Allāh from us. To make Allāh ﷻ happy is to obey Him in everything that He asked us. Obedience must have in it a secret that makes us to be always remembering Allāh ﷻ.

Ramaḍān is the month of fasting, where Allāh ﷻ said and as Prophet ﷺ said:

الصوم لي وانا أجزي به

Fasting is for Me and I will reward it.[30]

So no one can reward us except Allāh ﷻ. To be near each other, Allāh ﷻ said:

يد الله مع الجماعة

Allāh's Hand is with the group.[31]

Allāh's Hand is with the group of people, so we don't want to be scattered. Although we might be the same in number, if we are near then more reflection of different energy will be reflected on each other. In this month *inshāʾAllāh* we will be preparing to speak about different Islamic principles and subjects in order that we will learn our religion as much as

---

[30] *Ḥadīth Qudsī.*

[31] *Kanz al-ʿUmmāl.*

we can; especially about *dhikrullāh, Tawḥīd* and many other issues that come in front of us.

Allāh said on the tongue of the Prophet ﷺ, "Fasting is for Me and I will reward for it." Then if you are going to meet someone important, you are going to give them a nice gift. If you are going to meet a leader, your gift is going to be different, it will be nicer. If you are going to meet a king, whatever you give him as a gift he has a better one, as he has everything. But giving a gift is showing your love and respect and he will be happy with you when he sees you are trying your best. That is between servant to servant, from *'abd* to *'abd*, so what then do you think from servant to Allāh ﷻ? He says, "Fasting is for Me and I will reward for it." When we fast, our fasting must be nice and clean as the Prophet ﷺ said, "*Jinn* and *shayāṭīn* will be chained not to run after fasting people." That means he is giving us a hint that if you behave well, Shayṭān will be hooked and Allāh will put that chain on him by ordering his angels to put a chain around these *shayāṭīn* in order not to run after *Ummat an-Nabī* ﷺ.

What is the first important principle in Islam? [*Shahādah.*] You? [*Lā ilāha illa-Llāh.*] You? [*Tawḥīd.*] Good answer, first is *Tawḥīd*. The first principle that Allāh sent in the Message of Islam with Sayyīdinā Muḥammad ﷺ is to teach us *Tawḥīd*. That means Allāh does not like *shirk*. *Tawḥīd* means to make sure that your self, your *nafs* and your soul, is understanding that there is no Creator except Allāh ﷻ, by saying "*Lā ilāha illa-Llāh*" and "*Ash-hadu an lā ilāha illa-Llāh wa Ash-hadu anna Muḥammadu 'r-Rasūlullāh.*" So it is important to stress on *Kalimat at-Tawḥīd* because Allāh ﷻ said, *'Aẓam adh-dhunūb ash-shirk*, "The greatest of sins is *shirk*." *Shirk* is impurity. If you are not pure, you are not giving Allāh's rights to Him; therefore, Allāh will *yuḥarrim 'alayhim al-jinān*, prohibit those who do *shirk* to enter Paradise. This is very important, so take notes and learn and I will test you later.

So what prevents people from entering Paradise? *Ash-shirk billāh*, to deny the Oneness of Allāh ﷻ. You need to step on your *shirk*, meaning to step on everything that *yansub ilā nafsik*, you attribute to yourself; whereas everything good has to be attributed to Allāh because He gave it to you. What allows us to enter Paradise? *Tawḥīd. Shirk* prevents you from entering Paradise. So what is the key to Paradise? "*Lā ilāha illa-Llāh*" and "*Muḥammadun Rasūlullāh.*"

Prophet ﷺ said:

من قال لا اله الا الله دخل الجنة

Whoever says 'Lā ilāha illa-Llāh' enters Paradise.

Allāh loves that. Yes, you will commit sins, but first you have to establish within yourself the words *'Lā ilāha illa-Llāh.'* If you are saying *"Lā ilāha illa-Llāh"* but not acting on it, it will still save you from Hellfire, but you will not be recognized in Paradise as someone who is highly respected. So the key of Paradise is *Lā ilāha illa-Llāh* and do you have a key? The key if you look at it, it is straight and you cannot have a crooked key as it will not open. So it has to be straight, which means you are on *Sirāṭ al-Mustaqīm*, the Straight Path. If it is straight, also it might not open because it needs these teeth, if it doesn't have teeth it doesn't open. So as much as you have teeth and you are slowly moving on *Sirāṭ al-Mustaqīm* and entering your key inside the Heavenly Doors, it makes teeth. So without teeth you cannot enter Paradise; the key will go inside the ignition, but not ignite the car, so if we don't have teeth in the key of Paradise the door will not open.

What are the teeth of the key of Paradise? The key of *Sirāṭ al-Mustaqīm* is *'Lā ilāha illa-Llāh Muḥammadun Rasūlullāh,'* but it has teeth and you have to make sure they are perfect. That is where *Fiqh* comes. The *Fiqh ash-Sharī'ah* of Islam is what you have to have in your key in order to open the door of Paradise. The first of the teeth of keys of Paradise is *aṣ-ṣalāt*, and what is the second? *Zakāt.* And the third is *ṣiyām* and fourth is *Ḥajj*, and the fifth one is *jihād* and sixth is *amr bi 'l-ma'rūf wa 'n-nahīyy 'ani 'l-munkar*, and there are many more. So each tooth represents one principle of Islam and the first after *Tawḥīd* is:

ما بين الكفر والايمان ترك الصلاة

What is between disbelief and belief is the leaving of prayers.[32]

What is between unbelief, which prevents you to enter Paradise, and faith is to leave prayers. If you leave your prayers you are prohibited to enter Paradise. So *mā bayn al-kufr wa 'l-īmān tarku 'ṣ-ṣalāt*, between *kufr* and *īmān* is someone who does not pray. The difference between belief and disbelief is to leave the prayer. If you do the prayer you have *īmān*, but if

---

[32] Tirmidhī.

you leave prayer you have *kufr* although you recite *"Lā ilāha illa-Llāh,"* but you left out one major tooth on the key. So it might be one major tooth to the lock, so you are not praying and the key does not open the lock. Sometimes you say, "I am praying," but not all the prayers, so that is a partial tooth and the door will still not open.

The Importance of Ṣilat ar-Raḥim, Blood Relationships

How many of us are praying and how many are not praying, and what kinds of prayers are accepted and what kinds of prayers are not accepted? You might pray and it is not accepted and you might pray and it is accepted because there are differences. And also most important is what the Prophet ﷺ mentioned in many *aḥadīth* is *ṣilat ar-raḥim wa birr al-wālidayn*, the relationships, blood relationship and spiritual relationship. You must connect to your family. Don't say, "I don't talk to that one as he abused me."

The Prophet ﷺ said to Abū Hurayrah ﷺ, who asked him, *wa mā ḥusna 'l-khuluqi yā Rasūlullāh*, "What is the good manners?" and Prophet said, *an taṣila man qataʿk*, "It is to reconnect with the one who disconnected you."

أوصى النبي صلى الله عليه وسلم أبا هريرة بوصية عظيمة فقال: { يا أبا هريرة! عليك بحسن الخلق }. قال أبو هريرة رضي الله عنه: وما حسن الخلق يا رسول الله؟قال:

{ تصل مَنْ قطعك، وتعفو عمن ظلمك، وتُعطي من حرمك}

*The Prophet ﷺ advised Abū Hurayrah: O Abā Hurayrah! You must
have good manners. Connect with the one who cut you off,
forgive the one who oppressed you and give to the one
who prevented you from reaching your desires.*[33]

You have to connect to your relatives. (Speaking to a *murīd*.) You have to connect to your mother, she is asking about you and she is missing you. So you have to connect to each other in spiritual relations, like Muslims. If a group of people speak bad about you, never mind, step on your ego and be better than them. Prophet ﷺ said that is from the best character, *birr al-wālidayn*. Like today, many people think their parents are old-fashioned and "Why do I have to listen to them?" So *birr al-wālidayn* is to be good to your parents, to do something they like to be happy with you, and to remember

---

[33] al-Bayhaqī.

how much they were trying day and night to raise you up and you are going to be responsible if you raise them doing sins and running in the streets. You cannot bring children and say, "I don't care for them, they are doing drugs and drinking salt! I am not interested." No, you are responsible for them! You have to take care of them and look after them or else you will be asked by Allāh ﷻ. Anyone who makes *ṣalāt, ṣawm, zakāt, Ḥajj, jihād, amr bi 'l-maʿrūf wa 'n-nahīyy ʿani 'l-munkar* and *birr al-wālidayn*, Allāh will give him a key to open any level of Paradise.

إنما الأعمال بالنيات

Every action is according to (its) intention.[34]

So let us make intention, "Yā Allāh! We are trying our best with Your support, with support of the Prophet ﷺ, support of *awlīyāullāh*, support of scholars and each other, as we are weak servants, in order that we fulfill the obligations You have ordered us to do, we say:

أَطِيعُوا اللَّهَ وَأَطِيعُوا الرَّسُولَ وَأُوْلِي الأَمْرِ مِنكُمْ

Obey Allāh, obey the Prophet, and obey those in authority among you.[35]

And Allāh said:

إِنَّ اللَّهَ لاَ يَغْفِرُ أَن يُشْرَكَ بِهِ وَيَغْفِرُ مَا دُونَ ذَلِكَ لِمَن يَشَاء

Indeed, Allāh does not forgive association with Him, but He forgives what is less than that for whom He wills.[36]

Allāh does not like anyone to make *shirk* with Him. Anything else He will forgive, if He likes and He likes us to be Muslim, so don't let the words, "I am not Muslim" to pass your tongue as you don't know what will happen! So that key will open only for you if you have sins and *khaṭāyā* and *maʿāṣiyy*, it still has its residue on the key or if the key has been corrupted, even though you might think they are small sins, the key doesn't open the lock because it is corroded. You have the key, you have the teeth on it, but it is corroded with small sins that are still left there. So be sure to make

---

[34] Bukhārī.

[35] Sūrat an-Nisā, 4:59.

[36] Sūrat an-Nisā, 4:48.

istighfār every day 100 times so that Allāh will forgive you from your sins, because it needs repentance and *istighfār*!

Allāh will not let anyone enter Paradise until he is pure from all these small sins and the key is polished, so He will put us in punishment to purify us. So we cannot go into punishment, *yā Rabbī*, as we cannot take it, so forgive us! And He said those who die, the angels take their souls and they are *ṭayyibīn*, good people and pure people. Allāh will send them to Paradise:

وسيق الذين اتقوا ربهم إلى الجنة زمرا حتى إذا جاءوها وفتحت أبوابها
وقال لهم خزنتها سلام عليكم طبتم فادخلوها خالدين

And those who feared their Lord will be driven to Paradise
in groups until, when they reach it while its gates have been opened
and its keepers say, "Peace be upon you! You have become pure,
so enter it to abide eternally therein."[37]

The people who believe will be pushed to Paradise by angels and then you have the key, so they welcome you, "Come, come, come! This is for you! Enter it for Eternal Life!"

May Allāh put us in Paradise *fadkhulūhā khālidīn*, for Eternal Life! *Yā fawzan li 'l-mustaghfirīn astaghfirullāh!*

This is an introduction to what we will, *inshā'Allāh*, explain in Ramaḍān, *wa 'l-ʿabdu idhā qāma fi 'ṣ-ṣalāt ghār ash-shayṭānu minhu.*

May Allāh forgive us and may Allāh bless us.

Wa min Allāhi 't-tawfīq, bi ḥurmati 'l-ḥabīb, bi ḥurmati 'l-Fātiḥah.
And with Allāh is success. For the sake of the Beloved, for his sake we recite the opening chapter of Holy Qur'ān.

---

[37] Sūrat az-Zumar, 39:73.

Favors of the Month of Ramaḍān

A'ūdhu billāhi min ash-Shayṭāni 'r-rajīm. Bismillāhi' r-Rahmāni 'r-Rahīm.
Nawaytu 'l-arbā'īn, nawaytu 'l-'itikāf, nawaytu 'l-khalwah, nawaytu 'l-'uzlah,
nawaytu 'r-riyāḍa, nawaytu 's-sulūk, lillāhi Ta'alā fī hādha 'l-masjid.
Atī'ullāha wa atī'ū 'r-Rasūla wa ūli 'l-amri minkum. (4:59)

As-salāmu 'alaykum wa rahmatullāhi wa barakātuh. Bismillāhi 'r-Rahmāni 'r-Rahīm. Alhamdulillāhi Rabbi 'l-'Alamīn, wa 'ṣ-ṣalātu wa 's-salāmu 'ala ashrafi 'l-mursalīna Sayyidinā wa Nabīyyina Muḥammadin wa 'ala ālihi wa ṣahbihi ajma'īn. Alhamdulillāhi 'Lladhī hadāna li 'l-Islāmi wa mā kunnā li-nahtadīa law lā an hadānā 'Llāh, Alhamdulillāhi hamdan kāmilan kamā yuhibbu wa yarḍā. Wa lanā ash-sharaf haythu ja'alāna 'Llāhu min ummat al-Muṣṭafā.

O Muslims, brothers, sisters, Believers, viewers. In a very few days, *Ramaḍān* will be coming and we have to prepare ourselves for it. Allāh ﷻ has given us what He blessed us with in order to save ourselves in *Ramaḍān*, to be a fasting month that is accepted.

Devils are Chained and the Doors of Heaven Open

As the Prophet ﷺ said, Allāh ﷻ orders the angels to chain all *shayāṭīn* in *Ramaḍān*. Abū Hurayrah ؆ narrated that the Prophet ﷺ said:

إذا دخل رمضان فتحت أبواب الجنة وغلقت أبواب النار وسلسلت الشياطين

> *When Ramaḍān begins, the doors of Paradise are opened and*
> *the doors of Hell are closed and the shayāṭīn are tied with chains.*[38]

Idhā dakhala ramaḍān futihat abwāb as-samāwāt. As soon as *Ramaḍān* appears, as soon as it comes, Allāh ﷻ opens the doors of Heavens. He says, "Open the doors of Heavens!" How many doors, one door, two doors, three doors? Today they are renovating *Masjid al-Ḥarām*, they are renovating and they are going to make doors that through every door you look you see the *Ka'bah*. Allāh is saying in this *hadīth*, as the Prophet ﷺ mentioned, "When *Ramaḍān* comes, *futihat abwāb as-samāwāt*, the doors of Heavens will be opened." It means every person, *mu'min*, *muwāḥḥid*, Muslim, who says "*Lā*

---

[38] Bukhārī and Muslim.

ilāha illa-Llāh Muḥammadun Rasūlullāh," Allāh gave him a door. So it is not only one door or seven doors, but infinite numbers of doors will be opened for you in *Ramaḍān!* And when someone opens a door for you what do they say? "Welcome!" So Allāh is ordering the angels to welcome us, welcoming those who are fasting, welcoming those who are obeying Allāh ﷻ, welcoming those who are worshipping Allāh ﷻ, welcoming those who are doing good in their lives, welcoming those who don't make *shirk* in their lives.

And in order not to make a mistake, He closed the doors of Hellfire so you cannot make a mistake, "Which door is Paradise and which is door of Hellfire?" Hellfire is closed in *Ramaḍān,* as the Prophet ﷺ said:

إِذَا جَاءَ رَمَضَانُ فُتِّحَتْ أَبْوَابُ الْجَنَّةِ وَغُلِّقَتْ أَبْوَابُ النَّارِ وَصُفِّدَتَ الشَّيَاطِينُ

The doors of Heavens are opened and the doors of Hellfire are closed.

It means He is saying to us, "I am not letting you to go to *Jahannam,* I am closing that door, because it is *Ramaḍān* and you are fasting, you are obeying, you are trying to behave well, and you are saying '*Lā ilāha illa-Llāh,*' you are admitting Allāh's Oneness, that there is no Creator except Allāh ﷻ."

Wa sulsilati 'sh-shayāṭīn, Allāh's Prophet ﷺ is saying that Allāh orders the angels to chain all devils. Since there are no more devils and they are chained, since doors of *Jahannam* are closed, so what is our choice? Is there anything left? There is only the choice to enter the doors of Paradise to Allāh's Mercy! *Shukran, yā Rabbī, shukran lillāh!*

لَئِن شَكَرْتُمْ لَأَزِيدَنَّكُمْ

If you thank Me, I will give you more.
(Sūrat Ibrāhīm, 14:7)

لَا يُشْرِكُونَ بِي شَيْئًا

They do not associate anything with Me.[39]

---

[39] Sūrat an-Nūr, 24:55.

If you thank Allāh that He closed the doors of Hellfire and opened the doors of Paradise, He will give you more. So you see that door? If opened, it leads you to another door and so one door leads to another door and so in *Ramaḍān* you will be opening door behind door, behind door, and it never ends until the end of *Ramaḍān*. As we said before, every breath-in during *Ramaḍān*, Allāh will bring out from your breath-in or breath-out a smell better than musk and He increases our *ʿamal*. If you do one *ʿamal*, Allāh will reward you 10 or 700 times for every breath you have in *dunyā*, that you are breathing in or out. So Allāh is multiplying your rewards up to 700 levels. How many breaths are you doing each day? Too many, scientists count between 15,000 to 24,000, breaths in and breaths out. Allāh is rewarding and rewarding and rewarding!

How many hours are we fasting here? Seventeen. In equatorial countries, they fast from six to six, maximum from six to seven, so 12 hours. Here we are fasting 17-18 hours. Are you fasting more or not? (Yes.) Ok, are those who fast 12 hours going to get as much as those who fast 17 hours? It must be that a 17-hour fast is rewarded more than the 12 hour fast. Because you are fasting and breathing in and out, and on every breath-in and breath-out Allāh is rewarding because you are fasting. So it is better to fast more. There are some who fast 24 hours, they don't break fast. Do you fast 24 hours? He said, "No." There are some who do. One time I fasted 36 hours, from plane to plane to plane and still the sun was not coming down! And you have to wait at the airport and the sun is still up, up, up, it was 36 hours! Try it!

عَنْ أبِي سَعِيدٍ، عَن النَّبِيِّ صلى الله عليه وسلم قَالَ " مَنْ صَامَ يَوْمًا فِي سَبِيلِ اللَّهِ عَزَّ وَجَلَّ بَاعَدَ اللَّهُ وَجْهَهُ مِنْ جَهَنَّمَ سَبْعِينَ عَامًا " .

Whoever fasts one day in the cause of Allāh, the Mighty and Sublime, Allāh will separate his face from the Fire by (a distance of) seventy years.[40]

If you fast one day for Allāh's sake, for nothing else, it is not an obligation; for an obligation you will also be rewarded more, but if you voluntarily say, "I am going to fast that day for Allāh's sake..." *illā bāʿada'Llāhu bi dhālika 'l-yawm wajhahū ʿani 'n-nār*, that day Allāh will make

---

[40] *Sunan an-Nasāʾī.*

your face far away from Hellfire. That means no sins in that day will be written for you, Allāh will save you.

Prophet ﷺ said:

مَنْ صَامَ رَمَضَانَ إِيمَانًا وَاحْتِسَابًا غُفِرَ لَهُ مَا تَقَدَّمَ مِنْ ذَنْبِهِ

Whoever fasts during Ramaḍān with faith and seeking his reward
(from Allāh), all his past sins will be forgiven.[41]

"Whoever fasts Ramaḍān believing in Allāh ﷻ, Allāh will forgive him all his sins, meaning whatever he did the prior years Allāh will forgive." So that's why we have to pay attention in *Ramaḍān*, as Allāh said in Holy Qur'ān:

Allāh said about the people in *Ramaḍān*, they are dressed with the verse:

وَعِبَادُ الرَّحْمَنِ الَّذِينَ يَمْشُونَ عَلَى الْأَرْضِ هَوْنًا وَإِذَا خَاطَبَهُمُ الْجَاهِلُونَ قَالُوا سَلَامًا

The (true) servants of The Most Merciful are those who walk humbly
on the Earth and who, when the ignorant people behave
insolently towards them, say, "Peace be unto you."[42]

The servants are dressed with Allāh's Mercy, servants of the One Who is the Forgiver. It means that Allāh is putting you in the level of, "He will forgive you." How then do we have to behave? Allāh is describing the characteristics of those who are in *Ramaḍān*. He described them literally as, "Those who walk," but it means "those who behave with humility." It means they have no arrogance, no pride, no hatred to others; it means to be thankful, to connect with those who disconnected with you, to forgive those who oppressed you, to give to those who obstruct you, to be a person thinking, "This is what Allāh wants me to do, I have to do it."

Our problem is, we read the verses of Holy Qur'ān and read the *ḥadīth* but we don't focus on what we are reading or we don't act on what we are reading. Allāh is saying, *wa 'ibādu 'r-raḥmān alladhīna yamshūna 'ala 'l-arḍi hawnan*, "Those who themselves behave with humility, those who are humble." *Wa idhā khāṭabahumu 'l-jāhilūna qālū salāma*, "When some ignorant people speak with them they say, 'Peace be on you, we are not going to

---

[41] Bukhārī and Muslim.

[42] Sūrat al-Furqān, 25:63.

argue, may Allāh give you peace, may Allāh give us peace.'" *Wa idhā khāṭabahumu 'l-jāhilūna qālū salāma,* "When ignorant people speak with them," they say, "We are raising our hands, our ten fingers (in surrender)."

So we spoke last time about this is a way to enter into the most important part: *Ramaḍān* is to remember that there is a Creator, that there is an obligation we have to do for a Creator, for Allāh ﷻ. The one who is responsible for this *masjid* has to keep this *masjid* in order; you cannot look at the *masjid* and see something wrong and say, "O! Never mind." But there are honorable guests coming, so how do you have to keep the *masjid*? You have to keep it in good condition. Why didn't you keep it in good condition today? That means, "I am giving you *Ramaḍān,* you have to keep Me in your life," to keep *Ramaḍān* reminding you that you have to keep yourself in good condition in front of Allāh ﷻ!

So to keep yourself in good condition there are two ways. Either in order for Allāh to be happy with us, we have to eliminate *ash-shirk;* to enter Paradise you must not associate anything with Allāh ﷻ, He is the Creator and we are His Servants, and we explained that, and then you deserve Paradise. That's why, *wa sīq alladhīna 'ttaqaw,* "With *taqwā,* with sincerity."

وَسِيقَ الَّذِينَ اتَّقَوْا رَبَّهُمْ إِلَى الْجَنَّةِ زُمَرًا حَتَّى إِذَا جَاؤُوهَا وَفُتِحَتْ أَبْوَابُهَا وَقَالَ لَهُمْ خَزَنَتُهَا سَلَامٌ عَلَيْكُمْ طِبْتُمْ فَادْخُلُوهَا خَالِدِينَ

And those who feared their Lord will be driven to Paradise
in groups until, when they reach it while its gates have been opened
and its keepers say, "Peace be upon you! You have become pure,
so enter it to abide eternally therein."[43]

Fasting Cleans Bad Character

Ramaḍān is coming in two days or three days. Allāh is saying, "Those who have *taqwā,*" which means to be worshipping with sincerity, to be saying *"Lā ilāha illa-Llāh"* with sincerity, with purity, with love, with emotions to Allāh ﷻ, those people will bring them all the way to Paradise. So you want to go to Paradise you have to have *taqwā.* If you don't have *taqwā,* then you have the opposite of *taqwā, khubuth,* corrupted character. Anyone that has corrupted character has *khubuth,* then he can have corruption in what you

---

say, *fi 'l-aqwāl*, *fi 'l-ʿamal*, in what you act, *fi mā akal*, in what you eat and in what you drink. Allāh will take that *khubuth* and put it in Hellfire as that is the only way to clean it, only fire can clean it. So anyone who has *khubuth*, in Ramaḍān try to take it away from your life. That's why you always have to have your heart pure for Allāh ﷻ so that it doesn't go right and it doesn't go left! So keep your focus on Allāh, especially when you are praying as the Prophet ﷺ said:

إِنَّ اللَّهَ أَمَرَكُمْ بِالصَّلَاةِ فَإِذَا صَلَّيْتُمْ فَلَا تَلْتَفِتُوا ، فَإِنَّ اللَّهَ تَعَالَى يَنْصِبُ وَجْهَهُ لِوَجْهِ عَبْدِهِ فِي صَلَاتِهِ مَا لَمْ يَلْتَفِتْ

Verily Allāh has commanded prayer, so when a person is praying let him not look around, for surely Allāh turns His Face (mercy) towards His servant as long as he does not turn his face away.[44]

Prophet ﷺ said, "Allāh ordered us to pray." Why? One of the reasons is that, "When you are praying, *fa in ṣallaytū fa lā taltafitū*, don't let your eyes go right or left, but let your eyes remain only on where you are making *sajda*, because if you let your eyes go left or right Allāh is looking at you and it as if you are turning your face from Allāh right or left," and you are not focusing. That is why it is said:

الالتفات المنهي عنه في الصلاة قسمان: أحدهما: التفات القلب عن الله عز وجل إلى غير الله تعالى.

Turning your face from Allāh is of two branches: One is when you turn your heart from Allāh the Exalted and Glorious to other than Allāh.

You are between Allāh's Hands, you are praying and you turn your face right or left, looking with your eyes, and many people when they are praying are looking with their eyes right or left, which means, "...you are turning your face and your heart away from Allāh ﷻ."

الثاني: التفات البصر، وكلاهما منهي عنه

Secondly: "To look right or left with your eyes is prohibited and your prayer will be far from you," and it will be thrown in your face on the Day of Judgment.

---

[44] Abū Dāwūd.

O Muslims! This is also an introduction to come to what we will be discussing in *Ramaḍān*. We have to very careful where we are looking, how we are facing when praying. May Allāh forgive us. "We are opening in *Ramaḍān* doors after doors after doors." I was reading:

حم وَالْكِتَابِ الْمُبِينِ إِنَّا أَنزَلْنَاهُ فِي لَيْلَةٍ مُّبَارَكَةٍ إِنَّا كُنَّا مُنذِرِينَ فِيهَا يُفْرَقُ كُلُّ أَمْرٍ حَكِيمٍ أَمْرًا مِّنْ عِندِنَا إِنَّا كُنَّا مُرْسِلِينَ

Ḥā. Mīm. By the Book that makes things clear, We sent it down
during a blessed night for We (ever) wish to warn (against evil).
In the (night) is made distinct every affair of wisdom by Command
from Our Presence for We (ever) send (revelations).[45]

Most scholars say this night is 15th *Sha'bān*. Okay, this night is 15th of *Sha'bān*, but Allāh also said:

إِنَّا أَنزَلْنَاهُ فِي لَيْلَةِ الْقَدْرِ

We have indeed revealed this (Message) in the Night of Power.[46]

Allāh is saying, "We revealed the Holy Qur'ān in *Laylat al-Qadr*." So which one then? *Innā anzalnāhu fī laylatin mubārakatin innā kunnā mundhirīn,* "We have revealed the Holy Qur'ān in a blessed night," which is the 15th of *Sha'bān,* but then Allāh says in another verse, "We have revealed Holy Qur'ān on *Laylat al-Qadr.*" One night...we have to choose which night? And here Allāh is saying you cannot choose, "I have revealed the Holy Qur'ān to the Prophet ﷺ in 15th *Sha'bān,* on that night," and also, "I have revealed to Prophet the Holy Qur'ān on *Laylat al-Qadr,*" means Holy Qur'ān was revealed to the Prophet ﷺ two times.

One on the night of 15th *Sha'bān,* one on the night of *Laylat al-Qadr*. *Sha'bān,* as the Prophet ﷺ said:

رَجَبُ شَهْرُ اللَّهِ ، وَشَعْبَانُ شَهْرِي ، وَرَمَضَانُ شَهْرُ أُمَّتِي

Rajab is Allāh's month, Sha'bān is my month and
Ramaḍān is the month of my Ummah.[47]

---

[45] Sūrat ad-Dukhān, 44:1-5.

[46] Sūrat al-Qadr, 97:1.

[47] Abū'l-Fatḥ ibn Abī Fawāris in his *'Amalī* from al-Ḥasan.

Sha'bān is the month of Prophet ﷺ, "That month is my month," so Allāh revealed the Holy Qur'ān in that month according to the level of the Prophet ﷺ. *Ramaḍān* is the month of the *ummah*, *Laylat al-Qadr* is in that month which is for the whole *ummah*, Allāh revealed the Holy Qur'ān according to the level of the *ummah*. One according to the level of Prophet ﷺ; one according to the level the *ummah* can carry.

Sha'bān is before *Ramaḍān*, and that is why, as mentioned by *awlīyāullāh*, when it was revealed first in *Sha'bān* it was revealed from *al-'Alīm*, The Absolute Knower, to the Preserved Tablets and then it came out from the Preserved Tablets where it was hidden into *samā ad-dunyā*, the sky of the Earth, where Allāh "descends" on the 15th *Sha'bān* to see if anyone is seeking His favors and beseeching Him. And on that night, Allāh is giving. So the Holy Qur'ān with the secrets which Allāh wants Prophet ﷺ to know from its secrets was revealed in *Sha'bān* while those secrets that are for the *ummah* have been revealed in *Ramaḍān*.

This *Ramaḍān*, *awlīyāullāh* are expecting a lot of things coming up according to what has been revealed of Holy Qur'ān to the Prophet ﷺ, to his heart, and he informed *awlīyāullāh* and they are ready for many, many changes and events going to happen in the very near future. So prepare yourself to be honest in *Ramaḍān*, not to do anything Allāh doesn't like, to observe *Ramaḍān* correctly and *inshā'Allāh* things will be opened to your heart from Divine Knowledge and Heavenly Knowledge.

May Allāh forgive us and may Allāh bless us.

Wa min Allāhi 't-tawfīq, bi ḥurmati 'l-ḥabīb, bi ḥurmati 'l-Fātiḥah.
And with Allāh is success. For the sake of the Beloved, for his sake we recite the opening chapter of Holy Qur'ān.

The Greatest Favor Allāh Bestowed on Us

A'ūdhu billāhi min ash-Shaytāni 'r-rajīm. Bismillāhi' r-Rahmāni 'r-Rahīm.
Nawaytu 'l-arbā'īn, nawaytu 'l-'itikāf, nawaytu 'l-khalwah, nawaytu 'l-'uzlah,
nawaytu 'r-riyāda, nawaytu 's-sulūk, lillāhi Ta'alā fi hādha 'l-masjid.
Atī'ullāha wa atī'ū 'r-Rasūla wa ūli 'l-amri minkum. (4:59)

As Allāh ﷻ says in Holy Qur'ān, what is the biggest *ni'mat* that Allāh gave to us? People are wondering and thinking, what is that favor? Some people believe that there is a favor and for some people it doesn't even come to their mind that Allāh has favored them; they think that they have wealth because of their effort, but this wealth is going and ending by leaving it and dying. So what kind of wealth are you speaking about?

There is one wealth that Allāh gave to humanity, which there is no wealth above it that can be described, *al-ni'mata 'l-'Azīm*, the Greatest Favor that Allāh gave and it is through the *du'ā* of Sayyīdinā Ibrāhīm ﷺ when he looked in the future and saw what is going to happen, he asked Allāh ﷻ for the big favor that He will give humanity. And in *Sūrat al-Baqarah*, verse 129, Allāh ﷻ said:

رَبَّنَا وَابْعَثْ فِيهِمْ رَسُولاً مِّنْهُمْ يَتْلُو عَلَيْهِمْ آيَاتِكَ وَيُعَلِّمُهُمُ الْكِتَابَ وَالْحِكْمَةَ وَيُزَكِّيهِمْ إِنَّكَ أَنتَ الْعَزِيزُ الْحَكِيمُ

Our Lord! And send among them a messenger from themselves who will recite to them Your verses and teach them the Book and wisdom and purify them. Indeed, You are the Exalted in Might, the Wise.[48]

That is the greatest *ni'mat* that Allāh ﷻ has sent to us through the *barakah* of the *du'ā* of Sayyīdinā Ibrāhīm ﷺ, where he asked, "O Allāh, send to them a messenger from among themselves, who will show them Your Signs, *ayātika*, and he will recite it for them and *yu'allimahumu 'l-Kitāb*, he will teach them about the Book." So Sayyīdinā Ibrāhīm ﷺ knows about the Holy Qur'ān, *wa yu'allimahumu 'l-Kitāb*, "Teach them the Book and teach them the Holy Precious Words of Yours that are not *makhlūq*, not created, Your Ancient Words, *Kalāmullāh al-Qadīm*. So send them a messenger from themselves to show them Your Signs." Which Signs? He will tell them about

---

[48] Sūrat al-Baqarah, 2:129.

Your Signs. What are Allāh's Signs? If we want to take it in *dunyā*, Allāh ﷻ said:

لخَلْقُ السَّمَاوَاتِ وَالأَرْضِ أَكْبَرُ مِنْ خَلْقِ النَّاسِ

The creation of Heavens and Earth is indeed greater
than the creation of Mankind.[49]

"The creation of Heavens and Earth is more difficult than creation of human beings." We say human beings are the most complicated creature and Allāh says, "Yes, true, but the creation of Heaven and Earth is more great among Allāh's Signs." That means when we look to the stars, our eyes or our vision when we look to the stars goes back unable; you look down because you are unable to see them because you are unable to see what is there. With all of today's advanced technology we are unable to know what is there.

ثُمَّ ارْجِعِ الْبَصَرَ كَرَّتَيْن يَنقَلِبْ إِلَيْكَ الْبَصَرُ خَاسِئاً وَهُوَ حَسِيرٌ

Thy sight will return unto thee weakened and made dim.[50]

It means "you look then your sight will come down, unable to understand anything of these galaxies, stars and universes." Allāh sent Prophet ﷺ to recite Your Verses and Your Signs:

سَنُرِيهِمْ آيَاتِنَا فِي الْآفَاق وَفِي أَنفُسِهِمْ حَتَّى يَتَبَيَّنَ لَهُمْ أَنَّهُ الْحَقُّ

Soon will We show them our Signs in the (furthest) regions
(of the Earth) and in their own souls until it becomes
manifest to them that this is the Truth.[51]

"We are going to show them our Signs on the horizon," and today there are too many scientific signs that people find in the Holy Qur'ān. "Horizon" means in the future, as before they could not understand it.

سَنُرِيهِمْ آيَاتِنَا فِي الْآفَاق وَفِي أَنفُسِهِمْ

We are going to show them Our Signs in the horizons and in themselves.[52]

---

[49] Sūrah Ghāfir, 40:57.

[50] Sūrat al-Mulk, 67:4.

[51] Sūrah Fuṣṣilat, 41:53.

[52] Sūrah Fuṣṣilat, 41:53.

40

And today there are too many signs they are finding in science that they did not understand it before, but today they understand. Today you say an airplane carrying 300 passengers you believe it, but if you said that 300 years ago, something like a bird carrying 300 passengers, would you have believed? No, you wouldn't believe it. So the Prophet ﷺ gave only the knowledge of Sharīʿah and left the sciences for the future. So Sayyīdinā Ibrāhīm ﷺ is asking, "O Allāh, send them a messenger from within themselves!" Look how much Sayyīdina Ibrāhīm ﷺ loved *Ummat an-Nabī* ﷺ, the nation of *mu'mins*, Believers, to send from within themselves a messenger to teach them signs and sciences, *yatlū ʿalayhim ayātika wa yuʿallimahumu 'l-kitāb*. He put "teach them the sciences" on one side and "teach them the Book" on the other side. That means the sciences and Signs, *ayātillāh* are in the Book! When He says, *wa yuʿallimahumu 'l-kitāb*, it means "teach everyone the Holy Qur'ān." Did you understand *yuʿallimahum*, "in the future" he will teach them the Holy Qur'ān.

That means in reality, in the interpretational meaning of the verse, that the Prophet ﷺ is taking the responsibility of teaching every single person one by one the knowledge of the Book. He didn't say "to teach the Book," but rather "will teach the Book," emphasizing that the Prophet ﷺ will teach the Holy Qur'ān. So he took on his shoulders to teach the whole *ummah* the Holy Qur'ān, so that is why Allāh ﷻ said:

وَاعْلَمُوا أَنَّ فِيكُمْ رَسُولَ اللَّهِ

And know Allāh's Messenger is in you.[53]

You must know that the Prophet ﷺ is among you. That is why when he is with you and in you, he is teaching everyone the Holy Qur'ān while we are unaware. The body doesn't know, but the heart knows. So on Judgment Day, we will be coming and he was teaching us the Holy Qur'ān and we come knowing the Holy Qur'ān, even though you didn't learn when young. And if you don't learn Wisdom you cannot understand the Book, as in, "Teach them Your Book and Wisdom." *Wa 'l-ḥikmat*, then He teaches Wisdom, by the *duʿā* of Sayyīdina Ibrāhīm ﷺ, *yatlū ʿalayhim āyātika wa yuʿallimuhumu 'l-kitāba wa 'l-ḥikmata*, he teaches them Allāh's Signs, then the Book and the Wisdom.

---

[53] Sūrat al-Ḥujurāt, 49:7.

Sayyīdinā ʿAlī ﷺ said, "All Islam is built on one point; if you don't understand that point you cannot benefit in anything." The *Ṣaḥābah* ﷺ said, "Yā ʿAlī, what is that point?" He said, "The head of everything, every *ʿamal* you do, every intention you have, has to be based on one point, not two." And they said, "What is it? And he said, "That is Wisdom."

رَأسُ الْحِكْمَةِ مَخَافَةُ اللهِ

The head of Wisdom is fear of Allāh.

Fear that He will punish you if you disobey and also fear of being far from Him, that you will be far from the Divine Presence even though your love for Him might be more and more. So after he teaches the Signs that are in the universe and after he teaches them the Book then the Wisdom, then he purifies them, so anyone who wants to be purified must look into this verse very carefully to be on the track, *Ṣirāṭ al-Mustaqīm*. This verse shows us different tracks, different instruments, different machines, different understandings that are there to learn from Prophet ﷺ and be purified:

1. the Signs that Allāh wants us to know;
2. the Book;
3. the Wisdom;
4. to be purified.

These are the four principles that Sayyīdinā Ibrāhīm ﷺ asked Allāh to give to *Ummat an-Nabī* ﷺ and to humanity. And Allāh ﷺ said:

كَمَا أَرْسَلْنَا فِيكُمْ رَسُولاً مِّنكُمْ يَتْلُو عَلَيْكُمْ آيَاتِنَا وَيُزَكِّيكُمْ وَيُعَلِّمُكُمُ الْكِتَابَ
وَالْحِكْمَةَ وَيُعَلِّمُكُم مَّا لَمْ تَكُونُوا تَعْلَمُونَ

Just as We have sent among you a messenger from yourselves
reciting to you Our verses, and purifying you and teaching you
the Book and wisdom, and teaching you that which you did not know. [54]

Allāh is confirming another time, "We have sent from within you, from among you, from you, a messenger to teach you." First the *duʿā* of Sayyīdinā Ibrāhīm ﷺ came into reality in verse 151, in the time of the Prophet ﷺ as, "I sent a messenger," Allāh is saying, "from within you telling you about His Signs and he purifies you and teaches you the Book," which Sayyīdinā Ibrāhīm ﷺ asked and Allāh answered! Allāh ﷺ answers everyone:

---

[54] Sūrat al-Baqarah, 2:151.

اذْعُونِي أَسْتَجِبْ لَكُمْ

Call on Me, I will answer you.[55]

"Ask and I respond!" So He responded to the *du'ā* of Sayyīdinā Ibrāhīm ﷺ to send from themselves a messenger to teach them Allāh's Signs and recite His Book and teach them His Book and the Wisdom and to teach them what they don't know. Allāh mentioned 1400 years ago that He will teach them what they don't know, so technology and sciences are coming from the secret of that *āyah*, "He will teach you what you never knew about," and that is why they are discovering one after one different discoveries. From that one verse it is enough for *awliyāullāh* to pull the sciences from this verse, depending on each one's power. So after this, after teaching you Holy Qur'ān and Wisdom and teaching you what you never knew, what then you have to do? To say "Thank You," *an nashkurallāh.* What Did Allāh ﷻ say after this verse?

فَاذْكُرُونِي أَذْكُرْكُمْ وَاشْكُرُوا لِي وَلَا تَكْفُرُون

*Remember Me, I will remember you. Give thanks to Me
and do not be ungrateful towards Me.*[56]

"Remember Me and I remember you and love you, and thank Me, then you go to Paradise. Only remember Me, I don't want more than that: love Me, I love you; pray for Me and you go to Paradise." After all that He gave us only, "Remember Me! I don't want more than that." So one Bedouin came to the Prophet ﷺ and said, "Islam's Sharī'ah is too much for me. Give me something that is easy for me." And the Prophet ﷺ said, *ij'al lisānak raṭban bi-dhikrullāh,* "Keep your tongue moist with *dhikrullāh.*" As Allāh said, "Keep remembering Me on your tongue," as in the verse, *fadhkurūnī adhkurkum, w 'ashkurū lī wa lā takfurūn,* "Keep My Name on your tongue, keep asking Me, mentioning Me; I will give you what you want, but don't run away from Me." But what are we doing? We are running away from Allāh ﷻ. In another verse:

لَقَدْ مَنَّ اللهُ عَلَى الْمُؤْمِنِينَ إِذْ بَعَثَ فِيهِمْ رَسُولًا مِّنْ أَنفُسِهِمْ يَتْلُو
عَلَيْهِمْ آيَاتِهِ وَيُزَكِّيهِمْ وَيُعَلِّمُهُمُ الْكِتَابَ وَالْحِكْمَة وَإِن كَانُوا مِن قَبْلُ لَفِي ضَلَالٍ مُّبِين

---

*Certainly did Allāh confer (great) favor upon the Believers
when He sent among them a messenger from themselves,
reciting to them His verses and purifying them and teaching them
the Book and wisdom, although they had been before in manifest error.*[57]

Another time reminding us, first with Sayyīdinā Ibrāhīm's *du'ā* and then, "Allāh favored *mu'mins*, He sent a messenger from among themselves," then He sent a messenger from among themselves, showing them His Signs and teaching them the Book, purifying them and teaching them the *ḥikmah*, Wisdom and teaching them the *ḥikmah* even though they were ignorant before. He mentioned it another time in order to keep in our head to thank Allāh every day at least 100 times (by saying) "*shukran lillāh!*"

What did the Prophet ﷺ say?

إِنَّ فِي أَصْلَابِ أَصْلَابِ أَصْلَابِ رِجَالٍ مِنْ أَصْحَابِي رِجَالًا وَنِسَاءً مِنْ أُمَّتِي يَدْخُلُونَ الْجَنَّةَ بِغَيْرِ حِسَابٍ

*Verily in the loins of the loins of the loins of men from
my Companions are men and women of my Nation who
will enter Paradise with no account.*[58]

Aṣlābī means 'from within me'. "There are people going to come and from them more people are going to come and then also more people are going to come, and in them more people are going to come until the Day of Judgment, men and women from my *Ṣaḥābah*, from me and from them, men and women and they are going to enter Paradise with no account." What did he mean? He meant anyone who entered Islam *man kāna ila yawm al-qīyamah*, are going to enter Paradise with no account, men and women, as long as they are Muslim. So let us say, *Ash-hadu an lā ilāha illa-Llāh wa Ash-hadu anna Muḥammadan Rasūlullāh!*

So what are the most important things that we have to do? *Fadhkurūnī adhkurukum w 'ashkuru lī wa lā takfurūn*, most important is, "Remember Me and then thank Me," (by saying) "*Shukran, yā* Allāh!" "Mention Me and thank Me." The meaning of "*shukran, yā* Allāh," yes, we say "Thank You for Your favors," but what are the favors we have to take and what are the things we have to stop doing in order for Allāh to be happy with us? *An-*

---

[57] Sūrat Āli-'Imrān, 3:164.

[58] aṭ-Ṭabarānī.

nahīyy 'ani 'sh-shirk, to leave *shirk*, to tell ourselves and our ego not to associate itself with Allāh, not to let our ego associate anyone with Allāh. We all say *"Lā ilāha illa-Llāh"* but we still associate our ego with Allāh as when we do something good we say, "Oh, I did something good!" but whatever good you did is from Allāh ﷻ.

The Prophet ﷺ said:

أخوف ما أخاف على أمتي الشرك الخفي

What I fear most for my ummah is hidden shirk.

"The thing I fear most for my Nation is the hidden *shirk*." (We say), "I did this. I made this book. I did this artwork." No, Allāh inspired you to do that! So eliminate this from yourself. Today we teach our children pride and arrogance, saying, "Oh my son, be proud of yourself!" What to be proud of? Even *awlīyāullāh* who spent all their life in helping people and training them and building what they call today 'community centers', they were doing that hundreds of years ago, building *ribāṭs* and *zāwiyas* and feeding the poor. They were doing that and much better than what they are doing today, teaching what? Ping pong and chess and basketball. Is that what a community center is for or it is to polish our behavior? We have to eliminate the thinking that, "I did this, I did that." No, you didn't do anything! *Awlīyāullāh* do all things for humanity and the Prophet ﷺ did everything for humanity and used to say:

اللَّهُمَّ لَا تَكِلْنِي إِلَى نَفْسِي طَرْفَة عَيْنٍ وَلَا أَقَلَّ مِنْ ذَلِكَ

O Allāh! Don't leave me to my ego for the blink of an eye or less.

This the Messenger of Allāh ﷺ and still we say, "We did this and we did that." And the second (most important thing we have to do) is *al-amru bi 'l-iḥsān*, to call for goodness. What is *iḥsān*? To call for goodness, good manners, justice, a word of truth and to help those who need help, whatever help is needed and to prohibit wasting of favors. What is wasting of favors? Allāh favored you with wealth and you go and spend on something wrong instead of giving it to needy people. He gave you knowledge so go and teach it, He gave you Wisdom, go and teach it. Be nice in your talk, speak nicely, diplomatically, make people to be happy. Don't eat the money of orphans, help the orphans, build them shelters and give them money, make them happy.

I am sorry to say that now most of eastern countries are following the western countries, the father and mother making their children orphans while they are still alive, by what? By divorce. You need to think. A wife divorces the husband and the husband divorces the wife, they cannot stay together and after ten years they need a change. Now Eastern culture is following Western culture. What happens to their children? They become orphans, even though their parents are alive, the children don't know what to do. Even when the child becomes 18 years old, there is still deficiency in the mind, a circuit breaker that when two wires short the breaker shuts down immediately. When the children see the parents divorced, then their circuits shut down and they cannot understand any more. People come and they are proud, they come on TV saying, "I don't like my husband and I go with someone else!" They don't care. Where is the respect of 15, 16 years ago and the children everywhere become orphans? You have to be very careful not to make our children orphans while their parents are still alive, to lose their parents because they want to fight.

May Allāh forgive us and may Allāh bless us.

Wa min Allāhi 't-tawfiq, bi ḥurmati 'l-ḥabīb, bi ḥurmati 'l-Fātiḥah.
And with Allāh is success. For the sake of the Beloved, for his sake we recite the opening chapter of Holy Qur'ān.

Prophet ﷺ Will Teach Them the Holy Book and the Wisdom

A'ūdhu billāhi min ash-Shayṭāni 'r-rajīm. Bismillāhi' r-Raḥmāni 'r-Raḥīm.
Nawaytu 'l-arbā'īn, nawaytu 'l-'itikāf, nawaytu 'l-khalwah, nawaytu 'l-'uzlah,
nawaytu 'r-riyāḍa, nawaytu 's-sulūk, lillāhi Ta'alā fī hādha 'l-masjid.
Atī'ullāha wa atī'ū 'r-Rasūla wa ūli 'l-amri minkum. (4:59)

Madad yā Sayyidī, Sulṭān al-Awlīyā, yā Rasūlullāh, yā Raḥmatan li 'l-'Alamīn.
Yesterday we mentioned the du'ā of Sayyīdina Ibrāhīm ﷺ:

رَبَّنَا وَابْعَثْ فِيهِمْ رَسُولاً مِّنْهُمْ يَتْلُو عَلَيْهِمْ آيَاتِكَ وَيُعَلِّمُهُمُ الْكِتَابَ وَالْحِكْمَة
وَيُزَكِّيهِمْ إِنَّكَ أنتَ الْعَزِيزُ الحَكِيمُ

Our Lord! And send among them a messenger from themselves who will recite to
them Your verses and teach them the Book and wisdom and purify them. Indeed,
You are the Exalted in Might, the Wise.[59]

We explained that in many places in Holy Qur'ān, Allāh says He "sent from within Us a messenger that's taking care of everyone, *wa yuzakkīhim wa yu'allimukumu 'l-kitāba*, who will teach them Holy Qur'ān and purify them."

When someone says, "I take responsibility to teach you," it means, "I have to teach you and have to make you complete the Holy Qur'ān and memorize the Holy Qur'ān, and make you understand as much as you can from the level of the Holy Qur'ān." All this the Prophet ﷺ took on his shoulders after the *du'ā* of Sayyīdina Ibrāhīm ﷺ where he said in *Sūrat al-Baqarah* (2: 129), *wa yu'allimahumu 'l-kitāb*, "to teach them Holy Qur'ān," as we mentioned, besides what he said regarding, "to purify them, *yuzakkīhim.*" That means the whole meaning of spirituality entered in that word in Holy Qur'ān! If they ask you, "Where is spirituality in Holy Qur'ān?" say, "Allāh said in Holy Qur'ān from the *du'ā* of Sayyīdina Ibrāhīm, '*wa yuzakkīhim,*' to purify them."

"*Wa yuzakkīhim*" means all knowledge of good manners they need in their life from Holy Qur'ān, the Prophet ﷺ is responsible for carrying that message, to make sure everyone is purified and polished and that

---

[59] Sūrat al-Baqarah, 2:129.

everyone's four enemies are not running after him. These four are *dunyā*, the world; *nafs*, the self; *hawwā*, desire and Shayṭān, which all of you know. So when he said *"yuzakkīhim,"* it means "he must purify the self." That means when you are called on Judgment Day, the Prophet ﷺ will not take you without purifying you of all sins and you will be as if newly born, *wa yuzakkīhim. Wa yuʿallimahumu 'l-kitāba wa'l-ḥikmata wa yuzakkīhim,* "Teach them the Holy Book with all its meanings."

Wa 'l-ḥikmata, it is not enough to memorize the Holy Qur'ān. There are many *imams* who memorize the Holy Qur'ān, but they don't act on what the Holy Qur'ān is asking. There are many non-Muslims today who read the Holy Qur'ān and study it very well and pose questions to Muslims, but they don't act on it, so what is the benefit? It is to act on the issue! To say, *"Lā ilāha illa-Llāh"* is to enter Paradise, but do you say, *"Lā ilāha illa-Llāh"* and stop? No, you must say, *"Lā ilāha illa-Llāh Muḥammadun Rasūlullāh."* Like the Christians say, *"Lā ilāha illa-Llāh"* and stop, but they say that Sayyīdinā ʿĪsā ﷺ is the Son of God, *astaghfirullāh,* and that sentence is not acceptable. So what they say of *"Lā ilāha illa-Llāh"* is not acceptable from them. Also, the Jews say, *"Lā ilāha illa-Llāh,"* but some of them add after it, *uzayr ibnu'Llāh,* Uzayr is the son of Allāh, so that part is not accepted. So the whole thing is not accepted.

So *ʿulamā* and *imams* must not only teach Holy Qur'ān, but they need *ḥikmah,* wisdom, with it. Without wisdom you might not understand the Holy Qur'ān or you might understand the literal meaning, but not understand the meaning inside, which is what Allāh wants to describe, human beings and His Messenger, in a very eloquent way.

Here, Allāh is describing this *dunyā* and whatever appeared in it as a tree, *ka-shajaratin ṭayyibatin:*

أَلَمْ تَرَ كَيْفَ ضَرَبَ اللهُ مَثَلاً كَلِمَةً طَيِّبَةً كَشَجَرَةٍ طَيِّبَةٍ أَصْلُهَا ثَابِتٌ وَفَرْعُهَا فِي السَّمَاء تُؤْتِي أُكُلَهَا كُلَّ حِينٍ بِإِذْنِ رَبِّهَا وَيَضْرِبُ اللهُ الأَمْثَالَ لِلنَّاسِ لَعَلَّهُمْ يَتَذَكَّرُونَ

Have you not considered how Allāh presents an example,
(making) a good word like a good tree, whose root is firmly fixed
and its branches (high) in the sky? It produces its fruit all the time,

by permission of its Lord. And Allāh presents examples for
the people that perhaps they will be reminded.[60]

Allāh ﷻ is giving an example in Holy Qur'ān about who we are. He mentioned *"shajarah"* here:

اللَّهُ نُورُ السَّمَاوَاتِ وَالْأَرْضِ مَثَلُ نُورِهِ كَمِشْكَاةٍ فِيهَا مِصْبَاحٌ الْمِصْبَاحُ فِي زُجَاجَةٍ الزُّجَاجَةُ كَأَنَّهَا كَوْكَبٌ دُرِّيٌّ يُوقَدُ مِن شَجَرَةٍ مُّبَارَكَةٍ زَيْتُونِةٍ لَّا شَرْقِيَّةٍ وَلَا غَرْبِيَّةٍ يَكَادُ زَيْتُهَا يُضِيءُ وَلَوْ لَمْ تَمْسَسْهُ نَارٌ نُّورٌ عَلَى نُورٍ يَهْدِي اللَّهُ لِنُورِهِ مَن يَشَاء وَيَضْرِبُ اللَّهُ الْأَمْثَالَ لِلنَّاسِ وَاللَّهُ بِكُلِّ شَيْءٍ عَلِيمٌ

Allāh is the Light of the Heavens and Earth. The parable of His Light is as if there were a niche and within it a lamp: the lamp is in a glass, the glass like a Brilliant Star lit from a blessed tree, an olive tree that is neither of the East nor of the West, the oil of which is so bright that it would certainly give light of itself. Light upon Light! Allāh guides whom He wills to His Light: Allāh sets forth Parables for men: and Allāh knows all things.[61]

He ﷻ is describing the Light of the Prophet ﷺ, where the example of Allāh's Light is the Light of the Prophet ﷺ which has been created first before any Creation, and He described the Lamp, which to ignite, *yuqadu min shajaratin mubārakatin zaytūnatin lā sharqīyyatin wa lā gharbīyyatin*, it is from a tree not from East, not from West. Allāh sent a message 1400 years ago that "I can make a lamp shine without your technology. I can make a lamp," because the Prophet ﷺ is mentioned as *mathala nūrihi kamishkātin fīhā miṣbāḥ*, "the example of His Light is like a bundle in which is a lamp." That lamp is described as *al-miṣbāḥu fī zujāja*, "the lamp is inside of a crystal," *yuqadu min shajaratin zaytūnatin*, "Nūr of that light has suddenly been ignited from a tree, *lā sharqīyyatin wa lā gharbīyyatin*, not of East, not of West."

So Allāh doesn't need East and doesn't need West, the East who think they know everything and the West who think they know everything! He doesn't need them and everything in-between. So Allāh is describing that tree in *Sūrat Ibrāhīm* as 'ṭayyiba,' sweet, not sweet as in (dessert) sweets, but "full of goodness and love and emotions and good manners."

---

[60] Sūrat Ibrāhīm, 14:24-25.

[61] Sūrat an-Nūr, 24:35.

49

The Tree with Many Branches

That is the *shajarah* that has many branches, *aṣluhā thābitun wa far'uhā fi 's-samā*, the root of it is standing up and *wa far'uhā*, its branches are all going up, they don't go down.

Every tree has a life and everyone cutting the tree is cutting the life of the tree. So that tree has life in it, so the branches are coming out. Allāh is describing, after He described in many places, "I am sending a messenger from within you…and that messenger is like a tree: its roots are firm, strong and you see the branches are up, reaching to Heavens, asking Allāh ﷻ and making *tasbīḥ*." So you see branches up and branches down, and sometimes you see a branch half dead and you trim or cut it. So He wants to mention, *aṣluhā thābitun wa far'uhā fi 's-samā*, "The trunk is firm and good and the branches are going up." It means the trunk is Sayyīdinā Muḥammad ﷺ, the reality of the life of the tree is through the trunk, with all its roots going everywhere, and the branches are us, the human beings.

That is why we mentioned the *ḥadīth*:

إِنَّ فِي أَصْلَابِ أَصْلَابِ أَصْلَابِ رِجَالٍ مِنْ أَصْحَابِي رِجَالًا وَنِسَاءً مِنْ أُمَّتِي يَدْخُلُونَ الْجَنَّةَ بِغَيْرِ حِسَابٍ ثُمَّ قَرَأَ : وَآخَرِينَ مِنْهُمْ لَمَّا يَلْحَقُوا بِهِمْ .

Verily, in the loins of the loins of the loins of men
from my Companions are men and women of my Nation
who will enter Paradise with no account.[62]

"Inside the body, inside more of the body, inside more of the body…" there is the sperm, and that sperm and the egg are the reality of the connection together, in order to bring a healthy child. So what He is saying is, "From the womb of the womb of the womb of mothers there come men and women, *yadkhulūna al-jannata bi ghayri ḥisāb*, who enter Paradise with no account." That is the meaning of "*shajaratin ṭayyibatin aṣluhā thābitun wa far'uhā fi 's-samā tu'tī ukulahā kulla ḥīn*," a firm trunk with many branches, and you pick whatever branch you want and take the fruit of what you like. He said, *tu'tī ukulahā kulla ḥīn*, "In every time, every moment, it gives its fruit to those who want to carry." If you want to carry, then follow Sayyīdinā Muḥammad ﷺ!

---

[62] aṭ-Ṭabarānī.

قُلْ إِن كُنتُمْ تُحِبُّونَ اللَّهَ فَاتَّبِعُونِي يُحْبِبْكُمُ اللَّهُ وَيَغْفِرْ لَكُمْ ذُنُوبَكُمْ وَاللَّهُ غَفُورٌ رَّحِيمٌ

Say (O Muḥammad), "If you (really) love Allāh,
then follow me! Allāh will love you."[63]

Follow Sayyīdinā Muḥammad ﷺ and Allāh will love you! So that is the branch and that is the tree. When He described it as a trunk with all these branches on the trunk, this verse of Holy Qur'ān came to explain the *niʿmat* that is sent by Allāh from one generation to another generation and in every century people get the benefit from it, and it never stops until the Day of Judgment.

So, like Sayyīdinā Luqmān ؏, what did Allāh say about him in Holy Qur'ān in *Sūrat Luqmān*?

وَلَقَدْ آتَيْنَا لُقْمَانَ الْحِكْمَةَ أَنِ اشْكُرْ لِلَّهِ وَمَن يَشْكُرْ
فَإِنَّمَا يَشْكُرُ لِنَفْسِهِ وَمَن كَفَرَ فَإِنَّ اللَّهَ غَنِيٌّ حَمِيدٌ

And indeed We granted this wisdom to Luqmān, "Be grateful to Allāh."
And he who is grateful (to Him) is but grateful for the good of his own self,
whereas he who chooses to be ungrateful (ought to know that)
verily, Allāh is Self-Sufficient, Ever to be Praised![64]

In *Sūrah Luqmān*, Allāh said to Luqmān ؏ one thing and from that one thing many come under it. He said to him, "Yā Luqmān! We gave you wisdom," finished! If Allāh gave wisdom to anyone no need for more. *Awlīyāullāh* are struggling to get wisdom; if you get wisdom you get everything. *Wa laqad ātaynā Luqmāna al-ḥikmata*, "We gave him wisdom," to do what? *Ani 'shukr*, to praise Allāh and to thank Him, that's it! *Shukr* is from good manners, *akhlāqan ṭayyiba*. You can pray and you don't make *shukr*, but *shukr* is from the good manners, good characters. You pray and you say, "Alḥamdulillāh, yā Rabbī!"

One time the Prophet ﷺ was in a sad position from too many overwhelming problems and he said to Sayyīdinā Bilāl ؓ, *ariḥnā yā Bilāl*, "Relieve us, O Bilāl! Relieve us from what we are in." How? It means with *ṣalāt*, as the Prophet ﷺ said, "Take us into relief after these difficulties," and to take him where? To take him to pray. It means, "Call *adhān*." If you call

---

[63] Sūrat Āli-ʿImrān, 3:31.

[64] Sūrah Luqmān, 31:12.

adhān when you are unhappy or asking for something or you are sad, call *adhān* and pray and that difficulty will go away. When you are asking for something, immediately make *wuḍū* and pray and you will feel more at ease.

So Allāh ﷻ called Luqmān ؑ and told him, "I gave you wisdom to thank Me." So whatever you have acquired in this *dunyā* or you breathe in and out, you have to thank Allāh for it! Allāh gave you two ears and if someone took your ears what will you say? You would look at someone with ears and you have no ears. So *ḥikmah* teaches you to have ears, because with no ears you are deaf. Some people are blind and you are not blind, so what you have to say? "*Shukran, yā Allāh.*" Go to hospital and see all kinds of patients, and what do we have to say? "*Shukran, yā Allāh.*" So that is *ḥikmah*: you are eating and drinking and saying, "*Shukran, yā* Allāh!" That is why it is recommended to make *duʿā* before and after eating and drinking.

He said, *ani 'shukr lillāhi*, "Thank Allāh!" *Wa man yashkur fa-innamā yashkuru li-nafsihi.* Look how great Allāh is and generous! He said, *wa man yashkur*, "If you thank Me, it is not really for Me, it is for you." *Fa-innamā yashkuru li-nafsihi*, "He is thanking Me but in reality it is for him, because he is going to say, '*Shukran, yā* Allāh,' when he sees the others going for punishment." Like what we said, you have ears and they don't, so you say, "*Shukran yā* Allāh!" So the benefit of the *shukr* is not for Allāh, He doesn't need it, but you have to do it in order that you will be rewarded for it, *fa-innamā yashkuru li-nafsihi*, as if you are thanking for your own benefit.

وَاشْكُرُوا لِي وَلَا تَكْفُرُونَ

Give thanks to Me and do not be ungrateful towards Me.[65]

"Make *shukr* for Me and *lā takfurūn*." "*Lā takfurūn*" here is not in the meaning of real *kufr*, but it means, "Don't deny My favors." *Wa man kafara fa-inna'Llāha Ghaniyyun Ḥamīd.* "Whoever denies Allāh's Favors, He ﷻ is not interested as He is the Rich One."

There is no benefit for Him if you thank or not as it is for you. Also from *ḥikmah* is to run away from Shayṭān. Don't let Shayṭān to catch you, because if he catches you it's like cancer. If Shayṭān catches us we ask Allāh

---

[65] Sūrat al-Baqarah, 2:152.

to send His Mercy on us, because if Shayṭān catches us we are lost, as Allāh said in the Holy Qur'ān:

الشَّيْطَانُ يَعِدُكُمُ الْفَقْرَ وَيَأْمُرُكُم بِالْفَحْشَاء وَاللهُ يَعِدُكُم مَّغْفِرَةً مِّنْهُ وَفَضْلاً وَاللهُ وَاسِعٌ عَلِيمٌ

Satan threatens you with poverty and orders you to immorality,
while Allāh promises you forgiveness from Him and bounty.
And Allāh is all-Encompassing and Knowing.[66]

Shayṭān promises you and promises you, but then pulls the carpet from under you. It means he is *yaʻidukumu 'l-faqra*, he promises you to make you bankrupted, to make you in poverty or "*pauvre*" in French, it is easy. He makes you have no wealth as the Prophet ﷺ said to Ṣaḥābah ﷺ, "*Man il-muflis*? Who is the bankrupted?" Shayṭān is giving you bankruptcy, bankruptcy in everything to prevent you going to Paradise. He plays with you in *dunyā* to cut you from *Ākhirah, wa yāmurukum bi 'l-faḥshāi*, and he orders you to be corrupted, to do everything that is not accepted. And Allāh said, *w'Allāhu yaʻidukum maghfiratan minhu*, "And Allāh promises you forgiveness." Look at Allāh's Greatness! He didn't say, "Because you follow Shayṭān I am punishing you," but He said, "I am forgiving you, but come to Me! I'm promising you forgiveness, but come, don't run away! Break your relationship with Shayṭān and I will give you. Don't depend on him." *W'Allāhu Wāsiʻun ʻAlīm*, Allāh is the Greatest with a Vast Kingdom that never ends from pre-Eternal to post-Eternal!

And He said, "The example of the one who spends his money in Allāh's Way is like an ear of corn which Allāh increases as much as He likes."

مَّثَلُ الَّذِينَ يُنفِقُونَ أَمْوَالَهُمْ فِي سَبِيلِ اللهِ كَمَثَلِ حَبَّةٍ أَنبَتَتْ سَبْعَ سَنَابِلَ فِي كُلِّ سُنبُلَةٍ مِّئَةُ حَبَّةٍ وَاللهُ يُضَاعِفُ لِمَن يَشَاء وَاللهُ وَاسِعٌ عَلِيمٌ

The likeness of those who spend their wealth in Allāh's Way
is as the likeness of a grain which grows seven ears, in
every ear a hundred grains. Allāh gives increase manifold
to whom He will for Allāh is All-Embracing, All-Knowing.[67]

---

[66] Sūrat al-Baqarah, 2:268.

[67] Sūrat al-Baqarah, 2:261.

When you thank Allāh He will give you so much, but Shayṭān promises you and gives you nothing, he only takes from you. In that *āyah*, Allāh describes those who spend their wealth, their money in the way of Allāh as like a seed which gives a plant with seven shoots and in every shoot 100 grains. Shayṭān does not give you anything! Today people are so much in bad desires and they want to have everything in order to enjoy it. We are not saying it is easy to stop that, but repent. Allāh promises to give to you from His Vast Kingdom, from every good *'amal* you do, 700. Like for example, *astaghfirullāh*, we cannot give that as an example, but like someone who has 100 coins and Allāh says, "Thank Me and I will give you 70,000 coins by saying one time, '*Shukran lillāh*.'" Saying "*Shukran lillāh*" one time is enough. From 100-700 times or up to no end and no beginning! *Allāhu Akbar*! Because Allāh wants His servants to come to His Door.

May Allāh ﷻ forgive us and give us wisdom. Next time we will mention some of the wisdoms that happened to the *Salaf*, previous people, in their lives, some of their stories in order to understand more.

May Allāh forgive us and may Allāh bless us.

Wa min Allāhi 't-tawfīq, bi ḥurmati 'l-ḥabīb, bi ḥurmati 'l-Fātiḥah.
And with Allāh is success. For the sake of the Beloved, for his sake we recite the opening chapter of Holy Qur'ān.

"We Have Granted Luqmān Wisdom"

A'ūdhu billāhi min ash-Shayṭāni 'r-rajīm. Bismillāhi' r-Raḥmāni 'r-Raḥīm.
Nawaytu 'l-arbā'īn, nawaytu 'l-'itikāf, nawaytu 'l-khalwah, nawaytu 'l-'uzlah,
nawaytu 'r-riyāḍa, nawaytu 's-sulūk, lillāhi Ta'alā fī hādha 'l-masjid.
Atī'ūllāha wa atī'ū 'r-Rasūla wa ūli 'l-amri minkum. (4:59)

Whoever has been given wisdom, *faqad ūtīyya khayran kathīra*, Allāh promises that He is giving him 'a lot of favors,' which means He will give him something that...what does Shayṭān promise a servant? Allāh ﷻ says, "Shayṭān is giving you something of no value. Don't listen to your ego, your self, your Shayṭān, but listen to Allāh ﷻ," and that's why what you give to Allāh ﷻ is as He said in Holy Qur'ān:

مَّثَلُ الَّذِينَ يُنفِقُونَ أَمْوَالَهُمْ فِي سَبِيلِ اللهِ كَمَثَلِ حَبَّةٍ أَنبَتَتْ سَبْعَ سَنَابِلَ
فِي كُلِّ سُنبُلَةٍ مِّئَةُ حَبَّةٍ وَاللّهُ يُضَاعِفُ لِمَن يَشَاء وَاللّهُ وَاسِعٌ عَلِيمٌ

The likeness of those who spend their wealth in Allāh's Way
is as the likeness of a grain which grows seven ears, in
every ear a hundred grains. Allāh gives increase manifold
to whom He will for Allāh is All-Embracing, All-Knowing.[68]

Every one of us has recited this verse of Holy Qur'ān and knows about it, because whoever is fundraising puts, "Those who are spending their money in the Way of Allāh is like an example of a seed that brings a shoot of a hundred (grains), in every shoot there are a hundred seeds and Allāh will increase it as much as He likes and multiply it." So seven shoots come from every spending of one penny and Allāh will give, but there is really another meaning if we look into it. He said, *mathalu 'l-ladhīna yunfiqūna amwālahum fī sabīl 'Llāhi*, "The example of those people who spend their money in the Way of Allāh." How many forms of jihad are there, how many different kinds of jihad? People today have in their mind that there is one jihad, to fight, but the reality of the word "jihad" has been mentioned in many places of the Holy Ḥadīth of Prophet ﷺ, like in the ḥadīth:

---

[68] Sūrat al-Baqarah, 2:261.

أفضل الجهاد كلمة عدل عند سلطان جائر

Afḍal al-jihād kalimatu 'adlin 'inda sulṭānin jā'ir.
(in another version, aw kalimat al-ḥaqq.)

The best jihad is a word of justice (or a word of truth) before a tyrannical king.[69]

"The best of jihad is to say one word of truth in front of a tyrant leader." He said, "Best of jihad," so jihad has too many meanings and too many ways; they counted fourteen different kinds, one of them is holy war and the other thirteen are different types of struggling with your ego, your self. So when Allāh says, *mathalu 'l-ladhīna yunfiqūna amwālahum fī sabīli'Llāh*, "The example of those people who spend their money in the Way of Allāh," what is "your wealth"? What is your money? Money that will stay forever or money that will vanish in a period of a certain time? Which money is the verse mentioning here? Yes, it mentions different types of wealth being given in the Way of Allāh, for in the time of Prophet ﷺ and the Ṣaḥābah ؓ and holy war, your wealth was whatever you had, but the most important what you have is *ḥikmah*, what we discussed before, as Allāh said in *Sūrat Luqmān*:

وَلَقَدْ آتَيْنَا لُقْمَانَ الْحِكْمَةَ أَنِ اشْكُرْ لِلَّهِ وَمَن يَشْكُرْ فَإِنَّمَا يَشْكُرُ لِنَفْسِهِ وَمَن كَفَرَ فَإِنَّ اللَّهَ غَنِيٌّ حَمِيدٌ

And indeed We granted this wisdom to Luqmān, "Be grateful to Allāh."
And he who is grateful (to Him) is but grateful for the good of his own self, whereas
he who chooses to be ungrateful (ought to know that)
verily, Allāh is Self-Sufficient, Ever to be Praised![70]

Wa laqad ātaynā Luqmāna al-ḥikmat, "We gave Luqmān the Wisdom." So when you have wisdom you can differentiate between good and evil. A child doesn't have wisdom; that's why he grabs anything, might be something that will kill him or poison him, he doesn't mind it. He will drink it because there is no wisdom, but an adult already has some wisdom that he or she can distinguish between what is good and what is not good, but it is a limited wisdom. Everyone has a limited wisdom and Allāh ﷻ wants us,

---

[69] Related by Abū Sa'īd al-Khuḍrī.
[70] Sūrah Luqmān, 31:12.

if we have a higher Level of Wisdom, as Sayyīdinā Luqmān ؏ said to his
son:

وَإِذْ قَالَ لُقْمَانُ لِابْنِهِ وَهُوَ يَعِظُهُ يَا بُنَيَّ لَا تُشْرِكْ بِاللَّهِ إِنَّ الشِّرْكَ لَظُلْمٌ عَظِيمٌ

And (mention, O Muḥammad), when Luqmān said to his son while
he was instructing him, "O my son, do not associate (anything) with Allāh. Indeed,
association (with Him) is great injustice."[71]

It means you have wisdom, so don't make *shirk* and don't say,
"Everything to my self," as Prophet ﷺ said, "The most I fear for my *ummah*
is hidden *shirk*," that they refer attributes and everything to themselves (as if
they did it) when it has to be to Allāh ﷻ. So if you have wisdom, don't make
shirk. If you have wisdom don't say, "Allāh has a son!" Why, Allāh needs a
son? *Ḥāshā, astaghfirullāh!* Allāh doesn't need anything, everything is in
need for Allāh ﷻ! The whole Creation is in need for Allāh. He is not in need
of us, we need Him! So if we have wisdom, no *shirk*! If we have no *shirk*,
then we understand that there is a Creator and that means someone is going
to judge you. That is why Sayyīdinā Luqmān ؏ said this to his son when he
was advising him, and everyone must look into these *surahs*, such as *Sūrat
al-Baqarah, Sūrat al-Isrā', Sūrat al-Jumu'ah, Sūrat al-Luqmān* and there are too
many verses of wisdom, too many verses of *ḥikmah*, too many verses of
leaving *shirk*.

So when we leave *shirk*, it means we have established, we have planted
these (verses) in our heart and that is going to be a shoot. This, *alladhīna
yunfiqūna amwālahum*, "Those who spend their money, it is like a seed that
you plant and it gives you seven shoots," which means anything that you
do in this life you plant. If you have wisdom, you plant seeds into your
heart and every seed is giving seven shoots and every shoot is giving a
hundred seeds that Allāh will multiply. So one of them, Allāh is saying in
Holy Qur'ān that Luqmān ؏ was saying to his son:

---

[71] Sūrah Luqmān, 31:13.

وَاقْصِدْ فِي مَشْيِكَ وَاغْضُضْ مِن صَوْتِكَ إِنَّ أَنكَرَ الْأَصْوَاتِ لَصَوْتُ الْحَمِيرِ

*And be moderate in your pace and lower your voice (for) verily,
the worst of sounds is the braying of the donkey.*[72]

Allāhu Akbar! "*Waqṣid fī mashyika*" means be humble. "*Fī mashyika*" is when you walk, "*waqṣid fī mashyika*" means be humble and keep your eyes down, keep your ego down and don't be arrogant when you are walking between crowds. Allāh doesn't look at your image, but He looks at your hearts. *Waqṣid fī mashyīka*, "Be humble in your way, how you are walking in your journey in this life."

So the Wisdom grows up in your heart by planting seeds from the wealth that Allāh gave you, not the wealth of money, but the wealth of *ḥikmah*, wisdom in your heart. As much as you have wisdom, as much as you have seeds that you are planting on your journeys from *dunyā* to *Ākhirah*, you have to plant different seeds in it so that on the Day of Judgment these seeds will be coming out and Allāh is rewarding on every shoot, *wa 'Llāhu yuḍā'ifu liman yashā'u*, "Will multiply of rewards."

Waghḍuḍ min ṣawtika, "And when you speak don't speak with a loud tone." There are people that speak in a loud (contentious) tone, especially on talk shows. On the Muslim talk shows they speak and fight, throwing chairs on each other, and Allāh ﷻ is saying, "Speak low, don't speak loud, speak in a low voice," because me, you, everyone have to know that as soon as you open your mouth to speak, not a pure voice will come, but a voice that is full of pride, arrogance and *shirk*. Angels cannot be near you with the bad smell and a loud voice has a bad smell, so (if you do that) angels cannot approach you. Only when you speak the truth and you don't make a 'jerk' (of yourself), making everyone around you like in a Turkish bath, where everyone enters inside shouting, speaking, cursing; they don't know what they are saying! Don't be a like people in a Turkish bath, *hammam turkiye!* Allāh said, *waghḍuḍ min ṣawtika*, "Keep your voice in a low tone," which means "be humble," don't let your mouth to speak. You see some people always talking, whether or not something makes sense or doesn't make sense, they remain talking and they cannot stop!

Sayyīdinā 'Alī ؓ, what he said? "Keep quiet, keep silent." Zip your mouth, don't talk, because whenever you talk you are giving a bad smell.

---

[72] Sūrat Luqmān, 31:19.

The exception is, there is no bad smell when you recite Holy Qur'ān, when you read *ḥadīth*, when you do *qasīdah*, when you praise Allāh ﷻ, when you praise Prophet ﷺ, when you speak about the *Ṣaḥābah* ﻬ, when you speak about Islam, when you speak about *īmān*, when you speak about struggling against your Shayṭān, that's a good voice. Shout as much as you like, raise your voice as much as you like in such discussions, but not for *dunyā* shouting. People today are fighting, Allāh says, *waghḍuḍ min ṣawtika*, "Keep your voice low," which means don't fight, don't act something wrong, don't say things that you want to convince people of your idea and you don't accept their ideas, then you are fighting.

Inna ankar al-aṣwāti la-ṣawtu 'l-ḥamīr. He is describing the worst of voices, when they are loud is like the sound of a braying donkey. In the whole Qur'ān, Allāh mentioned one time the word "donkey." *Inna ankar al-aṣwāti la-ṣawtu 'l-ḥamīr,* "The worst and the most disgusting voice is the voice of Shayṭān, of *hamīr,* the donkey," which means ignorance. Why He ﷻ said "donkey?" In order to tell us, "Your voice when you are speaking loud and you are not speaking about something that is beneficial, only things that are *dunyā* issues, that is like a donkey," because the sound of the donkey is disgusting, like a donkey shouting by himself. When you see the donkey...I never saw donkeys here in this country, but in our countries in the Middle East, you see donkeys everywhere, also in Pakistan, for sure. In all Middle East countries, in Cyprus they have donkeys. You see the donkeys standing there, and suddenly (they bray), "Hee-haw, hee-haw!"

Grandshaykh, may Allāh bless his soul, said, "You hear the donkey saying this because at that moment Shayṭān comes to his ear and says, 'No more female donkeys on Earth, all of them died, there are only male donkeys now and you are left alone!'" So males have this bad sound; that doesn't mean that females don't have a bad sound, also they have. So Allāh is saying in Holy Qur'ān, "Don't have a loud voice to be disgusting like a donkey."

So when we have wisdom, we observe our tongue and what it is going to say; if you have no tongue you cannot say anything, you cannot express yourself except through movement if you have no tongue, but when you have a tongue, you begin backbiting everyone and spreading *fitna* and rumors for nothing. Shayṭān plays with us.

So what did Allāh say of Sayyīdinā Luqmān ؏? *Wa laqad ātaynā Luqmāna al-ḥikmah,* "We gave Luqmān the Wisdom." Read *Sūrah Luqmān* and get the wisdom that is written there. *Ani 'shukr lillāhi*, "Thank Me, I gave you wisdom." It means if we are children we have no wisdom: we might drink poison, we might burn ourselves and die, we might drown in an ocean, no wisdom. But when you have wisdom, when you grow up, slowly, slowly you have to know that Allāh gave you wisdom and you have to thank Him.

More Wisdom Comes with Thanking Allāh

Today they call wisdom "IQ," how much intelligence you have. Intelligence comes from what? From wisdom. So Allāh will give you wisdom and as much as you thank Him, *wa man yashkur fa-innamā yashkuru li-nafsihi*, "And whoever thanks Allāh ﷻ is thanking himself," which means, *wa man yashkur fa-innamā yashkuru li-nafsihi*, "Thanking for himself," he will find this wealth that we have mentioned about, that Allāh says, *mathalu 'Lladhīna yunfiqūna amwālahum fī sabīli'Llāh*, "The example of those who spend their wealth." It means all what Allāh gives to you and you thank Him is wealth that you will be saving, not wealth in *dunyā* that we will be leaving, but it will be wealth in *Ākhirah* waiting for you, calling you, "*Yā* Shaykh, come, come! Your rewards are here, saved in *Ākhirah*," in the Heavenly Bank that Shayṭān cannot touch, there you will find it!

In *Sūrat al-Baqarah*, 2:261, Allāh ﷻ says, "*Mathalu 'l-ladhīna yunfiqūna amwālahum fī sabīli'Llāhi*," and in Verse 268, He says:

الشَّيْطَانُ يَعِدُكُمُ الْفَقْرَ وَيَأْمُرُكُم بِالْفَحْشَاء وَاللّهُ يَعِدُكُم مَّغْفِرَةً مِّنْهُ وَفَضْلاً وَاللّهُ وَاسِعٌ عَلِيمٌ

Satan threatens you with poverty and orders you to immorality,
while Allāh promises you forgiveness from Him and bounty.
And Allāh is all-Encompassing and Knowing.[73]

Shayṭān's promises will make you poor, when he says, *wa yaʿidukumu al-faqra*, "O come to me, I will give you everything!" But that is not everything, that is poverty. He is giving you poverty, but showing you it is nice, meaning that he makes you *yuzayyin laka*, he decorates *dunyā* for you, which is going to be poverty for you if you are not in Allāh's Way. If you listen to Shayṭān, you cannot receive these rewards in *Ākhirah*; there is no reward for you. *Wa yāmurukum bi 'l-faḥshāi*, "And he calls you to

---

[73] Sūrat al-Baqarah, 2:268.

corruption," to be corrupted, *wa 'Llāhu ya'idukum maghfiratan minhu*, "and on the other hand, Allāh is promising you forgiveness." When you say, "*Shukran, yā Rabbī, astaghfirullāh*," Allāh gives you wealth, not for *dunyā*, and Shayṭān shows you wealth, but that wealth is poverty, "decorated. "Like someone has a cake, he says, "I bring a cake for you," and inside there is poison and on the outside is cream decorated with sprinkles, and he says, "Eat, eat, it's nice, eat! I gave you the best cake that has ever been done," but inside is full of dirty things, poison that will kill you.

Allāh ﷻ is saying, "Come to Me, I give you forgiveness." Which way do we prefer, the Way of Allāh or the way of the Shayṭān? All of this is coming from wisdom. So having wisdom, and the highest Level of Wisdom is the Level of Moral Excellence, *Maqām al-Iḥsān*, Prophet ﷺ said, "Because wisdom gives you *akhlāq*, *akhlāq* gives you wisdom." So wisdom gives you to have moral excellence and as much as you have a higher Level of Wisdom, then you have a higher Level of Moral Excellence. So who has the highest Level of Wisdom in this universe? Prophet ﷺ. So then who has the highest Level of Moral Excellence? Prophet ﷺ, where Allāh ﷻ said:

$$وَإِنَّكَ لَعَلَى خُلُقٍ عَظِيمٍ$$

You are of the most exalted character.[74]

"You are of the highest level that no one of human being or angel can reach, *yā* Muḥammad, *wa innaka la-'alā khuluqin 'aẓhīm!* You are of the highest level of good manners and characters, there is no one above." He said, "*Wa innaka la-'alā khuluq*"; *khuluq* means "good character," *akhlāq*, and under *akhlāq*, *subḥānAllāh*, we used to study in the school when we were young this book, *Tahdhīb al-Akhlāq*, about good manners and how to polish your character. When we were young they used to give to us books called *Tahdhīb al-Akhlāq* and they have pictures on how you have to be, to speak with people, how to eat, how to walk, and all these different examples of having good manners. Today, no more we see such a book in English, French, German, Italian, European, American or Arabic, it is not required any more. Before, it was required for us and when we were in elementary and intermediate school we had to study *akhlāq*, every week you had two hours. Now? No *akhlāq* now. Now no *akhlāq*, they are proud of dating and if

---

[74] Sūrat al-Qalam, 68:4.

you don't date they make you to look bad, but in Allāh's Eyes you look the best and that's what you need!

So Allāh said, "You have the highest level of character," *wa innaka la-'alā khuluqin 'āzhīm*. He added at the end *'āzhīm*, "great," which means, "There is no limitation of your good manners." Why is that like that? Because the Prophet ﷺ said:

ادبني ربي فأحسن تأديبي

Allāh taught me and gave me the best manners.

"Allāh disciplined me, taught me good manners," and when Allāh taught His Prophet ﷺ good manners, He taught him from a Heavenly Level, from *Qāba Qawsayni aw Adnā*. Allāh perfected him, *Adabanī rabbī fa-ahsana tā'dībī*, "Allāh perfected my character." He is confirming that, "Yes, for sure He made me of the best character."

That's why Prophet ﷺ said:

انما بعثت لاتمم مكارم الاخلاق

I have been sent to perfect the best of conduct (your behavior and character).[75]

"I have been sent *hasran*, "exclusively," *innamā*, "I have been sent exclusively to perfect the manners of a human being." It means Prophet ﷺ took it as his responsibility and that means on the Day of Judgment we will appear like stars on dark nights, every *mu'min* will appear like that because Prophet ﷺ took on his shoulders the responsibility to perfect our manners and to bring us clean to *Ākhirah* in the Presence of Allāh!

That's why in Holy Qur'ān, Allāh ﷻ said:

لَقَدْ كَانَ لَكُمْ فِي رَسُولِ اللَّهِ أُسْوَةٌ حَسَنَةٌ لِمَنْ كَانَ يَرْجُو اللَّهَ وَالْيَوْمَ الْآخِرَ وَذَكَرَ اللَّهَ كَثِيرًا

*Indeed in the Messenger of Allāh you have an excellent example
for anyone whose hope is in Allāh and the Last Day
and (who) remembers Allāh often.*[76]

"You have in Prophet an example, a way, *'usw*, the best example, the best way for those who want *Ākhirah*," *liman kāna yarju 'l-Llāha*, "For those who want *Ākhirah* and Allāh," take an example from Prophet ﷺ. *Laqad kāna*

---

[75] Bazzār.

[76] Sūrat al-Aḥzāb, 33:21.

lakum fī Rasūlullāhi uswatun ḥasanatun liman kāna yarju 'Llāha wa 'l-yawm al-ākhirah wa dhakara 'Llāha kathīran is saying, "You have a good example in Prophet ﷺ." So the other verse, is confirming:

قُلْ إِن كُنتُمْ تُحِبُّونَ اللَّهَ فَاتَّبِعُونِي يُحْبِبْكُمُ اللَّهُ وَيَغْفِرْ لَكُمْ ذُنُوبَكُمْ وَاللَّهُ غَفُورٌ رَّحِيمٌ

Say (O Muḥammad), "If you (really) love Allāh,
then follow me! Allāh will love you."[77]

Since in the previous verse in *Sūrat al-Aḥzāb*, He is saying to you, "You have a best example in the Prophet ﷺ," and in Sūrat Āli-'Imrān He is saying, "Since you have that, follow Muḥammad ﷺ; follow his way, don't follow any other way, there is no other way." Either you follow Prophet ﷺ and you will be saved or you don't follow Prophet ﷺ and then it is in Allāh's Judgment, He judges and we don't say anything.

May Allāh ﷻ forgive us and bless us in this early morning and make all your days good all around the world!

May Allāh forgive us and may Allāh bless us.

Wa min Allāhi 't-tawfīq, bi ḥurmati 'l-ḥabīb, bi ḥurmati 'l-Fātiḥah.
And with Allāh is success. For the sake of the Beloved, for his sake we recite
the opening chapter of Holy Qur'ān.

---

[77] Sūrat Āli-'Imrān, 3:31.

Prophet's ﷺ Character is the Holy Qur'an

A'ūdhu billāhi min ash-Shaytāni 'r-rajīm. Bismillāhi' r-Rahmāni 'r-Rahīm.
Nawaytu 'l-arbā'īn, nawaytu 'l-'itikāf, nawaytu 'l-khalwah, nawaytu 'l-'uzlah,
nawaytu 'r-riyāda, nawaytu 's-sulūk, lillāhi Ta'alā fi hādha 'l-masjid.
Atī'ullāha wa atī'ū 'r-Rasūla wa ūli 'l-amri minkum. (4:59)

Allāhu 'l-Ghaniyy! Allāh's Richness cannot be limited, His Greatness cannot be limited and His Generosity cannot be limited. That is why no one can partner with Him, no one can associate with Him as everyone is a servant to Allāh ﷻ.

We mentioned in the previous session that Allāh ﷻ said in Holy Qur'ān:

يُؤْتِي الْحِكْمَة مَن يَشَاء وَمَن يُؤْتَ الْحِكْمَة فَقَدْ أُوتِيَ خَيْرًا كَثِيرًا وَمَا يَذَّكَّرُ إِلاَّ أُوْلُوا الأَلْبَابِ

He gives wisdom to whom He wills, and whoever has been
given wisdom has certainly been given much good.
And none will remember except those of understanding.[78]

"Anyone to whom Allāh gives wisdom," which means that Allāh is happy with that person as wisdom will only indicate one thing, which Sayyīdinā 'Alī ؑ mentioned to the Sahābah ؓ, that the whole Qur'ān, which consists of 6,666 verses, points to one direction. Although some scholars say that there are 6,236 verses, but we take from the majority of scholars, those scholars in the previous period. So all the 6,666 verses indicate one major principle: there is no one who can be united with Allāh ﷻ and no one can be with Allāh in the physical meaning. That means there is no acceptance of *Wahdat al-Wujūd* in Islam, the combination of existence, the unity *with* Allāh; there is no such thing, as Allāh is *lā sharīka lahu!* So the one to whom Allāh gives wisdom understands that there is no unity with Allāh ﷻ.

---

[78] Sūrat al-Baqarah, 2:269.

Without Wisdom, no Manners and Without Manners, no Wisdom

Those who speak about unity are not understanding the reality of Islam. The one who knows wisdom, *ḥikmat*, as Sayyīdinā 'Alī ؏ said to the *Ṣaḥābah* ؇, it's based on one thing: that you always fear from the one who is above you, is it not? You do not fear the one below you, but the one above as they might harm you. Above all these universes, Who is The One that owns them? We must fear Him, as everything is in His Hands and He owns everything! That is why Sayyīdinā 'Alī ؏ said that Holy Qur'ān is indicating one thing: fear of Allāh ﷻ as He is the Creator and you are the servant.

راس الحكمة مخاة الله

The head of wisdom is fear of Allāh ﷻ.

When you can understand that fear, you can polish all your bad manners, so wisdom takes you to manners. Without wisdom, you have no manners and without manners you have no wisdom. It is a basic principle in Islam that wisdom equals or gives you good manners. No good manners, no wisdom. So then everyone has the tendency to judge themselves whether they have wisdom or not by judging their manners, (asking themselves), "Do I have manners or I don't have manners? If I think I do, then I have wisdom. If I feel that I have no manners, then I have no wisdom."

Do you really accept that your ego has manners? Do you really accept that our egos are clean from dirtiness? No way! That is why our wisdom is shaky. I do not want to say that there is no wisdom, but that wisdom is barely above zero, barely. It might even be minus zero!

That is our problem and our situation that we are falling in. That is why it is said, *'alā anna 'l-ḥikmata fī istilāḥi 'l-qur'ān wa ta'abīrihi lahā ṣilatun 'amīqatun wathīqatun bi 'l-akhlāq*, "Wisdom, according to the explanation of Holy Qur'ān, has a very deep and strong relationship with good manners." That is why when Sayyida 'Ayesha ؇ was asked about the moral excellence and manners of the Prophet ﷺ, "*Kayfa khuluq an-Nabī ﷺ?*" she said just two words that were enough for the *Ṣaḥābah* ؇ and everyone to understand, which has been narrated by *Muslim*.

She said:

كَانَ خُلُقُهُ القُرءان

His character was the Qur'ān.[79]

"His manners were the Holy Qur'ān." That means everything in Holy Qur'ān that Allāh revealed to the Prophet ﷺ, everything in the 6, 666 verses in Holy Qur'ān, scholars can pull out a description of the Prophet's ﷺ good manners and characters. Imagine, think about it. *Kāna khuluquhu 'l-Qur'ān,* "His manners were the Holy Qur'ān." So this means that the reality and secrets of 6,666 verses are in the heart of the Prophet ﷺ.

That is why Allāh ﷻ said:

وَإِنَّكَ لَعَلى خُلُقٍ عَظِيمٍ

You are of the most exalted character. [80]

Allāh is saying, "You are of greatest, most tremendous characters and manners because your manners and your character, *yā* Muḥammad ﷺ, are the Holy Qur'ān, *kāna khuluqhu 'l-qur'ān.*

So what is greater than the Holy Qur'ān? Is there anything in this Creation? The Holy Qur'ān is not created and is Allāh's Ancient Words, and Allāh's Greatness is above everything. Everything is under Allāh's Greatness, everything in this universe, and even though this universe is so perfect it is still under Allāh's Creation as it cannot be greater than the Creator. The Creation cannot be greater than the Creator. The Holy Qur'ān is Allāh's Ancient Words, which means they are not created like the universe, the Heavens, galaxies, stars, Earth, trees, whatever planets you are seeing, nature, deserts, jungles, under sea, under oceans, living species, fish...everything that you can imagine that is created is not yet a drop from what we understand of the Creation! The Greatness of Allāh cannot be described through His Creation, still creation is coming and never ending, and the Holy Qur'ān is still above them all. So it means what do these 6,666 verses contain? Whatever they contain of secrets, they describe the manners of the Prophet ﷺ!

---

[79] Muslim.

[80] Sūrat al-Qalam, 68:4.

Sayyida 'Ayesha ﷺ said, "*Kāna khuluquhu 'l-Qur'ān*," "his character was the Qur'ān" not "*Kāna khuluquhu ka 'l-Qur'ān*," "his character was like the Qur'ān." She said, "*Kāna khuluquhu 'l-Qur'ān*," *khuluquhu*, which means Allāh dressed him with the Holy Words of Allāh ﷻ, he became perfect. When Allāh dressed him with the revelation of Holy Qur'ān when he was a prophet and when Sayyīdinā Adam ﷺ was between soul and body or between water and clay, Allāh dressed him with the Holy Qur'ān.

كنت نبي و ادم بين الماء و الطين

I was a prophet when Adam was between water and clay.

كنت نبيا وآدم بين الروح والجسد

I was a prophet while Adam was between soul and body.

We Dressed Him with the Heavenly Dress of Holy Qur'ān

حم وَالْكِتَابِ الْمُبِين إِنَّا أَنزَلْنَاهُ فِي لَيْلَةٍ مُّبَارَكَةٍ إِنَّا كُنَّا مُنذِرِين
فِيهَا يُفْرَقُ كُلُّ أَمْرٍ حَكِيمٍ أَمْرًا مِّنْ عِندِنَا إِنَّا كُنَّا مُرْسِلِينَ

*Hā. Mīm. By the Book that makes things clear, We sent it down
during a blessed night for We (ever) wish to warn (against evil).
In the (night) is made distinct every affair of wisdom by Command
from Our Presence for We (ever) send (revelations).*[81]

Innā anzalnāhu fī laylatin mubārakatin, "We sent it down on a blessed night." Why "*layla*," why "in a night," why not, *innā anzalnāhu fī nahārin mubārakatin*, "We revealed the Holy Qur'ān on Prophet ﷺ on a *laylatin mubārakatin*, a blessed night." It means, "We have revealed the Holy Qur'ān to Prophet ﷺ when everything was in '*adam*, the state of non-existence," described as "darkness," not darkness of sins, but darkness that there is nothing before it, no existence. So the interpretation of this verse is, "We have revealed when there was no Creation except the Light of Prophet ﷺ, We dressed him with the Heavenly Dress of Holy Qur'ān." That is big, it means where there was nothing!

الرَّحْمَنُ عَلَّمَ الْقُرْآنَ

---

[81] Sūrat ad-Dukhān, 44:1-5.

(God) Most Gracious! It is He Who has taught the Qur'ān.
He has created Man.[82]

By Himself, Allāh ﷻ, with His Greatness He taught the Holy Qur'ān directly to the Prophet ﷺ. That is why the Prophet ﷺ was able to reach *Qāba Qawsayni aw Adnā*, with the power of Holy Qur'ān. Burāq was pulling power from the Holy Qur'ān, moving with Prophet ﷺ. Jibrīl ﷺ was not able to reach where the Prophet ﷺ reached. So Allāh dressed Prophet ﷺ when everything was in *'adam* except the Light that Allāh created from His Light, the Light of the Prophet ﷺ, because light = existence and darkness = no existence. That is why He said, "In a night." *Innā anzalnāhu fī laylatin mubārakatin* and in another verse, *inna anzalnāhu fī laylati 'l-qadri*, always at night, *layla*, where there was nothing that could be seen. When you don't see anything it is *'adam*. Put the light off, you don't see anything. Can you see anything? No.

Let us do an experiment. Put the light off. Is there anything? No existence. Light on = existence: they appeared, everything appeared although you didn't move the camera. Put the light off and move the camera. Is there anything? Put the light on and keep moving the camera. You see everything, they pop up. So there is no existence except the Light of the Prophet ﷺ and Allāh dressed him with 6,666 verses, *Kāna khuluquhu 'l-qur'ān*, "His character became dressed with the Secrets of Holy Qur'ān" as *Muḥammadun Rasūlullāh* ﷺ, Muḥammad the the Messenger of Allāh ﷺ. What you want more? That means He is *Khalifatullāh*, representing the Divine Presence, *Muḥammadun Rasūlullāh* ﷺ, he is the Messenger of Allāh! A messenger represents the one who is sending him. Either He sent His Messengers through Jibrīl ﷺ or, like Sayyīdinā Mūsā ﷺ, *Kalīmullāh*, but he was *Kalīmullāh* on Toor Sina (Mount Sinai):

إِذْ قَالَ مُوسَى لِأَهْلِهِ إِنِّي آنَسْتُ نَارًا

When Moses said to his family, "Indeed, I have perceived a fire."[83]

فَلَمَّا أَتَاهَا نُودِي يَا مُوسَى إِنِّي أَنَا رَبُّكَ فَاخْلَعْ نَعْلَيْكَ إِنَّكَ بِالْوَادِ الْمُقَدَّسِ طُوًى

---

[82] Sūrat ar-Raḥmān, 55:1-3.

[83] Sūrat an-Naml, 27:7.

But when he came to the fire a voice was heard, "O Moses! Indeed I am your Lord!
Therefore, (in My Presence) remove your shoes, (for) you are
in the sacred valley, Ṭūwā.[84]

Allāh said directly to him when he was looking for some warmth, when his family was in Ṭūr Sīnā moving from Yemen back to Egypt, he felt they were cold and said, "I see some lights there, some fire; let me go there," and Allāh spoke with him, *Kalīmullāh* ﷺ. It was not necessary to send him, but He spoke to him at Toor Sina and He spoke with the Prophet ﷺ from where? The only prophet invited to *Qāba Qawsayni aw Adnā*. It was not anymore "in here" or "there" or "there" or "there," but Allāh spoke directly to the Prophet ﷺ in *Qāba Qawsayni aw Adnā*, that no one can reach, because he was pure, *khuluquhu 'l-Qur'ān*.

Allāh dressed him when He created his Light, where it is mentioned in many *aḥadīth* and in *Muṣannaf 'Abdu 'r-Razzāq*, that the first thing Allāh created was the Light of Prophet ﷺ.

رواه عبد الرزاق بسنده عن جابر بن عبد الله بلفظ قال قلت: يا رسول الله، بأبي أنت وأمي، أخبرني عن أول شيء خلقه الله قبل الأشياء. قال: يا جابر، إن الله تعالى خلق قبل الأشياء نور نبيك من نوره»،...

When Jābir ﷺ asked, "Let my father and mother be sacrificed for you,
O Prophet of Allāh! What is the first thing that Allāh ﷻ created?"
The Prophet ﷺ said, "The first thing that Allāh ﷻ created is the Light of your
Prophet from His Light, O Jābir..."[85]

That Light was dressed with the Heavenly Dress, enabling him to move to *Qāba Qawsayni aw Adnā* and Allāh spoke to him ﷺ, with no veils. That is what many scholars say and among them are Īmām Nawawi ق. So that one who has wisdom gives the meaning of the relationship of *akhlāq*; they are related. If there is wisdom there is *akhlāq*, no wisdom no *akhlāq*. So the one whom Allāh *khuluquhu 'l-Qur'ān*, dressed with the Holy Qur'ān, Allāh wanted everyone to follow him, to follow the role model, the one whose Light was created first, the one who was a prophet before Adam's creation in Heavenly Power. *Awwala mā khalaq Allāh nūru Nabīyyika yā Jābir*, the first of Allāh's Creation is the Light of Prophet ﷺ, then:

---

[84] Sūrat ṬāHā, 20:11-12.

[85] *Muṣannaf 'Abdu 'r-Razzāq.*

كنت نبيا وآدم بين الروح والجسد

I was a prophet while Adam was between soul and body.

So the one that's like that, Allāh ﷻ has sent him and Allāh has said about him in Holy Qur'ān:

لَقَدْ كَانَ لَكُمْ فِي رَسُولِ اللَّهِ أُسْوَةٌ حَسَنَةٌ لِمَنْ كَانَ يَرْجُو اللَّهَ وَالْيَوْمَ الآخِرَ وَذَكَرَ اللَّهَ كَثِيرًا

Indeed in the Messenger of Allāh you have an excellent example
for anyone whose hope is in Allāh and the Last Day
and (who) remembers Allāh often.[86]

"There was for you from Prophet ﷺ the role model," meaning, there is no other role model for you. He ﷺ is the one who wants *liman kāna yarjū 'Llāha wa 'l-yawma 'l-Ākhirah*, "The one who wants to be saved in the Last Days," and *dhakara 'Llāha kathīra*, "The one who is always remembering Allāh too much." He said '*kathīra*,' He didn't limit it, He didn't say 10 times, 100 times, 1,000 times, "always your tongue is wet with *dhikrullāh*." Like when the Bedouin came to the Prophet ﷺ and said, *qad kathura 'alayya shara'i al-Islam*, "There are too many conditions and principles with Sharī'ah and Islam so give me something easy!" and the Prophet ﷺ said, "Keep your tongue wet with *dhikrullāh*, *ija'al lisānak raṭban min dhikrillāh*."

عن عبد الله بن بسر رضي الله عنه أن رجلا قال: يا رسول الله إن شرائع الإسلام قد كثرت علي فأخبرني بشيء أتشبث به؟ قال لا يزال لسانك رطبا من ذكر الله" الترمذي.

A man came to the Prophet ﷺ and said, "O Rasūlullāh! The rules of Islam
became heavy on me, so give me news of something which I can maintain." Prophet
ﷺ said, "Make your tongue wet with dhikrullāh."[87]

So the one who wants Allāh, *liman kāna yarjū'Llāh*, who wants Allāh ﷻ the Creator, no associating anyone with Him, no partner with Him, no son for Him, nothing, no *shirk*, he wants *al-Yawmu 'l-Ākhirah* to be saved in the Day of Judgment, and the one who remembers Allāh so much, "Follow Muḥammad ﷺ, he is your role model." Follow the Prophet ﷺ as he is, Allāh gave him, *fī rasūlillāhi uswatan ḥasanah*, "Follow him, then you be saved."

That is why He ﷻ said:

---

[86] Sūrat al-Aḥzāb, 33:21.

[87] Tirmidhī.

قُلْ إِن كُنتُمْ تُحِبُّونَ اللّٰهَ فَاتَّبِعُونِي يُحْبِبْكُمُ اللّٰهُ وَيَغْفِرْ لَكُمْ ذُنُوبَكُمْ وَاللّٰهُ غَفُورٌ رَّحِيمٌ

*Say (O Muḥammad), "If you (really) love Allāh,
then follow me! Allāh will love you."*[88]

"Say (O Muḥammad!), 'If you really love Allāh ﷻ then follow me!'" *Yuhbibkumullāhu*, "If you follow me then Allāh will love you." If you really say you love Allāh, then follow Muḥammad ﷺ! Allāh will love you and if Allāh loves you, what will happen? He will give you wisdom, *wa man ūtiya al-ḥikmata faqad ūtiya khayran kathīra*, "The one who gets the wisdom will get the most favors," endless favors in *dunyā* and *Ākhirah*, with no limitation!

Allāh said, *faqad ūtiya khayran kathīra*. You may not know what you have been given, but Allāh gave and gives and is giving non-stop! When you love Allāh, follow Muḥammad ﷺ, then Allāh loves you and when Allāh loves you, *kuntu sama'uhulladhī yasma'u bihi wa baṣarahulladhī yubṣiru bihi*, until the end of the *ḥadīth*:

فَإِذَا أَحْبَبْتُهُ كُنْتُ سَمْعَهُ الَّذِي يَسْمَعُ بِهِ وَبَصَرَهُ الَّذِي يُبْصِرُ بِهِ، وَيَدَهُ الَّتِي يَبْطِشُ بِهَا وَرِجْلَهُ الَّتِي يَمْشِي بِهَا،

*When I love him, I will become the ears with which he hears,
the eyes with which he sees, the hand with which he acts,
and the legs with which he walks; (and other versions include,
"and the tongue with which he speaks.")*[89]

When Prophet Spread the Wisdom it Changed the Universe!

This wisdom that Allāh gives, Prophet ﷺ spread it to his *Ṣaḥābah* ؓ and changed the whole universe, the meaning of everything! *Inshā'Allāh* we will come to it later. May Allāh give us the *barakah* of Prophet ﷺ, to keep us under the arms of Prophet ﷺ, under the wing of Prophet ﷺ! 'Wing' is not meaning physical wings, but spiritual wings. *Allāh, Allāh. Subhān-Allāh. Inshā'Allāh khayr.* May Allāh accept our fasting, changing it from imitational fasting to real fasting.

---

[88] Sūrat Āli-'Imrān, 3:31.

[89] *Ḥadīth Qudsī*, Bukhārī.

May Allāh forgive us and may Allāh bless us.

Wa min Allāhi 't-tawfīq, bi ḥurmati 'l-ḥabīb, bi ḥurmati 'l-Fātiḥah.
And with Allāh is success. For the sake of the Beloved, for his sake we recite
the opening chapter of Holy Qur'ān.

Prophet Muḥammad ﷺ is the
Best Role Model for Humanity

A'ūdhu billāhi min ash-Shayṭāni 'r-rajīm. Bismillāhi' r-Raḥmāni 'r-Raḥīm.
Nawaytu 'l-arbā'īn, nawaytu 'l-'itikāf, nawaytu 'l-khalwah, nawaytu 'l-'uzlah,
nawaytu 'r-riyāḍa, nawaytu 's-sulūk, lillāhi Ta'ala fī hādha 'l-masjid.
Atī'ullāha wa atī'ū 'r-Rasūla wa ūli 'l-amri minkum. (4:59)

O brothers and sisters, both present and absent, and viewers, listeners or
leaders, as we mentioned in the previous session that Allāh ﷻ said in the
Holy Qur'ān:

لَقَدْ كَانَ لَكُمْ فِي رَسُولِ اللَّهِ أُسْوَةٌ حَسَنَةٌ لِمَنْ كَانَ يَرْجُو اللَّهَ وَالْيَوْمَ الآخِرَ وَذَكَرَ اللَّهَ كَثِيرا

Indeed in the Messenger of Allāh you have an excellent example
for anyone whose hope is in Allāh and the Last Day
and (who) remembers Allāh often.[90]

To those who would like to get Paradise in *dunyā, fi 'd-dunyā ḥasanah*, to
get some good in *dunyā* and *Ākhirah*, and to those whom their movement
and goal is Allāh ﷻ, nothing else, no desires, they have penetrated the
minefield of desires and their only desire is Allāh. One example of that is
when Sayyīdinā Abū Yazīd al-Bistāmī ق, one of the big scholars and one of
the greatest saints, we don't want to call them saints, but *awlīyā, walīyullāh*,
as Allāh ﷻ described them in Holy Qur'ān:

ألا إنَّ أوْلِيَاء اللَّهِ لا خَوْفٌ عَلَيْهِمْ وَلاَ هُمْ يَحْزَنُونَ

Behold! Verily on the Friends of Allāh there is no fear,
nor shall they grieve; they who have attained faith
and have always been conscious of Him.[91]

"*Awlīyā* will never be sad and will never get anything that may harm
them. Allāh loves them," because they follow the footsteps of Prophet ﷺ. So
if we want, those who want Allāh ﷻ and those who want to be saved in the
Last Days, we have to be at a level that Sayyīdinā Bayāzīd al-Bistāmī ق
reached in his *du'ā* and *munajāt*. He was so close to the Station of *Ḥuḍūrullāh*,

---

[90] Sūrat al-Aḥzāb, 33:21.
[91] Surah Yunus, 10:62-63.

meaning he had Allāh's Greatness present in his heart and in his mind. One day he asked, "*Yā Rabbī*," as everyone does:

اذْعُونِي أَسْتَجِبْ لَكُمْ

Call on Me, I will answer you.[92]

"Ask Me, I will respond to you, I give to you," and he was asking and saying, "*Yā Rabbī*! Open for me Your Door!" Everyone's wish and desire is for Allāh to open His Door as this is the greatest pleasure, the greatest desire that you will enter, where no one entered except a few. These associations are for this reason and that is why the *Ṣaḥābah* ﷺ were with the Prophet ﷺ always, in order to reach that level. So Allāh ﷻ kept him asking and asking, because Allāh loves someone who keeps asking in *ilḥā*, to be persistent and to be always continuously asking Him non-stop. Even though he doesn't see that his *du'ā* has been responded to, Allāh ﷻ for sure is raising that person higher and higher until the time comes that it opens to his eyes from the Heavenly Kingdom!

So Abū Yazīd ق was asking and Allāh ﷻ ordered a voice from angels to say to him, "O Abayāzīd! You are asking for Allāh to open His Door for you, He will open." He was so happy to hear that voice; sometimes you can hear voices through your ears, but without sound coming to your heart and we call it inspiration. Allāh sends messages through His Angels to everyone's heart to correct themselves and these messengers take the responsibility to make sure that what he or she is asking for reaches Allāh's Servant.

So Abayāzīd ق was asking Allāh to open His Door for him and the answer came, "*Yā* Abayāzīd, you want Our Door to be opened? No problem but on one condition, O My beloved servant!" The voice came, *utruk nafsaka wa ta'al.* So clear and so easy, the answer came to him in two words, "Leave yourself," because the self always likes to associate with Allāh and to say, "I did this and I did that, I am proud." When the Prophet ﷺ saw the greatness of this situation, he said, "I don't say I am this or, *yā Rabbī*, don't leave me to my self for the blink of an eye!" That is the Prophet ﷺ, who said to us:

---

[92] Sūrat Ghāfir, 40:60.

قُلْ إِنَّمَا أَنَا بَشَرٌ مِّثْلُكُمْ

Say, "I am but a man like yourselves."[93]

"Say to them (O Muḥammad), you are a servant, you are a human being like them," because Prophet ﷺ was saying this out of humbleness before Allāh's Greatness. When Allāh opens to him that door, how can he find himself there? There is no more 'himself' there, there is nothing there except Allāh ﷻ, in that level. So *awlīyāullāh* and all of us like to follow, as Allāh ﷻ said:

لَقَدْ كَانَ لَكُمْ فِي رَسُولِ اللَّهِ أُسْوَةٌ حَسَنَةٌ لِمَنْ كَانَ يَرْجُو اللَّهَ
وَالْيَوْمَ الآخِرَ وَذَكَرَ اللَّهَ كَثِيرًا

Indeed in the Messenger of Allāh you have an excellent example
for anyone whose hope is in Allāh and the Last Day
and (who) remembers Allāh often.[94]

"You have in Prophet ﷺ a role model," so we have the role model, but are we following it? No one is! We might struggle and all of us are trying, but we struggle in order to be able to follow the role model. Allāh did not create us in this *dunyā* for nothing, only to run after *dunyā!* Allāh created us to run...it's a cycle: first, you were in the Presence of Allāh ﷻ as a soul, then Allāh sent you to *dunyā*, "Look! I have saved you as a soul in My Presence, your soul is pure. I am sending you to *dunyā* to know My Favors on you." If Allāh would not send us to *dunyā*, how would we know His Favors? And the biggest favor is that Allāh created us, or as we said in previous sessions, we will be like '*adm*, not existing. Now there are Creations that are not in existence and they will be created in the future, but as long as they are non-existent they are in '*adm*, Absolute Nothingness. That is what all beliefs, not only Islam, run towards, to try to reach the Ocean of Nothingness, the ocean of "I am nothing and there is nothing, only the Creator."

So Allāh sent him a message, "If you want to come to Me, come! *Laqad kāna lakum fī Rasūlullāhi uswatun ḥasanah*, There is a role model for you already. It is open, but leave your desires, then come."

Our desires put us in problems and difficulties. *Dunyā* desires put us in problems and difficulties and also *Ākhirah* desires put us in a higher level of

---

[93] Sūrat al-Kahf, 18:110.

[94] Sūrat al-Aḥzāb, 33:21.

77

problems and difficulties, as they it is more valuable. Something more valuable is more difficult to get, but something less valuable is easy to get.

"Muḥammad ﷺ is a Jewel"

Muḥammad is a man, but not like other men! He is a gem and human beings are stones. [95]

"Muḥammad ﷺ is a human being, but not like any other human being; he is a jewel," and the rest are what? "Rocks, pebbles," Muḥammad al-Busayri ق said in *al-Burdah ash-Sharīfah*. So people of *dunyā* collect pebbles and sell them. How many times do they go and buy them for construction in trucks and sell them cheap, of no value. Also those who collect diamonds go underground even though they know that the mine might fall on them, but they still go. What do they get? Valuable rocks.

Muḥammad basharun wa laysa ka 'l-bashari, "Muḥammad ﷺ is a man, but not like other men!" *Bal hūwa yāqūtatun,* "He is a gem, a jewel and the rest are rocks." So we are running after rocks and what is the benefit? If we run after the Prophet ﷺ, as Allāh said, "Follow Muḥammad ﷺ, he is the role model, he left his desires completely," of course *Qāba Qawsayni aw 'Adnā* is open to him.

So what did Allāh say to Bayāzīd? "Leave your desires and come! Leave what I don't like and you don't like. I don't like *dunyā* desires, I send a test for My servants so leave it." Is it easy? Yes it is, but to step on it is not, as Shayṭān will not let you.

So our responsibility, as Allāh ﷻ said, "You have a role model," who said to us in many *aḥadīth* that will be mentioned in the coming sessions, that there are many different exits on the highway. Prophet ﷺ is mentioning every exit through his *Sunnah*, saying, "Be careful, red-flag, red light." Be careful. So what is the *ḥadīth* for? It is to polish you. Ṣaḥābah ﷺ were living with the Prophet ﷺ, so he was polishing them directly, but we are not sitting with the Prophet ﷺ. We need to follow his *Sunnah*, it means through his *ḥadīth* what he was teaching his Ṣaḥābah. That is why Allāh ﷻ said, "Follow Muḥammad ﷺ as he is the role model."

---

[95] Shaykh Muḥammad al-Busayri, *al-Burdah ash-Sharīfah*.

What did Bayāzīd ق say? *Kayfa al-wuṣūlu ilayk*, "How do we reach the Divine Presence, Your Happiness or Your Love?"

The answer came, "Leave your self and come to Me."

And he said, "*Yā Rabbī*, how can I leave my self?"

Allāh ﷻ said, "Don't go too far to find obstacles, it is so easy. Make your self a dump for My servants, that self that is always trying to take you towards badness. You cannot crush it until you make yourself a dump where everyone is dumping their badness on you."

It will crush it because it is very difficult to accept something you don't like from someone else. No, your self immediately will want to explode on you, like a rocket full of anger! That is why in previous times they used to be more pious. Today piety is gone, so you see Shayṭān's work is too much on *Ummat an-Nabī* ﷺ. Forget about other religions, we are speaking about Islam. Your desire will not allow you. That is where it is very difficult to crush it or step on it to reach the Divine Presence. It will come like an enemy against you saying, "No." That is why we see the *ẓulma*, darkness coming down on everyone. You see problems between husband and wife, divorce everywhere. It was less in the Muslim world previously, but now you find divorce in every house because there is no harmony, no acceptance of the other and lots of shouting.

وأوصى النبي صلى الله عليه وسلم أبا هريرة بوصية عظيمة فقال: يا أبا هريرة! عليك بحسن الخلق. قال أبو هريرة رضي الله عنه: وما حسن الخلق يا رسول الله؟ قال: تصل مَنْ قطعك، وتعفو عمن ظلمك، وتُعطي من حرمك٩٦

As the Prophet ﷺ said to Sayyīdinā Abū Hurayrah ﷺ: "You must keep good character," and he asked, "What is the good character?" And the Prophet ﷺ said:

1. Ta'fū 'amman ẓalamak, 'To forgive the one who oppressed you,' not to come and oppress each other, but to forgive; *Laqad kāna lakum fi Rasūlullāhi uswatun ḥasana*, "You have the best role model in the Prophet ﷺ."

2. Taṣila man qata'k, 'To connect with the one who disconnected with you.' If he disconnected with you, try to be the better one who connects back.

3. Tu'ṭī man ḥaramak, 'To give to the one who blocked you from getting what you like.' You see him in need of something and in the previous time he

---

96 Narrated by Bayhaqī.

did something harmful; for example, he stole your project from which you were going to make lot of income and behind your back he made money from that. Prophet ﷺ said, "Never mind, give him what he needs. He tried to block you, no problem, but give him what he wants."

Allāhu Akbar! How do you give to the one who took the bite from your mouth? That is the meaning: he snatched it from you, and the Prophet ﷺ is saying, "Never mind, give him what he wants." What kind of character? No limit of... that is why Allāh ﷻ said, "The Prophet ﷺ is a role model." To reach the level of role model is to crush the self.

Abū Yazīd ق said, "How do I crush myself?" and the Voice said, "Make yourself a dump for My servants." It means show humility, show humbleness for My servants; not you come like a rocket, angry from one word from your husband or wife or children as you cannot carry each other. To those who like *Ākhirah*, that is what you have to do! Those who don't want *Ākhirah*, *dunyā* is open to do what they want, but those who want *Ākhirah* and want the Last Day and remember Allāh all their life, their role model is Prophet ﷺ! But those who don't believe in *Ākhirah* and the Last Day, they have different beliefs and don't believe in the Day of Resurrection and don't remember Allāh so much, so they have *dunyā*; take it and go!

So Bayāzīd ق made himself a dump for Allāh's servants and how did he do that? He was a scholar, so he went to a city and on the *Jumu'ah* prayer on the *minbar*, the pulpit, he said, "O people! I am coming this *Jumu'ah* to tell you that you have to make *sajda* to me!" He was putting himself in problems in order to crush his desires and he cannot crush his desire by himself. So this world is a world of *kufr* and it is not accepted. So what did the *'ulamā* do? They decided to stone him. Look how far he went to crush himself, getting stoned, and the people didn't know he is doing it to carry it to become a dump for their sins. He surrendered to Allāh to be killed or not through Allāh's Hands through the stoning and they were stoning him until he fainted. It is good there were no doctors at that time or they would have put too many machines and said, "No, the heart is still beating" (and the stoning would have continued)! Every century has its own ways. He fainted and they thought he died. That is Allāh's Will. He wants His servant to come to Him, He likes that. He is testing him, and so what they wanted to do with him? They threw him in the dump because what he said is *kufr*, so how they could make *Ṣalāt al-Janaza* on him? There was no cleaning or anything, they just took him and threw him in the dump.

Then he was happy he was in that dump. For seven days he stayed unconscious and people were throwing trash on him. He opened his eyes and was looking for something to eat as he was hungry and he found nothing. Like today, when someone goes into a coma they are put in the ICU and hooked up to machines. What is the ICU going to do for you? They put machines, but if they would not then everyone would know that you only need Allāh's Support and Power; it changes the meaning. So he was looking and found a bone with a little bit of meat on it. It was smelly and full of white worms, but he still took it to eat.

One dog came and said, "Grrrrr! What are you doing in my home? What are you doing?" Grandshaykh ق was telling the story. Allāh gave Bayāzīd ق the ability to know and understand the dog was saying, "This is my territory."

Bayāzīd ق said to the dog, "I am a guest in your territory, let me," and the dog backed up.

That is a sign that animals will understand. When you crush your ego and your desires, you can understand all kinds of languages and voices that come. Whenever people open their mouth to speak, you can understand the different languages. So he stayed there some time until he recovered and then he went out. It is a long story, and then he had a problem on the boat and they accused him of things that were incorrect and many other issues, so he left. When the *Ṣaḥābah* ﷺ heard that Allāh said in Holy Qur'ān that they have a role model in the Prophet ﷺ, what did they do? Why are they called "Ṣaḥābah." They made *ṣuḥbah* around the Prophet ﷺ and established friendship with him. They were around him like soldiers, whatever Prophet ﷺ said was an order and they immediately complied.

Allāh ﷻ said:

قُلْ إِن كُنتُمْ تُحِبُّونَ اللَّهَ فَاتَّبِعُونِي يُحْبِبْكُمُ اللَّهُ وَيَغْفِرْ لَكُمْ ذُنُوبَكُمْ وَاللَّهُ غَفُورٌ رَّحِيمٌ

Say (O Muḥammad), "If you (really) love Allāh,
then follow me! Allāh will love you." [97]

---

[97] Sūrat Āli-'Imrān, 3:31.

"If you really love Allāh, follow me," but follow in what? Follow in the role mode, and what is that? It is wisdom, as we mentioned in the previous sessions. The Ṣaḥābah ❀ began to acquire wisdom by sitting with the Prophet ﷺ daily, and we can say it is like when a child sees his mother and father, where does he run and sit? In their lap. They were described as "sitting in the lap of Prophet ﷺ."

فنشأ في أحضانه جيل تحلى بأفضل الأخلاق

Fanasha'ā fī aḥḍānihi jīlun taḥalla bi afḍali 'l-akhlāq, "It came to appear now a new generation that has been decorated with the best of manners," because they were raised in the lap of the Prophet ﷺ.

Do you want to be raised in the lap of the Prophet ﷺ? Leave yourself and come to him! He will take you to Allāh ❀. So because of that Allāh gave the Ṣaḥābah ❀ the best of *akhlāq*; their character was to run away from evilness or evil-doers and leave all kinds of bad characteristics. There are 800 forbiddens, bad characteristics in us as *awlīyāullāh* say, and Holy Qur'ān mentioned them and in their hearts that was all cleared. That is why Allāh said, "Let it be known that *anna fikum Rasūlullāh*, "The Prophet ﷺ is among you, with you and in you," and because, "You are in the lap of the Prophet ﷺ, Allāh made you to love *īmān*, faith." It means they didn't have faith before, until they were in the lap of the Prophet ﷺ, growing. That is why Allāh ❀ said:

وَاعْلَمُوا أَنَّ فِيكُمْ رَسُولَ اللَّهِ لَوْ يُطِيعُكُمْ فِي كَثِيرٍ مِّنَ الْأَمْرِ لَعَنِتُّمْ وَلَكِنَّ اللَّهَ حَبَّبَ إِلَيْكُمُ الْإِيمَانَ وَزَيَّنَهُ فِي قُلُوبِكُمْ وَكَرَّهَ إِلَيْكُمُ الْكُفْرَ وَالْفُسُوقَ وَالْعِصْيَانَ أُوْلَئِكَ هُمُ الرَّاشِدُونَ

And know Allāh's Messenger is in you. If he were to obey you in much of the matter, you would be in difficulty, but Allāh has endeared to you the faith and has made it pleasing in your hearts and has made hateful to you disbelief, defiance and disobedience. Those are the (rightly) guided.[98]

So because you follow the role model, *'uswatun ḥasanah*, Allāh made them to be raised in the lap of the Prophet ﷺ and dressed you. What did He dress us with? He dressed the Ṣaḥābah ❀ with *īmān*, faith. It is not easy to be dressed with faith. It is like the neighbor of Sayyidinā Mūsā ❀ who believed

---

[98] Sūrat al-Ḥujurāt, 49:7.

82

in him and accepted him. One time he said to Sayyīdinā Mūsā 🕊, "Next time you go to *Ṭūr Sīnā,* ask Allāh to grant me *īmān* as I don't have it."

Sayyīdinā Mūsā 🕊 said, "How do you not have *īmān* when you believe in me?"

He said, "No, that is not enough, *yā* Mūsā, ask Allāh 🕊."

Sayyīdinā Mūsā 🕊 went to *Ṭūr Sīnā* and asked, "*Yā Rabbī,* my neighbor is asking for *īmān.*"

Allāh said, "Go tell him I am sending him *īmān.*"

Sayyīdinā Mūsā 🕊 went back to his neighbor and knocked at the door and there was no answer. He tried again, but no answer, so he opened the door and saw his neighbor sitting still, not moving at all. He was in a heavenly coma.

Mūsā 🕊 said, "*Yā Rabb*! What is this? I asked for *īmān* for him, You made him finished."

Allāh replied, "That is one *dharrah,* one atom's weight of the *īmān* that Prophet 🕊 is carrying in the Last Days that I sent to him and he is in a *ḥāl,* trance!"

So the Ṣaḥābah 🕊 were raised in the lap of Prophet 🕊 and Allāh said, "I gave them *īmān.*" He not only gave to them, but *wa zayyanahu fī qulūbikum,* "He decorated their heart with it." *Wa karraha ilaykumu 'l-kufra wa 'l-fusūqa wa 'l-ʿiṣyāna,* "and made them disgusted by all forms of *kufr,* unbelief, corruption and disobedience." So they were obedient, not corrupted, but good servants of Allāh 🕊. *Ūlāika humu 'r-rāshidūn,* "Those are the wise ones."

May Allāh forgive us and may Allāh bless us.

Wa min Allāhi 't-tawfīq, bi ḥurmati 'l-ḥabīb, bi ḥurmati 'l-Fātiḥah.
And with Allāh is success. For the sake of the Beloved, for his sake we recite the opening chapter of Holy Qur'ān.

The Best Century

Alḥamdulillāh alladhī ja'alanā min ummat an-Nabī al-Muṣṭafā ﷺ. *Alḥamdulillāh* that He made us from the Nation of Muḥammad ﷺ and He showed us that the Prophet ﷺ is the role model, and we explained that in the previous session where Allāh ﷻ said:

لَقَدْ كَانَ لَكُمْ فِي رَسُولِ اللَّهِ أُسْوَةٌ حَسَنَةٌ لِمَنْ كَانَ يَرْجُو اللَّهَ وَالْيَوْمَ الآخِرَ وَذَكَرَ اللَّهَ كَثِيرا

Indeed in the Messenger of Allāh you have an excellent example
for anyone whose hope is in Allāh and the Last Day
and (who) remembers Allāh often.[99]

"You have in the Prophet ﷺ a perfect role model," and the *Ṣaḥābah* ﵃ were following that according to the *āyah* that we mentioned before, *Sūrat Āli-'Imrān*:

قُلْ إِن كُنتُمْ تُحِبُّونَ اللَّهَ فَاتَّبِعُونِي يُحْبِبْكُمُ اللَّهُ وَيَغْفِرْ لَكُمْ ذُنُوبَكُمْ وَاللَّهُ غَفُورٌ رَّحِيمٌ

Say (O Muḥammad), "If you (really) love Allāh,
then follow me! Allāh will love you."[100]

"If you love Allāh follow me, Allāh will love you," and so they were following Sayyīdinā Muḥammad ﷺ in every footstep; every step he used to do or did they were following the same way according to their *īmān*. Also, here *"al-īmān"* plays a big role in the personality of people. That is what we can see when Prophet ﷺ asked the *Ṣaḥābah* ﵃ to donate for charity purposes for their needs at that time. Sayyīdinā Abū Bakr aṣ-Ṣiddīq ﵁ brought a lot of his wealth and so did Sayyīdinā 'Umar ﵁, Sayyīdinā 'Uthmān ﵁ and Sayyīdinā 'Alī ﵁. Prophet ﷺ asked Sayyīdinā Abū Bakr aṣ-Ṣiddīq ﵁, "What

---

[99] Sūrat al-Aḥzāb, 33:21.

[100] Sūrat Āli-'Imrān, 3:31.

did you leave for your family?" He said, "I left Allāh and His Prophet, I brought everything for you." So (that was the evidence that) his *imān* was at a very high level and very strong; his belief in the Prophet ﷺ was so strong and that is why he was called "aṣ-Ṣiddīq," because anything the Prophet ﷺ asked or said, he was the first one to comply, to accept immediately without question or doubts. Then the Prophet ﷺ asked Sayyīdinā 'Umar ؓ what he left for his family, and he said, "I brought half and left half." The Prophet ﷺ said, "*Yā* 'Umar! Your *imān* is half that of Sayyīdinā Abū Bakr aṣ-Ṣiddīq ؓ."

So this is showing that they have levels, even though the Prophet ﷺ said, "If there will be a prophet after me, 'Umar ؓ will be a prophet." Similarly, Sayyīdinā 'Uthmān ؓ, Sayyīdinā 'Alī ؓ and other *Ṣaḥābah* ؓ have levels according to their personality and because they had strong faith in Prophet ﷺ and following him, Allāh gave them wisdom that led them to purify themselves, because wisdom leads to *akhlāq*, to the best of characters, and the best of characters leads to wisdom. So you cannot have *akhlāq* without wisdom and you cannot have wisdom without *akhlāq*, and both of them lead to a strong belief in the *'aqīdah* of Islam that Allāh is One, He is the Creator and Sayyīdinā Muḥammad ﷺ is His Messenger. In Islam there are three different levels, not like what everyone not paying attention to the highest level, they are only paying attention to the first level, the Five Pillars of Islam, which is good, but then we have the Six Pillars of *Imān*, which is a different level, and then we have the one Pillar of *Iḥsān*, the Level of Moral Excellence, which is the highest level.

Prophet Imparted the Highest Character to His Companions

That is why the *Ṣaḥābah* ؓ were raised 'in the lap' of the Prophet ﷺ; he raised them by talking to them, where they spent every day in *ṣuḥbah*, association with him. Every day Prophet ﷺ was counseling them, teaching them, prohibiting them from entering into bad characters, to backbite and spread rumors, and he used to tell them:

الفتنه نائمه لعن الله من ايقضها

Fitna is dormant and Allāh cursed the one who awoke it.

So he took them all the way to prepare them for the next stage, the stage after Prophet ﷺ, and always the Prophet ﷺ was present in their hearts and minds: when they walked to work, when they sat in the *masjid*, when they sat with their families, when they ate. They always they had a presence with the Prophet ﷺ, not like us today where people come to the *masjid* to listen and they sleep, their eyes are closed, sleeping. The *Ṣaḥābah* ؓ never closed their eyes, their eyes were always open. Even though they did not sleep for 24 hours, especially in Ramaḍān where people don't sleep, they never closed their eyes.

And Allāh said:

وإعلموا أن فيكم رسول الله

And know Allāh's Messenger is in you.[101]

Allāh is saying that He is favoring them and promoting them and praising them, that, "You must know, O *Ṣaḥābah* ؓ of Prophet, that the presence of the Prophet ﷺ is in you, is with you, is in you!" That is why the Prophet, *allāhumma ṣallī ʿalā Sayyidinā Muḥammad* ﷺ said:

خَيْرُ النَّاس قرْنِي ثُمَّ الَّذِينَ يَلُونَهُمْ ثُمَّ الَّذِينَ يَلُونَهُمْ

The best of Mankind are my generation (or my century), then the one that follows it, then the one that follows it.[102]

Khayru 'n-nāsi qarnī, "The best of people are those who were in my time, that century that is around me, coming from my birth to my leaving *dunyā*." And the *Ṣaḥābah* ؓ continued, "The first century was the best century." And Allāh ﷻ said in Holy Qur'ān:

كُنتُمْ خَيْرَ أُمَّةٍ أُخْرِجَتْ لِلنَّاس تَأْمُرُونَ بِالْمَعْرُوفِ وَتَنْهَوْنَ عَنِ الْمُنكَرِ وَتُؤْمِنُونَ بِاللَّهِ

You are the best of nations evolved for Mankind, enjoining what is right, forbidding what is wrong and believing in Allāh.[103]

"You were the best *ummah* that Allāh has sent," and the best of the best as the Prophet ﷺ said, "The best of them are those in my century or my time, *khayru 'n-nāsi qarnī*, because you learned from the Prophet ﷺ and Allāh put the love of the Prophet ﷺ in your heart and you followed him, *tāmurūna b i'l-maʿrūfi*, you learned from him and *wa tanhawna ʿani 'l-munkari*, you call for good and prohibit what is bad." Calling for good is not easy; you might

---

[101] Sūrat al-Ḥujurāt, 49:7.

[102] Bukhārī, Muslim, Tirmidhī.

[103] Sūrat Āli-ʿImrān, 3:110.

face a lot of difficulties because people have no understanding or knowledge about Islam, especially today, for what Islam is standing for. Islam is standing,

O Muslims, viewers, wherever you are! Islam is calling for *ma'rūf*, *tāmurūna bi 'l-ma'rūf*, call people to what is good! So if Allāh is saying that we were the best of *ummah* that has been sent to humanity, calling for good, and calling for good is always faced by struggle. What happened when the Prophet ﷺ was calling for good? The Quraysh, Abū Lahab and Abū Jahl were opposing and abusing the Prophet ﷺ every day, and abusing those who believed in him, torturing them, beating them, killing them and still they never changed, standing forth like pine trees, green in summer, green in winter, standing firm; their beliefs never changed. We are from them, we are from their wombs, *min aslābi, aslābi rijāl...* As Prophet ﷺ said:

إِنَّ فِي أَصْلَابِ أَصْلَابِ رِجَالٍ مِنْ أَصْحَابِي رِجَالًا وَنِسَاءً مِنْ أُمَّتِي يَدْخُلُونَ الْجَنَّةَ بِغَيْرِ حِسَابٍثُمَّ قَرَأَ : وَآخَرِينَ مِنْهُمْ لَمَّا يَلْحَقُوا بِهمْ .

Verily in the loins of the loins of the loins of men from my Companions are men and women of my Nation who will enter Paradise with no account.[104]

"There will be from the womb of the womb of the womb of people who are the best, and they will enter Paradise with no account." And many of them are descended from the Ṣaḥābah ﷺ who traveled all around the world and entered new countries and had children.

عَنْ عَبْدِ اللَّهِ , قَالَ : قَالَ رَسُولُ اللَّهِ صَلَّى اللَّهُ عَلَيْهِ وَسَلَّمَ : خَيْرُ النَّاس قَرْني ثُمَّ الَّذِينَ يَلُونَهُمْ ثُمَّ الَّذِينَ يَلُونَهُمْ

The best of people are my century, then the one after them, then the one after them. [105]

Ibn Mas'ūd ﷺ described the Ṣaḥābah ﷺ:

كما قال ابن مسعود رضي الله عنه: "أولئك أصحاب رسول الله صلى الله عليه وسلم كانوا أبر الناس قلوباً، وأعمقهم علماً، وأقلهم تكلفاً"

Those were the Companions of the Prophet of Allāh ﷺ; they were the most pious and sincere people among humanity in their hearts and they were the

---

[104] aṭ-Ṭabarānī.

[105] Bukhārī.

deepest in Islamic knowledge (they memorized much and understood exceptionally well. If the Prophet ﷺ mentioned a ḥadīth one time, they memorized it) and they were the most simple in their needs."

The Ṣaḥābah ﷺ are only looking for their needs to the minimum level of life, of needs, not like today everyone is living a very high standard of life in technology, in cars, in everything. They were happy even if they only had dates in their home. Today are we happy with dates only? We are asking food and sweets and cakes and meat and all kinds of vegetables when they were not able to see vegetables always and not able to see meat always.

أحدثك كأنك تنظر إليهم : فرسان بالنهار ، رهبان بالليل ، ما يأكلون في ذمتهم إلا بثمن ، ولا يدخلون إلا بسلام ، يقفون عَلى من حاربهم حتى يأتوا عليهم

I will describe them to you as if you are actually looking at them. They are valiant horsemen by day, monks by night and they never take anything from their non-Muslim subjects without paying its full p[106]rice. They never see anyone without first greeting with Salām and they remain glued to anyone they meet in combat until the matter is settled."

It was mentioned by non-Muslims...they were describing the Ṣaḥābah as soldiers in daytime and monks in the night, where *"ruhbān"* means dedicated worshippers at night. They don't eat if they don't make money to eat; they don't eat except in their sweat. They were sweating in order eat, not to get it free. "They don't enter except by saying, *'Salāmu ʿalaykum;'* they don't enter without bringing peace with them, they come with peace." Are we like that today? No. In another *riwāyah*:

أَنَّهُمْ يَقُومُونَ اللَّيْلَ ، وَيَصُومُونَ النَّهَارَ

They were standing in prayer all night and fasting the days.[107]

Now we wait for *Ramaḍān* to finish quickly in order to eat.

---

[106] *Ṭārīkh Dimashq* of ibn ʿAsākir.

[107] ad-Daynūrī.

Who Has the Strongest Faith?

So they filled history, big history, their time is a history for everyone to learn from what they were doing. That is why the Prophet ﷺ asked the Ṣaḥābah ؓ in a ḥadīth:

وَعَنِ ابْنِ عَبَّاسٍ أَنَّهُ قَالَ لِجُلَسَائِهِ يَوْمًا : أَيُّ النَّاسِ أَعْجَبُ إِيمَانًا ؟ قَالُوا : الْمَلَائِكَةُ . قَالَ : وَكَيْفَ لَا تُؤْمِنُ الْمَلَائِكَةُ وَالْأَمْرُ فَوْقَهُمْ يَرَوْنَهُ ؟ قَالُوا : الْأَنْبِيَاءُ . قَالَ : وَكَيْفَ لَا يُؤْمِنُ الْأَنْبِيَاءُ وَالْأَمْرُ يَنْزِلُ عَلَيْهِمْ غُدْوَةً وَعَشِيَّةً ؟ قَالُوا : فَنَحْنُ . قَالَ : وَكَيْفَ لَا تُؤْمِنُونَ وَأَنْتُمْ تَرَوْنَ مِنْ رَسُولِ اللَّهِ مَا تَرَوْنَ ؟ ثُمَّ قَالَ : قَالَ رَسُولُ اللَّهِ ـ صَلَّى اللَّهُ عَلَيْهِ وَسَلَّمَ " : ـأَعْجَبُ النَّاسِ إِيمَانًا قَوْمٌ يَأْتُونَ مِنْ بَعْدِي يُؤْمِنُونَ بِي وَلَمْ يَرَوْنِي . أُولَئِكَ إِخْوَانِي حَقًّا "

"Who has the strongest faith in their heart?" They answered, "The Prophets!" Prophet ﷺ said, "How will they not have strong faith when revelation comes to them?" They said, "Then it is the angels!" Prophet ﷺ said, "How will they not have strong faith when they are in the Divine Presence?" They answered, "Us, your Ṣaḥābah!" Prophet ﷺ said, "How will they not have strong faith when you also see

me?" He ﷺ said, "The best of people will come at the End of Time, and they will not see me, but they still believe in me. They are my brothers, truly."[108]

"Who is the most astonishing, those who have strong *īmān* in Allāh ﷻ?" And the Ṣaḥābah ؓ were thinking, though they have deep knowledge, but they did not get that. *Man ashaddu 'n-nāsi īmānan, man 'ajab al-khalqu īmānan,* "Who is the strongest and most astonishing people to have *īmān*?" They said, "Yā Rasūlullāh! The angels." The Prophet ﷺ said, "How can the angels not have strong *īmān* when they are seeing what they are seeing in Paradise? That is not astonishing or amazing." Then they said, "Yā Rasūlullāh! The prophets." And Sayyidinā Muḥammad ﷺ said, "How can prophets not have strong *īmān* when they receive the Message and they are messengers and they see Jibrīl ؏ coming to them?" Then they said, "There is no one left except us, your Companions, *yā Rasūlullāh.*" The Prophet ﷺ said, "How are my Companions not going to have amazing, strong *īmān* when they are seeing me among them?" Then they said, "Yā Rasūlullāh, we don't know." He said, "Allāh ﷻ is creating, coming after me people whom they never saw me and believed in me without seeing me. They have the strongest *īmān*, they are the astonishing ones, because they are not seeing. You are seeing and you have *īmān*, but they have strongest *īmān* as they are not seeing."

---

[108] Saḥih Bukhārī.

Only from century to century, *imāms* were bringing and explaining, and they accepted everything, that is how they got strong *īmān*. So with the presence of the Prophet ﷺ among the Ṣaḥābah ؓ, he planted in them the seed of Islam, the seed of *iḥsān* and the seed of *īmān*, and that seed flourished. The Prophet ﷺ spent with them teaching them all kinds of knowledge, but what happened is that the Prophet ﷺ left *dunyā* and there was no more *waḥiyy*, no more revelation, it stopped. Until today there is no more revelation and until the Day of Judgment there will be no more revelation, but there is knowledge that the Prophet ﷺ left behind in the hearts of his *Ṣaḥābah* ؓ: how he was in his time, how he used to act, how he used to solve problems with the *Ṣaḥābah* ؓ, how he dealt with them and how they dealt with their families, how to do *muʿamalāt* and dealings with each other in trade.

Prophet ﷺ never left one single issue except he explained it, and because of that, *thumma badʿa ʿilmu 'l-ḥadīthi yaqtaṣir ʿalā ʿilmi 'l-aḥkām, ʿalā marri 'z-zamān wa bi taʿsīriʿ 'l-awāmi li 't-tabiʿīyya ijtimaʿīyya wa 't-tashrīʿyya*, the knowledge of *ḥadīth* became the source of all *tashriʿ*, the constitution of Muslims came from Holy Qurʾān and from Holy Ḥadīth. Every issue that happened in society and needed explanation came from what the Prophet ﷺ said in his *aḥadīth* that *Ṣaḥābah* had collected and kept in their hearts and wrote them. From that verdicts came, different *fatwās* came, different explanation of *Fiqh* came, and that is how the *Fiqh* of the *ḥadīth* of the Prophet ﷺ began to appear. From that we begin to see the time slowly, slowly coming to different schools of thought.

So that knowledge of *ḥadīth* became the important source of everything they needed in their life and you began to see all these knowledgeable people, scholars, sincere and pious people were busy writing it, explaining it and putting it in order for people to understand what they need from it and apply it in their lives. So they were shifting more towards this aspect of Islamic *Fiqh* and paying it more attention than to *al-Maqām al-Iḥsān*, the Moral Excellence. In any case, Moral Excellence is in the life and in the heart of every Muslim and it will be polished when you polish your knowledge of *Fiqh*! This is how it happened that we began to look for *aḥadīth* of the Prophet ﷺ, as the Prophet ﷺ is not there, but he is present in his *aḥadīth*, and as Allāh ﷻ said:

وَاعْلَمُوا أَنَّ فِيكُمْ رَسُولَ اللَّهِ

And know Allāh's Messenger is in you.[109]

"You must know that the Prophet ﷺ is with you, among you, between you, in you!"

What did Sayyīdinā 'Umar Ibn 'Abdul-'Azīz ؓ used to say? Look at their knowledge, which we don't have today.

كان آخر خطبة خطبها عمر بن عبد العزيز أن حمد الله وأثنى عليه ثم قال: أما بعد أيها الناس إنكم لم تخلقوا عبثا ولن تتركوا سدى وإن لكم معادا ينزل الله فيه للحكم بينكم والفصل بينكم فخاب وخسر وشقي عبد أخرجه الله من رحمته وحرم جنة عرضها السماوات والأرض ألم تعلموا أنه لا يأمن عذاب الله غدا إلا من حذر هذا اليوم وخافه وباع نافدا بباق وقليلا بكثير وخوفا بأمان ألا ترون أنكم من أصلاب الهالكين وسيكون من بعدكم الباقين حتى تردون إلى خير الوارثين ثم إنكم في كل يوم تشيعون غاديا ورائحا إلى الله عز وجل قد قضى نحبه وانقضى أجله حتى تغيبوه في صدع من الأرض في بطن صدع غير ممهد ولا موسد قد فرق الأحباب وباشر التراب وواجه الحساب مرتهن بعمله غني عما ترك فقير إلى ما قدم فاتقوا الله قبل انقضاء مواثيقه ونزول الموت بكم ثم جعل طرف ردائه على وجهه فبكى وأبكى من حوله

Sayyīdinā 'Umar ibn 'Abdul-'Azīz in his final sermon said: "O Mankind!
You were not created for nothing; Allāh created you for something important.
He ﷻ didn't leave you free, He sent down to you a principle, a constitution.
You are going to have an Appointment, a Day that Allāh ﷻ will bring you
all together and judge you."

Allāh didn't create you and leave you wild, and free in the wilderness. Today can you be free? They say, "Freedom of speech, freedom of speech...." You can be free to speak, free to say what you want, but if you don't accept the constitution you will be put in prison, so where is that 'freedom?' There is no freedom in reality, because we are wild; if they let us free we would be so wild and violent and extreme, just as we are seeing today.

"And Allāh ﷻ will bring you together on a Day and judge you of what you have done, because He has put for you a constitution for you to see what you have to follow."

Follow the Holy Qur'ān and the *aḥadīth* of Prophet ﷺ as he is the role model, so you have to follow what he came with:

---

[109] Sūrat al-Ḥujurāt, 49:7.

تَأْمُرُونَ بِالْمَعْرُوفِ وَتَنْهَوْنَ عَنِ الْمُنكَرِ وَتُؤْمِنُونَ بِاللهِ

Enjoining what is right, forbidding what is wrong and believing in Allāh.[110]

You have a duty to call for good and to leave bad! He is going to judge you, and those who did good in their life will go to Paradise and those who did not do good in their life, Allāh will judge them and whatever Allāh gives them of judgment Allāh knows better.

"A disaster will come up on the servant of Allāh who does not follow what the Prophet ﷺ said, he will be judged and he will be out of Allāh's Mercy. (May Allāh protect us!) And that person will be out of everything, naked from all his *'amal*, and he will be out of Allāh's Paradise that is bigger than Heavens and Earth (which means bigger than this universe) but safety tomorrow is for those who fear Allāh ﷻ." (Those who fear Allāh ﷻ will have safety, because when you fear Allāh ﷻ you stop doing what is bad.) They sold for something that is worth nothing they get something big. (That means, he sold his *dunyā* for his *Ākhirah*,) And gave up something that is going to be annihilated for something that will be eternal. (meaning: he left *dunyā* for *Ākhirah*.) And he carried difficulties in *dunyā* in order to get ease and relaxation in *Ākhirah*. Don't you see yourself among those people who are going to lose if you don't listen to what the Prophet ﷺ said?"

Finally, he ends saying, "One day you are going to be taken away from *dunyā*, naked, nothing on you, and you are going to be put in a hole, and you are going to have a bad smell coming from you and they will put you deep in the Earth without a pillow, without a mattress, and everything is taken from you, and you are going to leave the beloved one, and you are going to face the Judgment of Allāh ﷻ."

We will continue tomorrow *inshā'Allāh*, with what Imām Aḥmad ﷺ said in his *Musnad* and what is in the *Saḥīḥ* of Tirmidhī about this issue.

Wa min Allāhi 't-tawfīq, bi ḥurmati 'l-ḥabīb, bi ḥurmati 'l-Fātiḥah.

When you want to sleep, go home or the level of the *ṣuḥbat* will go down. Go over there and sleep. I want to see you near me and focused. When you are together, Allāh's Hand is with the group, then Shayṭān cannot affect you. I have to address someone when I am speaking,

---

[110] Sūrat Āli-'Imrān, 3:110.

(otherwise) I cannot speak. If that happens next time, I will stop. Come sit close, not far away! Better to go stay with chickens, they are outside! If you are not interested in *ṣuḥbat,* okay, we will stop *ṣuḥbat* and just pray *Fajr* and *Tahajjud.*

May Allāh forgive us and may Allāh bless us.

Wa min Allāhi 't-tawfīq, bi ḥurmati 'l-ḥabīb, bi ḥurmati 'l-Fātiḥah.
And with Allāh is success. For the sake of the Beloved, for his sake we recite the opening chapter of Holy Qur'ān.

Why the Armies of Shayṭān are Angry with Human Beings

A'ūdhu billāhi min ash-Shayṭāni 'r-rajīm. Bismillāhi' r-Raḥmāni 'r-Raḥīm.
Nawaytu 'l-arbā'īn, nawaytu 'l-'itikāf, nawaytu 'l-khalwah, nawaytu 'l-'uzlah,
nawaytu 'r-riyāḍa, nawaytu 's-sulūk, lillāhi Ta'alā fī hādha 'l-masjid.
Atī'ullāha wa atī'ū 'r-Rasūla wa ūli 'l-amri minkum. (4:59)

A'ūdhu billāhi min ash-Shayṭāni 'r-rajīm. Bismillāhi 'r-Raḥmāni 'r-Raḥīm. Ash-hadu an lā ilāha illa-Llāh wa ash-hadu anna Muḥammadan 'abduhu wa ḥabībuhu wa rasūluh, ṣall-Allāhu ta'ala 'alayhi wa 'alā ālihi wa ṣaḥbihi ajma'īn. What usually happens is that we have to first say, "As-salāmu 'alaykum wa raḥmatullāhi wa barakātuh."

Viewers, listeners, audience and everyone: what is Shayṭān upset with? Why is he upset from us? Why are the devils, the army of Iblees, upset with human beings? They are upset because Allāh ﷻ said in the Holy Qur'ān:

وَلَقَدْ كَرَّمْنَا بَنِي آدَمَ

We have honored the Children of Adam.[111]

Allāh is saying, "We have honored human beings and We have given them superiority over everyone." So Shayṭān gets jealous as he doesn't like that. When he gets jealous he comes to fight us, especially when *'abdallāh*, the servant of Allāh ﷻ, stands up for worshipness. When *Ummat an-Nabī* ﷺ, *Ummat al-Ḥaqq, Ummat aṭ-Ṭarīq al-Mustaqīm, al-Ummat alladhī sharafahullāhu 'azza wa jalla*, the *ummah* that Allāh honored, stands up to pray and worship, he gets upset because he knows that the servant of Allāh is between Allāh's Hands!

When the servant is praying, he has to understand that Allāh is looking at him. Shayṭān tries to always deviate us from focussing on the Divine Presence, on Allāh ﷻ and Prophet ﷺ, on the Holy Qur'ān and *ḥadīth* and on the creation of Heavens and Earth. Allāh said in the Holy Qur'ān:

---

[111] Sūrat al-'Isrā, 17:70.

إنَّ فِي خَلْقِ السَّمَاوَاتِ وَالأرْضِ وَاخْتِلافِ اللَّيْلِ وَالنَّهَارِ لآيَاتٍ لأُوْلِي الألْبَابِ الَّذِينَ يَذْكُرُونَ اللَّهَ قِيَامًا وَقُعُودًا وَعَلَى جُنُوبِهِمْ وَيَتَفَكَّرُونَ فِي خَلْقِ السَّمَاوَاتِ وَالأرْضِ رَبَّنَا مَا خَلَقْتَ هَذَا بَاطِلاً سُبْحَانَكَ فَقِنَا عَذَابَ النَّارِ

Behold! In the creation of Heavens and Earth, and in the alternation of night and day, there are indeed signs for men of understanding, those who remember Allāh (always, and in prayers) standing, sitting and lying down on their sides, and contemplating the creation of the Heavens and the Earth, (saying), "Our Lord! You have not created (all) this without purpose! Glory to You! Give us salvation from the torment of the Fire."[112]

Shayṭān doesn't like those who remember Allāh ﷻ, but Allāh is saying, "Those who remember Me, *wa yatafakkarūn*, and begin to think about the creation of Heavens and Earth, *yatafakkarūna fī khalqi 's-samāwāti wa 'l-arḍ.' Allāhu Akbar*, how small we are! When you look inside of this solar system, not outside, the entire Earth might be as small as the head of a pin! When it is in the galaxy it doesn't even appear, you cannot see it. It is in the closest galaxy to us, which carries billions and billions of stars. Scientists say that there are 80 billion stars in this galaxy, and there are thousands and thousands of galaxies that Allāh has created. So we are in a tiny place that has lots of significance, yet it is very, very small in existence. In that smallness Allāh ﷻ is showing His Greatness that, "I can make the small big and honor them, even though they are very small."

That is why when the Prophet ﷺ was in the Divine Presence and saw what he saw in *Maqām Qāba Qawsayni aw Adnā*, he was feeling shy to say in front of the Divine Presence, "*Yā Rabbī!* I am here," and he ﷺ said:

قُلْ إِنَّمَا أَنَا بَشَرٌ مِّثْلُكُمْ

Say, "I am but a man like yourselves."[113]

Prophet ﷺ knows the *'Ulūm al-Awwalīn wa 'l-Akhirīn*, he knows what we do not. He has the understanding of Heavenly Knowledge which Allāh grants to whom He likes, as in the case of Sayyīdinā Khiḍr ؏ and Sayyīdinā Mūsā ؏. Allāh granted to one of His servants, Sayyīdinā Khiḍr ؏, *'Ilm al-Ladunnī*, Heavenly Knowledge which He did not give to Sayyīdinā Mūsā ؏,

---

[112] Sūrat Āli-'Imrān, 3:191-192.
[113] Sūrat al-Kahf, 18:110.

even though he was one of the *Ūlu 'l-ʿAzam*, the Five Great Prophets, but Allāh gave them both what He gave.

That Heavenly Knowledge is what everyone is seeking, so that is why our hearts must always be focused on Allāh ﷻ, meaning on His Creation, "Those who remember Allāh standing, sitting and laying down, and reflect on the creation of Heavens and Earth."

Alḥamdulillāh, the focus of all the talks that we give in this Ramaḍān is to show that Allāh doesn't like anyone to be associated with Him or in partnership with Him. He is The Greatest, if we can say, there is no limit to His Greatness! We will never understand Allāh's Greatness except through His Oneness, by looking at His Creation. So if you look at the Creation, you can see the Oneness of Allāh ﷻ in everything. Can you make a star? If you bring all the scientists and all the prophets, can they create a star? [No.] So that means we are nothing. We cannot understand the Greatness of Allāh ﷻ and also the Greatness that He brought His Prophet ﷺ through the atmosphere without any harm to him, passing through the entire universe to reach the Station of *Qāba Qawsayni aw Adnā* in moments! Can anyone do that? So Allāh wants us to look at His Creation and understand that He is The One Who can do that.

Your heart must focus on Allāh through His Creation. He doesn't like you to focus on anyone except Him so, if in your worship, especially during your *ṣalāt,* you don't focus on where you make *sajda* and put your forehead on the ground declaring your *ʿubūdiyya,* servanthood to Allāh, but instead you look right or left, your prayer will curse you and say, "You didn't give Allāh His Right in the prayer." So many people don't know that during prayer they must keep their focus on the place of *sajda,* as that is the *Maqām al-ʿUbūdiyya.* What is the difference between bowing and putting your head on the floor in *sajda?* Bowing shows respect, not more than that, while the *sajda* shows servanthood, (demonstrating), "*Yā Rabbī,* I am Your servant! I am putting my forehead on the ground and I dare to raise it until You forgive me my sins!"

So Allāh ﷻ does not like your heart to move right or left by moving your eyes right or left as some people do. Be careful, because Shayṭān will come during your prayers in order to distract you from where you must focus your heart and your eyes, as anyone who focuses his eyes will be respected and honored. Anyone who gets distracted during prayer by looking back and forth during prayers must bring his eyes back to the location of the *sajda,* thinking on the creation of Heavens and Earth, as Allāh said in the Holy Qur'ān, *Wa yatafakkarūna fī khalqi 's-samāwāti wa 'l-arḍ*, "They reflect on the creation of the Heavens and Earth." Then say, "O Allāh! I am making *sajda* for You."

It is related in Īmām Āḥmad's *Musnad* and by at-Tirmidhī from a *ḥadīth* of al-Hārith al-Ashʿarī ﷺ, that the Prophet ﷺ said:

إِنَّ اللَّهَ أَمَرَ يَحْيَى بْنَ زَكَرِيَّا بِخَمْسِ كَلِمَاتٍ أَنْ يَعْمَلَ بِهَا وَيَأْمُرَ بَنِي إِسْرَائِيلَ أَنْ يَعْمَلُوا بِهَا وَإِنَّهُ كَادَ أَنْ يُبْطِئَ بِهَا فَقَالَ عِيسَى إِنَّ اللَّهَ أَمَرَكَ بِخَمْسِ كَلِمَاتٍ لِتَعْمَلَ بِهَا وَتَأْمُرَ بَنِي إِسْرَائِيلَ أَنْ يَعْمَلُوا بِهَا فَإِمَّا أَنْ تَأْمُرَهُمْ وَإِمَّا أَنَا آمُرُهُمْ . فَقَالَ يَحْيَى أَخْشَى إِنْ سَبَقْتَنِي بِهَا أَنْ يُخْسَفَ بِي أَوْ أُعَذَّبَ فَجَمَعَ النَّاسَ فِي بَيْتِ الْمَقْدِسِ فَامْتَلَأَ الْمَسْجِدُ وَقَعَدُوا عَلَى الشُّرَفِ فَقَالَ إِنَّ اللَّهَ أَمَرَنِي بِخَمْسِ كَلِمَاتٍ أَنْ أَعْمَلَ بِهِنَّ وَآمُرَكُمْ أَنْ تَعْمَلُوا بِهِنَّ أَوَّلُهُنَّ أَنْ تَعْبُدُوا اللَّهَ وَلَا تُشْرِكُوا بِهِ شَيْئًا وَإِنَّ مَثَلَ مَنْ أَشْرَكَ بِاللَّهِ كَمَثَلِ رَجُلٍ اشْتَرَى عَبْدًا مِنْ خَالِصِ مَالِهِ بِذَهَبٍ أَوْ وَرِقٍ فَقَالَ هَذِهِ دَارِي وَهَذَا عَمَلِي فَاعْمَلْ وَأَدِّ إِلَيَّ فَكَانَ يَعْمَلُ وَيُؤَدِّي إِلَى غَيْرِ سَيِّدِهِ فَأَيُّكُمْ يَرْضَى أَنْ يَكُونَ عَبْدُهُ كَذَلِكَ وَإِنَّ اللَّهَ أَمَرَكُمْ بِالصَّلَاةِ فَإِذَا صَلَّيْتُمْ فَلَا تَلْتَفِتُوا فَإِنَّ اللَّهَ يَنْصِبُ وَجْهَهُ لِوَجْهِ عَبْدِهِ فِي صَلَاتِهِ مَا لَمْ يَلْتَفِتْ وَآمُرُكُمْ بِالصِّيَامِ فَإِنَّ مَثَلَ ذَلِكَ كَمَثَلِ رَجُلٍ فِي عِصَابَةٍ مَعَهُ صُرَّةٌ فِيهَا مِسْكٌ فَكُلُّهُمْ يَعْجَبُ أَوْ يُعْجِبُهُ رِيحُهَا وَإِنَّ رِيحَ الصَّائِمِ أَطْيَبُ عِنْدَ اللَّهِ مِنْ رِيحِ الْمِسْكِ وَآمُرُكُمْ بِالصَّدَقَةِ فَإِنَّ مَثَلَ ذَلِكَ كَمَثَلِ رَجُلٍ أَسَرَهُ الْعَدُوُّ فَأَوْثَقُوا يَدَهُ إِلَى عُنُقِهِ وَقَدَّمُوهُ لِيَضْرِبُوا عُنُقَهُ فَقَالَ أَنَا أَفْدِيهِ مِنْكُمْ بِالْقَلِيلِ وَالْكَثِيرِ . فَفَدَى نَفْسَهُ مِنْهُمْ وَآمُرُكُمْ أَنْ تَذْكُرُوا اللَّهَ فَإِنَّ مَثَلَ ذَلِكَ كَمَثَلِ رَجُلٍ خَرَجَ الْعَدُوُّ فِي أَثَرِهِ سِرَاعًا حَتَّى إِذَا أَتَى عَلَى حِصْنٍ حَصِينٍ فَأَحْرَزَ نَفْسَهُ مِنْهُمْ كَذَلِكَ الْعَبْدُ لَا يُحْرِزُ نَفْسَهُ مِنَ الشَّيْطَانِ إِلَّا بِذِكْرِ اللَّهِ "

Indeed Allāh ﷻ commanded Yaḥyā ibn Zakarīyyā ﷺ (John the Baptist) with five commandments to abide by and to command the Children of Israel to abide by them, but he was slow in doing so. So ʿĪsā ﷺ said, "Indeed Allāh commanded you with five commandments to abide by and to command the Children of Israel to abide by. Either you command them or I will command them."

So Yaḥyā ﷺ said, "I fear that if you precede me in this, then the Earth may swallow me or I will be punished." So he gathered the people in Jerusalem and they filled (the masjid) and sat upon its balconies. So he said, "Indeed Allāh has commanded me with five commandments to abide by and to command you to abide by. The first of them is that you worship Allāh and not associate anything with him. The parable of the one who associates others with Allāh is that of a man who buys a servant with his own gold or silver, then he says to him, 'This is my home and this is my business, so take care of it and give me the profits.'

So he takes care of it and gives the profits to someone other than his master. Which of you would live to have a servant like that? And Allāh commands you to perform ṣalāt, and when you perform ṣalāt then do not turn away, for Allāh is facing the face of His worshipers as long as he does not turn away. And He commands you with fasting, for indeed the parable of fasting is that of a man in a group with a sachet containing musk. All of them enjoy its fragrance. Indeed the breath of the fasting person is more pleasant to Allāh than the scent of musk.

And He commands you to give charity. The parable of that is a man captured by his enemies, tying his hands to his neck, and they come to him to cut his neck. Then he said, 'I can ransom myself from you with a little or a lot,' so he ransoms himself from them. And He commands you to remember Allāh, for indeed the parable of that is a man whose enemy quickly tracks him until he reaches an impermeable fortress in which he protects himself from them. This is how the worshiper is: he does not protect himself from Shayṭān except by the remembrance of Allāh."[114]

This *ḥadīth* will tell us what is necessary and what has been asked of nations before us. Allāh ﷻ ordered Sayyīdinā Yaḥya ﷺ, the son of Sayyīdinā Zakarīyyā ﷺ, five words. He ordered him to order the people of Banī Isrā'īl, which is for them and for us as Prophet ﷺ is mentioning it. So it is also for us that we have to be careful in accepting these five different principles that Allāh ordered Sayyīdinā Yaḥya ﷺ, son of Sayyīdinā Zakarīyyā ﷺ to implement.

Sayyīdinā Yaḥya ﷺ was a little bit late in implementing the order of Allāh ﷻ, so Sayyīdinā 'Īsā ﷺ said to him, "If you are going to be late and not quickly implement and order the people, I am going to do that," although Allāh ordered Sayyīdinā Yaḥya ﷺ to do it, but Yaḥya ﷺ was delaying it perhaps because at that time he saw that people were reluctant to worship and he was frightened, so he delayed. Sayyīdinā 'Īsā ﷺ stepped in to do it and said, "Allāh ordered five orders for you and for Banī Isrā'īl, *fa imma an tāmurahum wa imma anā āmuruhum*, "Either you order them or I will."

So that is an order, *aṭī'ullāh*, and anyone who does not fulfill an order is in a real problem. So we have to fulfill what Allāh ﷻ ordered us. Allāh said:

---

[114] Tirmidhī, Āḥmad.

وَمَا آتَاكُمُ الرَّسُولُ فَخُذُوهُ وَمَا نَهَاكُمْ عَنْهُ فَانتَهُوا وَاتَّقُوا اللّهَ إِنَّ اللّهَ شَدِيدُ الْعِقَابِ

And whatever the Prophet brought take and whatever he forbade do not do.
And fear Allāh, for Allāh is strict in Punishment.[115]

Meaning, "Take without doubt and hesitation what the Prophet ﷺ gives, immediately fulfill it, and leave what he forbids you." That is an order, so what do we have to do? *Sami'nā wa ata'nā,* "We listen and obey." Sayyīdinā Yaḥyā ﷺ said, "Yā 'Īsā ﷺ, I am worried and afraid that if you declare it to people before me, that means I delayed Allāh's Order, then Allāh might open the Earth and pull me inside, *yakhsifa bihi 'l-arḍ!*"

Does that happen? Yes. Allāh ﷻ said in the Holy Qur'ān:

إِنَّ قَارُونَ كَانَ مِن قَوْمِ مُوسَى فَبَغَى عَلَيْهِمْ وَآتَيْنَاهُ مِنَ الْكُنُوزِ مَا إِنَّ مَفَاتِحَهُ لَتَنُوءُ بِالْعُصْبَةِ أُولِي الْقُوَّةِ إِذْ قَالَ لَهُ قَوْمُهُ لَا تَفْرَحْ إِنَّ اللَّهَ لَا يُحِبُّ الْفَرِحِينَ

Qārūn was doubtless of the people of Moses, but he acted insolently towards them.
Such were the treasures We had bestowed on him that their very keys would have
been a burden to a body of strong men, behold, his people said to him, "Exult not,
for Allāh loveth not those who exult (in riches).
(*Sūrat al-Qaṣaṣ,* 28:76)

Allāh gave Qārūn richness and he became arrogant. Anyone who becomes arrogant, Allāh ﷻ will order the Earth to swallow him. People were saying, "Qārūn has money and we have nothing." Allāh showed them that wealth does not give you any benefit and the Earth swallowed him up. This happened recently in Florida when the Earth opened and swallowed a person. That is a sign for us, that if you are standing anywhere and if Allāh wants it can happen at any moment. It is to show us that it is true that the Earth may open at any time and take one person, as people say, "How can the Earth open and take only one person?" Yes, Allāh can make the Earth to open and take only one person, there doesn't need to be an earthquake that takes everyone. The Earth can take one person by himself from among many.

So Sayyīdinā Yaḥyā ﷺ said, "No my brother 'Īsā ﷺ, I do not want the Earth to swallow me." He called all the people to *Masjid* al-Aqsa, which was the focus in Jerusalem and it was full, and he said, *Inna 'Llāha tabāraka wa*

---

[115] Sūrat al-Ḥashr, 59:7.

ta'ala amaranā bi khamsi kalimātin, "Allāh has ordered me five orders and I am asking you to do them as He ordered me to do."

The First Order

You must not make *shirk*, associate anyone with Allāh, and that is what Shayṭān doesn't like from us. Allāh has no child or spouse and does not need one, as He is Unique. How can you claim that a man with his mother became gods? When they were asking, that, Allāh gave an example, "Does a god go to the restroom?" *Ḥāsha.* He is not in need for it. Allāh ﷻ said eloquently in the Holy Qur'ān:

$$كَانَا يَأْكُلَانِ الطَّعَامَ$$

They had both to eat their (daily) food.[116]

When you eat food what do you have to do? Go to the restroom! So the first of the five words was to not make *shirk* and we will explain that later in detail, in the *aḥadīth* describing *shirk* and the verses from Holy Qur'ān that are related to it in the coming sessions. *Āwwalahunna an ta'bud-Allāha wa lā tushrikū bihi shay'an.* He gave the example of that as the person who got a helper to help him and he paid him with gold or *waraq*, paper. He said, "This is my home. You will do my work as you are entitled to do."

When someone hires you, what must they do? They must do whatever they are ordered. So the one making *shirk* is like the one who is hired to help and does the work, but he does not give the benefit (credit) of the work to the Lord or employer and instead, gives it to someone else. So that means when you associate someone with Allāh ﷻ, it is as if you are giving the benefit of what you are doing to someone other than Allāh. So what will happen if you hire someone to do work and agree to pay him, but he gives the benefit to someone else? You will fire him! Similarly, Allāh will fire us when we put someone in His position. That is why Allāh does not like *shirk* and it is not allowed in Islam. You cannot make *sajda* to a shaykh; you may respect him as much as you like, but you cannot make *sajda* to anyone other than Allāh ﷻ.

Sayyīdinā Muḥammad ﷺ always *yanhā*, forbade *sajda* to anyone other than Allāh. If Allāh ordered it that is something else, as when people say,

---

[116] Sūrat al-Mā'ida, 5:75.

"How did Allāh order the angels to make *sajda* to Sayyīdinā Adam ﷺ?" That is something else, because it was an order to them and it was not a *sajda* of worship, but a *sajda* of respect. They were making *sajda* of *iḥtirām*, respect, and not *sajda* of *'ubūdīyya* to Sayyīdinā Adam ﷺ, due to the Light of the Prophet ﷺ in his forehead. Allāh was showing the angels, "This is My Prophet ﷺ." He asked them to make *sajda* in the meaning of respecting Allāh's Beloved One, where He said:

إِنَّ اللَّهَ وَمَلَائِكَتَهُ يُصَلُّونَ عَلَى النَّبِيِّ يَا أَيُّهَا الَّذِينَ آمَنُوا صَلُّوا عَلَيْهِ وَسَلِّمُوا تَسْلِيمًا

Verily, Allāh and His angels send praise on the Prophet. O Believers!
Pray upon him and greet him with a worthy salutation.[117]

Can you have a guide? Yes you can, as people want to learn. You need a teacher, because you cannot learn without a teacher. You need to have someone who knows more than you. Why did Sayyīdinā Mūusāa ﷺ go to Sayyīdinā Khiḍr ﷺ? Although Sayyīdinā Mūsā ﷺ is higher and there is no comparison, but Sayyīdinā Khiḍr ﷺ had some knowledge that Mūsā ﷺ wanted to know about. So yes, you can have a guide and it does not mean that you are committing *shirk*. Also, you can go to the Prophet ﷺ and ask for forgiveness in his presence, as the Ṣaḥābah ﷺ have done that. It is in the Holy Qur'ān:

وَلَوْ أَنَّهُمْ إِذ ظَّلَمُوا أَنفُسَهُمْ جَآؤُوكَ فَاسْتَغْفَرُوا اللَّهَ وَاسْتَغْفَرَ لَهُمُ الرَّسُولُ لَوَجَدُوا اللَّهَ تَوَّابًا رَّحِيمًا

If they had only, when they were unjust to themselves, come to you and asked
Allāh's forgiveness, and the Messenger had asked forgiveness for them, they would
have found Allāh indeed Oft-returning, Most Merciful.[118]

"If only when they oppressed themselves they had come to the Prophet ﷺ and asked Allāh's Forgiveness and the Prophet ﷺ asked forgiveness for them, they would have found Allāh Forgiving and Merciful."

---

[117] Sūrat al-'Aḥzāb, 33:56.
[118] Sūrat an-Nisā, 4:64.

Prophet ﷺ said:

أنا في قبري حي طري، من سلم علي سلمت عليه

I am in my grave alive and supple. Whoever greets me I greet him back.

ما من أحد يسلم عليَّ إلا رد الله عليَّ روحي حتى أسلم عليه

No one prays on me, except that Allāh will send back my soul to me to return his greeting.[119]

So Prophet ﷺ can reach us and we can reach him. Although we cannot see, but when we say, "*Yā Sayyidī, yā Rasūlullāh,*" he intercedes for us. When we come to Prophet ﷺ asking for forgiveness, he asks Allāh on our behalf. Do you think Allāh will not respond? That is not *shirk*! You are asking Allāh ﷻ and Prophet ﷺ is helping you. It is like someone who is elderly and cannot walk without a cane, so we help them walk. We are handicapped, like someone with a broken leg who needs a wheelchair or crutches, we need help and that is not *shirk*.

So Allāh does not like *shirk*. Do not associate a partner to Allāh ﷻ or take someone as the Creator other than Allāh. The Creator is One and Sayyīdinā Muḥammad ﷺ is the Best of Creation. Allāh created the Prophet ﷺ from *Nūr*, from His Light, from the attribute of Allāh ﷻ *an-Nūr*.

So we have to listen to what Prophet ﷺ is saying to us, in many *aḥadīth* about *shirk* and how to avoid it and how not to fall into the trap of Shayṭān. Shayṭān wants you to make *shirk* in order to make Allāh hate you, so you must be careful.

The Second Order

The second order that was given by Allāh ﷻ is to make *ṣalāt*. And what kind of *ṣalāt*? He said, *Fa idhā ṣallaytum fa lā taltafitū*, "When you pray don't look left and right, focus." Like yesterday a deaf person came, he cannot hear and cannot talk. So when you are in your *ṣalāt*, make yourself deaf, don't hear what is going on around and don't talk. Can we do that? We hope to, but we are struggling. Make yourself just like someone who is deaf and cannot hear. Try to learn how not to listen to what is going on around you, because it distracts your *ṣalāt*. So that is why you should not pray after jama'ah, run

---

[119] Abū Dāwūd.

away and go to your house and pray, because your focus will be better there. Pray in jama'ah and if not, pray at home. Try to focus on your prayer in your room, not hearing anything from the left or the right, or else your prayer will be running away from you and it will be thrown in your face and say, "I am not accepting your prayer!" We will explain that tomorrow.

May Allāh forgive us and may Allāh bless us.

Wa min Allāhi 't-tawfīq, bi ḥurmati 'l-ḥabīb, bi ḥurmati 'l-Fātiḥah.
And with Allāh is success. For the sake of the Beloved, for his sake we recite the opening chapter of Holy Qur'ān.

Five Commands of Prophet Yaḥyā ﷺ and Prophet Muḥammad ﷺ

A‘ūdhu billāhi min ash-Shayṭāni ‘r-rajīm. Bismillāhi’ r-Raḥmāni ‘r-Raḥīm.
Nawaytu ‘l-arbā‘īn, nawaytu ‘l-‘itikāf, nawaytu ‘l-khalwah, nawaytu ‘l-‘uzlah,
nawaytu ‘r-riyāḍa, nawaytu ‘s-sulūk, lillāhi Ta‘ālā fī hādha ‘l-masjid.
Atī‘ūllāha wa atī‘ū ‘r-Rasūla wa ūli ‘l-amri minkum. (4:59)

كل أمر ذي بال لا يبدأ فيه ببسم الله الرحمن الرحيم فهو أقطع أو(فهو ابتر)

*The Prophet ﷺ said, "Any action which does not begin with ‘Bismillāhi ‘r-Raḥmāni
‘r-Raḥīm’ is cut off; it has no continuity."*[120]

As-salāmu ‘alaykum wa raḥmatullāhi wa barakātuh. Today we were going to
continue the *ḥadīth* of al-Hārith al-Ash‘arī ﷺ narrated by Īmām Āḥmad and
Īmām Tirmidhī. We mentioned the first part in the previous session, that
Allāh ﷻ has ordered Sayyīdinā Yaḥyā ibn Zakarīyya ﷺ five words: first, it is
harām to make *shirk* with Allāh ﷻ, as we explained, and the second order is
that Allāh ﷻ has ordered people for *ṣalāt, wa amarakum bi ‘s-ṣalāt;* Allāh ﷻ
said to them that it is an obligation from Him to do your worshipness in
your prayers. That is why the Prophet ﷺ said:

ما بين الكفر والايمان ترك الصلاة

What is between disbelief and belief is the leaving of prayers.[121]

Ṣalāt is what is between belief and unbelief; either you are on this side a
believer or on other side an unbeliever. To be a believer is to pray, to be an
unbeliever is to drop your *ṣalāt.*

Prophet ﷺ said:

الصلاةُ عمودُ الدين

Prayer is the pillar of the religion.[122]

---

120 Āḥmad, *Musnad.*

121 Tirmidhī.

122 Bayhaqī.

We cannot lean on anything except on our prayers. There are the five obligations in Islam that Allāh ordered us and the Prophet ﷺ has mentioned the great importance of prayer:

عنْ عمرو بن سعيد القرشي، قالَ : " كُنْتُ عِنْدَ عُثْمَانَ فَدَعَا بِطَهُورٍ ، فقالَ سَمِعْتُ رَسُولَ اللَّهِ صلَّى اللَّهُ عَلَيْهِ وَسَلَّمَ ، يَقُولُ : مَا مِن امْرِئٍ مُسْلِمٍ ، تَحْضُرُهُ صَلَاةٌ مَكْتُوبَةٌ ، فَيُحْسِنُ وُضُوءَهَا ، وَخُشُوعَهَا ، وَرُكُوعَهَا ، إِلَّا كَانَتْ كَفَّارَةً لِمَا قَبْلَهَا مِنَ الذُّنُوبِ ، مَا لَمْ يُؤْتِ كَبِيرَةً ، وَذَلِكَ الدَّهْرَ كُلَّهُ "

Sayyīdinā 'Uthmān ﷻ heard the Prophet ﷺ say, "There is not any Muslim person who prepares for the obligatory prayers, and perfects its ablution and its reverence and its bowing except that it would be expiation for whatever of sins occurred prior to that prayer, as long as it is not a grave sin, and that covers all of time."[123]

And it is better to renew the *wuḍū* on every prayer as a cleansing process. Immediately renew *wuḍū* and go for the prayer, and that prayer must be performed right with the details of *khush'u, rukū', qiyām, sujūd* and all parts, and not like a rooster pecking in prayer, but you must give all the *arkāns* of *ṣalāt,* and not go up and down quickly and recite incorrectly. So these are important aspects to Muslims, as *ṣalāt* is a very important *rukn* in Islam. And Prophet ﷺ said:

صَلَاةُ الْجَمَاعَةِ تَفْضُلُ صَلَاةَ الْفَذِّ بِسَبْعٍ وَعِشْرِينَ دَرَجَةً

The prayer in congregation is 27 times superior to the prayer offered by a person alone. [124]

The prayer in *jama'ah* is 27 times better than a prayer prayed alone. That means when you pray *Ẓuhr* in *jama'ah,* it is 27times praying *Ẓuhr.* We will go into that discussion of the *Bāb as-Ṣalāt* later. So the second declaration that Allāh gave to Sayyīdinā Yaḥyā ﷺ is that He ordered his people for *ṣalāt* and the Prophet ﷺ said:

نَّ اللَّهَ أَمَرَكُمْ بِالصَّلَاةِ فإِذَا صَلَّيْتُمْ فلَا تَلْتَفِتُوا ، فإِنَّ اللَّهَ تَعَالَى يَنْصِبُ وَجْهَهُ لِوَجْهِ عَبْدِهِ في صَلَاتِهِ مَا لَمْ يَلْتَفِتْ

Fa idhā ṣallaytum fa lā taltafitū fa inna 'Llāha yanṣibu wajhahu li-wajhi 'abdihi fī ṣalātihi mā lam yaltafit, "When you pray, don't look right or left with

---

[123] Muslim.

[124] Bukhārī.

your eyes for Allāh ﷻ looks to His servant face-to-face when His Servant is praying (looking towards the place where he makes *sajda)*, but if you look right or left, then Allāh will stop looking at you" and you will lose that importance, that Reality or that Light which Allāh is dressing you with and shining you with from His Mercy, His Beauty and His Love when you are looking forward and thinking about Allāh ﷻ and making your prayer without gossips or *dunyā* in your ear and without looking right or left.

Then Sayyīdinā Yaḥyā ﷺ said, "Allāh ordered us for *siyām*." Look, here we see him presenting the Five Pillars of Islam. The first one is not to make *shirk* (by believing in) *Tawḥīd* by saying, "Ash-hadu an lā ilāha illa-Llāh wa Ash-hadu anna Muḥammadu 'r-Rasūlullāh," then prayers, then *ṣiyām*, and of course *zakāt*, which is not in this narration of *ḥadīth*. He described the *ṣiyām* as a person between a group of people with a basket of musk, perfume that everyone is smelling and wants to have. The person holding it is happy with that smell and doesn't want to let it go. Everyone around him is trying to get some nice smell from it.

Prophet ﷺ said:

ولخلوف فيه أطيب عند الله من ريح المسك

*And the breath (of an observer of fast) is sweeter to Allāh
than the fragrance of musk.*[125]

Wa inna rīḥa 'ṣ-ṣāim aṭyab min rīḥa 'l-misk. The musk is one of the finest and very precious perfumes that comes from the deer and everyone wants to have that fragrance. Prophet ﷺ said, "The smell of the mouth of the fasting person is better to Allāh ﷻ than the smell of musk." This means after *'Asr* or *Ẓuhr* it is not advisable, as the Prophet ﷺ prohibited or did not approve, for people to put perfumes when they are fasting because the smell of the mouth of the fasting person to angels and Paradise is better than the best perfumes in this world. So Allāh is giving importance to fasting by saying:

الصوم لي وانا أجزي به

Fasting is for Me and I will reward it.[126]

---

[125] Muslim.

[126] *Ḥadīth Qudsī.*

The reward of fasting is not brought by angels, but is given directly by Allāh 鐵. "I am The One Who will reward for it and dress My servant with the smell of Heavens when he is fasting." So that is why when it is said *wa inna khalūf aṣ-ṣaim aṭyab min aṭ-ṭīb*, "The smell of the mouth of a fasting person is better than musk," it means Allāh will dress the fasting person with heavenly smells.

So the first order is *shirk*, second *ṣalāt*, third *ṣiyām*, and fourth *ṣadaqah*. *Wa amarakum bi 'ṣ-ṣadaqatī*, "He ordered you for charity," and, *fa innaka mathalu dhālika mathalu rajulin asarahu 'l-ʿadū fa awsaqū yadayhi ila ʿunuqihi wa qaddamuhu li yaḍriba ʿunuqahu fa qāl, anā aftadī minkum bi 'l-qalīl wa 'l-kathīr fafadā nafsahu minhum*, "Charity is like someone who gets caught by the enemy and they tie his hands to his neck, causing him to not breathe, speak or move, which also makes the sound of his voice to change," like mine just changed (Mawlānā demonstrates with hands around his to neck.) They tie his neck and want to kill him and he says to them, "Please, I will give you what I have and you take it and leave me alone. I will give you whatever I have and I will be free." It means here that you give a little and Allāh gives you a lot. He gave them a little and they gave him his life; you give a little charity and Allāh gives you Paradise.

The wealth of *dunyā* is not necessarily just money, as charity can even be a smile in the face of your brother as the Prophet 鐵 said, "It is from *īmān*." So *ṣadaqah* is any charity: if you visit a homeless person or smile in his face, or visit a sick person and give him *maʿnawiyyāt*, spiritual uplifting, he will be happy and that is a *ṣadaqah*. Going to a *masjid* and leaving your work is a *ṣadaqah*; anything you do and give in Allāh's Way, no matter how small, is a *ṣadaqah*. So you give a little, and Allāh gives you a lot!

And he ordered you to remember Allāh 鐵 in every *ʿamal* you do.

أَنَا جَلِيسُ مَنْ ذَكَرَنِي

I sit with him who remembers me.[127]

وأنا معه إذا ذكرني فإن ذكرني في نفسه ذكرته في نفسي، ومن ذكرني في ملأ ذكرته في ملأ خير منه

---

[127] Āḥmad, Bayhaqī.

"I will be with the one who remembers Me. If he mentions Me in a group (such as this one), I will mention him in a group in Paradise better than his group, I will mention him in My Presence."

O Muslims! Mention Allāh by saying, "*Lā ilāha illa-Llāh Muḥammadun Rasūlullāh ʿalayhi afḍalu ʾṣ-ṣalāt wa ʾs-salām. Yā Sayyidī, yā Rasūlullāh! Yā shafīʿ al-mudhnibīn, anẓurnā bi naẓrati ʾl-maḥabbah, wa bi naẓarati ʾl-ʿafwa, wa qadimnā ilā ḥuḍūri ʾLlāhi ʿazza wa jall, maghfūran lanā min ṭarafi ʾl-ḥaqq. Wa law annahum idh ẓalamū anfusahum jaʾūka f ʾastaghfarūllāha w ʾastaghfara lahumu ʾr-rasūlu la-wajadū ʾLlāha tawwāba ʾr-raḥīma. Naqūl astaghfirullāh, astagfirullāh, astagfirullāh!*"

The example of the person doing *dhikrullāh* is that of a man whom the enemy is trying to catch and the enemy is very fast, until he reached a fortress and hides himself there. So the one who remembers Allāh ﷻ is like someone running and every time he says, "Allāh," or "*Lā ilāha illa-Llāh Muḥammadun Rasūlullāh*," it is as if Allāh is giving him a fortress, immediately dressing him as if he is inside a fortress from Shayṭān. Shayṭān is running after everyone to catch them and so Allāh will protect *dhākirullāh*, those who remember Him, through a heavenly fortress which Shayṭān cannot penetrate.

Then the Prophet ﷺ said to the *Ṣaḥābah* ﷺ after mentioning that story of Sayyīdinā Yaḥyā ﷺ and the Five Orders of Allāh to him, at the end of that *ḥadīth* Prophet ﷺ said:

. قَالَ النَّبِيُّ صلى الله عليه وسلم " وَأَنَا آمُرُكُمْ بِخَمْسٍ أَمَرَنِي اللَّهُ بِهِنَّ السَّمْعُ وَالطَّاعَةُ وَالْجِهَادُ وَالْهِجْرَةُ وَالْجَمَاعَةُ فَإِنَّهُ مَنْ فَارَقَ الْجَمَاعَةَ قِيدَ شِبْرٍ فَقَدْ خَلَعَ رِبْقَةَ الْإِسْلَام مِنْ عُنُقِهِ إِلاَّ أَنْ يَرْجِعَ وَمَنِ ادَّعَى دَعْوَى الْجَاهِلِيَّةِ فَإِنَّهُ مِنْ جُثَا جَهَنَّمَ " .
فَقَالَ رَجُلٌ يَا رَسُولَ اللَّهِ وَإِنْ صَلَّى وَصَامَ قَالَ " وَإِنْ صَلَّى وَصَامَ فَادْعُوا بِدَعْوَى اللَّهِ الَّذِي سَمَّاكُمُ الْمُسْلِمِينَ الْمُؤْمِنِينَ عِبَادَ اللَّهِ

The Prophet ﷺ said, "And I command you with five that Allāh ﷻ commanded me: listening and obeying, fighting to defend Islam from aggression, migration, and the congregation. For indeed, whoever parts from the community the measure of a

---

hand-span, then he has cast off the yoke of Islam from his neck, unless he returns, and whoever calls with the call of *jāhiliyyah* (ignorance) then he is from the coals of Hell." A man said, "O Messenger of Allāh! Even if he performs *ṣalāt* and fasts?" So he ﷺ said, "Even if he performs *ṣalāt* and fasts. So call with the call that Allāh named you with: Muslims, Believers, worshippers of Allāh.[129]

"Wa anā amūrukum bi khams, Allāhu amaranī bihinn, I order you five which Allāh ordered me to do them and I order you to do them as well."

Prophet ﷺ ordered the *Ṣaḥābah* ﷺ to do them and then us, as well. Are we doing them? Let us see.

The First Order

The first order is *"as-samaʿ."* What is *as-samaʿ*? It means to listen, not just to hear in our ear, but, as we say, "Listen to me!" It means, "Accept what I am saying to you," *i.e.* accept what Allāh ﷺ and what Prophet ﷺ is saying to you. So "listen" to what Prophet ﷺ is teaching us and to what Allāh is revealing to us. Therefore, it is mentioned, *"Samiʿnā wa ataʿanā."* After *samaʿ* who remembers Allāh ﷺ and then does voluntary worship, as Prophet ﷺ mentioned in the *ḥadīth*:

عن أبي هريرة قال قال رسول الله صلى الله عليه وسلم إن الله قال من عادى لي وليا فقد آذنته بالحرب وما تقرب إلي عبدي بشيء أحب إلي مما افترضت عليه وما يزال عبدي يتقرب إلي بالنوافل حتى أحبه فإذا أحببته كنت سمعه الذي يسمع به وبصره الذي يبصر به ويده التي يبطش بها ورجله التي يمشي بها وإن سألني لأعطينه ولئن استعاذني لأعيذنه وما ترددت عن شيء أنا فاعله ترددي عن نفس المؤمن يكره الموت وأنا أكره مساءته ولا يزال عبدي يتقرب إلي بالنوافل حتى أحبه، فإذا أحببته كنت سمعه الذي يسمع به وبصره الذي يبصر به، ويده التي يبطش بها ورجله التي يمشي بها،

Whoever comes against a saint of Mine, I declare war on him. And My servant does not approach Me with anything more beloved to Me than what I obligated him with, and My servant does not cease to approach Me through voluntary worship until I will love him. When I love him, I will become the ears with which he hears, the eyes with which he sees, the hand with which he acts, and the legs with which he walks (and other versions include, "and the tongue with which he speaks.")[130]

---

129 Tirmidhī, Āḥmad.
130 *Ḥadīth Qudsī*, Bukhārī.

Whom do we listen to mostly? [Ourselves.] Good answer! You are focusing, the others are not, good answer, We listen to ourselves and don't listen to anyone else. Allāh ﷻ wants us to listen to Him. So when you listen, Allāh will give you a special hearing, the power of listening; you will not be listening to yourself anymore, but to Allāh ﷻ. And this is being given by doing what? By doing *nawāfil*. How? By increasing your *nawāfil*, do more of whatever you are doing.

The Second Order

The second order is *aṭ-ṭaʿat*, "Allāh ordered me to obey." Islam is obedience. If you want to be a *mu'min*, a Muslim, be obedient to Allāh, as He has said in the Holy Qur'ān:

أَطِيعُوا اللَّهَ وَأَطِيعُوا الرَّسُولَ وَأُوْلِي الأَمْرِ مِنكُمْ

Obey Allāh, obey the Prophet, and obey those in authority among you.[131]

Allāh is saying in Holy Qur'ān, "*Aṭīʿullāh.*" I heard it from Grandshaykh, may Allāh bless his soul, saying that this verse of Holy Qur'ān carries a lot of power in it and as soon as you recite it, Allāh will dress you with the light of that *āyah*:

يَا أَيُّهَا الَّذِينَ آمَنُوا أَطِيعُوا اللَّهَ وَأَطِيعُوا الرَّسُولَ وَأُوْلِي الأَمْرِ مِنكُمْ فَإِن تَنَازَعْتُمْ فِي شَيْءٍ فَرُدُّوهُ إِلَى اللَّهِ وَالرَّسُولِ إِن كُنتُمْ تُؤْمِنُونَ بِاللَّهِ وَالْيَوْمِ الآخِرِ ذَلِكَ خَيْرٌ وَأَحْسَنُ تَأْوِيلاً

O you who have believed! Obey Allāh and obey the Messenger
and those in authority among you. And if you disagree over anything,
refer it to Allāh and the Messenger, if you should believe in Allāh
and the Last Day. That is the best (way) and best in result.[132]

That *āyah* is full of power and energy. As soon as you read it, Allāh will dress you from that *āyah* to put you on the track of obedience. And the verse continues, "If you disagree on something, then send it back to Prophet ﷺ." *Fa-in tanāzaʿtum fī shay'in faruddū hu ila'Llāhi wa 'r-rasūl*, "If you disagree on something, send it," or, "look back to what Allāh ﷻ is saying in Holy Qur'ān and what the Prophet ﷺ is saying in holy *ḥadīth* and Allāh will open for you, because this is *itaʿat*, obedience, as Allāh said, "Take it back to Allāh, take it

---

[131] Sūrat an-Nisā, 4:59.

[132] Sūrat an-Nisā, 4:59.

back to Prophet ﷺ." Allāh will inspire you what you need to do because you are accepting His *Ilhām* to you. So *ita'at* is a powerful work on the ego to make it submit to Allāh ﷻ, because the Prophet ﷺ used to say:

اللَّهُمَّ لَا تَكِلْنِي إِلَى نَفْسِي طَرْفَةَ عَيْنٍ وَلَا أَقَلَّ مِنْ ذَلِكَ

O Allāh! Don't leave me to my ego for the blink of an eye or less.

"O Allāh! Don't leave me to myself for the blink of an eye," because immediately our self wants us to obey it and not to obey Allāh and His Prophet. So the Prophet ﷺ said it, although he does not need to do so, but he is teaching us. We have to be careful not to render all our matters to our ego, but to Allāh and His Prophet; this will be *ita'at*, obedience. When you render to His Prophet ﷺ you will be safe, because Shayṭān can no longer play with you, as you are now looking at the meaning of it and how you are going to handle the situation according to the Holy Qur'ān and holy *ḥadīth*.

O Muslims! We need heavenly power to enlighten all of us, to make peace in our heart and in our lives. This life is ending, people come and go, but one day we are all going to be between the Hands of Allāh ﷻ and He will bring us back to judge us.

Bayāzīd al-Bistāmī ق, one of the great scholars of Islam, said, "I always look at people from a certain view and learn from that wisdom, I look and I respect." People asked him, "Why you are respecting the young one?" He said, "I respect the young one because he has less sins than me," a young one like 15 or 20 years younger. He would say about anyone who was younger than him, "I look at him that he is younger than me, so he has less sins than me." And he said, "I look at the one older than me and respect him also, more than I respect myself, because he has more *'ibādah* than me. So this one has less sins than me and this one has more *'ibādah* than me, therefore I have to respect everyone on the right and on the left."

He said, "*Yā Rabbī*, open for me Your Door! I want to come there, I want to come to be with your Beloved One, to be with Sayyīdinā Muḥammad ﷺ!" Allāh said to him when Abū Yazīd ق asked Him, *kayf al-wuṣūlu ilayk yā Rabbī*, "What is the way to reach Your Divinely Presence, Your Love, Your *'Ishq*, Your *Ḥuḍūr*, Your *Fanā* and Your Presence? How can I reach *'ishq* of Prophet ﷺ, *fanā'* of Prophet ﷺ and *Ḥuḍūr* of Prophet ﷺ, to be in the presence of the Prophet ﷺ? How can I reach that?" He heard a voice in his heart saying, *itruk nafsaka wa ta'al*, "Leave your self and come." That is the Door! Don't look right or left, don't waste your time.

One *ḥadīth* from Prophet ﷺ is enough to teach the whole *ummah*, the whole universe and to fill everyone with *barakah*, don't underestimate the power of Prophet ﷺ! The *barakah* of that *ḥadīth* is enough for this life and the next. That gives us also an understanding that one word or even one letter of Holy Qur'ān can make us happy in *dunyā* and *Ākhirah*, but there is a condition, "Leave your self and come."

Sayyīdina Mūsā ؏ went to Sayyīdina Khiḍr ؏, although he is higher than him, but he went. He left his self and went and tried to accept what Khiḍr ؏ is doing. We must also try. Then about Sayyīdina Khiḍr ؏, Allāh ﷻ said:

$$وَعَلَّمْنَاهُ مِن لَّدُنَّا عِلْمًا$$

And We had taught him knowledge from Our Own Presence.[133]

If we leave our selves, meaning disobedience to Allāh, He will give us His Paradises and His *'Ilm ladunnīyy*, the Heavenly Knowledge. Allāh is not closing it, He will give, but let us take it. It is there, hanging between Earth and Heaven. "Come to Me and take it!" Allāh is saying, *Utruk nafsaka wa ta'al*, "Leave your self and come."

O Muslims! When we leave our selves, that means we reach the level of humility and humbleness. The Prophet ﷺ was on the highest and perfect manners, and that means to be humble. When he was humble, Allāh raised him. He dressed Prophet ﷺ with the best character and the best character is to be humble with everyone. If we are humble all the problems of this world will be solved. And when we are humble, we will listen and obey, *as-sama' wa 't-ṭa'at*.

The Third Order

The third order is *al-jihād*. First to listen, then to obey, and third to struggle in the Way of Allāh, struggle in any way: in education, in work, in worshipness, in *tazkiyyah*, in cleanliness, in Purification of the Self, in accepting others, in listening and obeying or in disobeying your ego, your self and Shayṭān, all of this is *jihād*. It is not as they think today that *jihād* is only to fight. No, jihad is from 13 or 14 different categories and only one of

---

them is fighting, and it has principles that allow you to fight. The rest of them are different kinds of struggle between good and evil. Allāh ﷻ said:

$$\text{فَأَلْهَمَهَا فُجُورَهَا وَتَقْوَاهَا}$$

He inspired the self of its good and its bad.[134]

Allāh showed us that you are going to struggle between *fujūr* and *taqwa*. He showed us the *fujūr* and the *taqwā* of the *nafs*. The *fujūr* is the corruption, rebelliousness and hypocrisy; hence, everything that Allāh does not like. On the other hand, *taqwā* is what Allāh likes.

The Fourth Order

The fourth important order is migration, *al-hijra*. You don't find one *walī* or pious person who stayed where they were born. No, they made *hijra*. The first one to make migration was the Prophet ﷺ with all his *Ṣaḥābah* ﷺ from Mecca, which he loved the most, but left Mecca *fī sabīlillāh* and went to Madinah and was buried there. *'Alā sākinihā afḍal aṣ-ṣalāt wa 's-salām*, upon its holy inhabitant the best prayers and greetings of peace! He inhabited Madinah. We cannot say "buried," but, "he inhabited and overtook" Madinah and his *barakah* is everywhere. *Yā Sayyidī, yā Rasūlullāh, yā Raḥmatan li 'l-'Alamīn, yā Shafī'al-Mudhnibīn, yā Sayyidi 'r-Rusul, yā Ḥabībullāh!*

$$\text{إِنَّمَا الْأَعْمَالُ بِالنِّيَّاتِ وَإِنَّمَا لِكُلِّ امْرِئٍ مَا نَوَى ، فَمَنْ كَانَتْ هِجْرَتُهُ إِلَى اللَّهِ وَرَسُولِهِ ،}$$
$$\text{فَهِجْرَتُهُ إِلَى اللَّهِ وَرَسُولِهِ ، وَمَنْ كَانَتْ هِجْرَتُهُ إِلَى دُنْيَا يُصِيبُهَا أَوْ امْرَأَةٍ يَتَزَوَّجُهَا ، فَهِجْرَتُهُ}$$
$$\text{إِلَى مَا هَاجَرَ إِلَيْهِ}$$

Deeds are only by intentions, for each man is only for which he has intended.
And so whoever makes hijra for Allāh and His Messenger ﷺ, then indeed his hijra
is only to Allāh and His Messenger, but whoever makes hijra is for the world he
wishes to acquire or a woman he seeks to marry, then his hijra is only
to that which he has actually immigrated.[135]

Everything is according to intentions. Your *niyyah* is to migrate to Allāh and His Prophet ﷺ. "Migrate" means to make *'amal*, migrate from bad to good. If you cannot migrate physically then migrate spiritually, make *hijra*

---

[134] Sūrat ash-Shams, 91:8.
[135] Bukhārī and Muslim.

from *'amāl ad-danīyya il al-'amālu ṣāliḥa*. So migration is one of the *sunnah* of Prophet ﷺ and anyone who migrates from one place to another, it will be written for him as if he complied with the order of the Prophet ﷺ.

The Fifth Order

The fifth and last order is *al-jama'ah*, to be with the group of the Muslim and not be alone. *Al-Muslimu akhu 'l-Muslim*, "The Muslim is the brother of the other Muslim." Come back together and you will be strong and powerful. It is like someone who has a hundred sticks or twigs and beating with just one does nothing, but if you put all of them together and hit, it will give you pain. So don't be alone! Be where there is goodness. Don't be alone with Shayṭān, but be with the *jama'ah* who are remembering Allāh ﷻ.

Jābir ibn 'Abdullāh ؓ narrated:

قَالَ جَابِرُ بْنُ عَبْدِ اللهِ : خَرَجَ عَلَيْنَا النَّبِيُّ صلي الله عليه وآله وسلم فقالَ: يَا أَيُّهَا النَّاسُ، إِنَّ لِلّهِ سَرَايَا مِنَ الْمَلَائِكَةِ تَحِلُّ وَتَقِفُ عَلَى مَجَالِسِ الذِّكْرِ فِي الْأَرْضِ. فَارْتَعُوا فِي رِيَاضِ الْجَنَّةِ. قَالُوا: وَأَيْنَ رِيَاضُ الْجَنَّةِ؟ قَالَ: مَجَالِسُ الذِّكْرِ. فَاغْدُوا وَرُوْحُوا فِي ذِكْرِ اللهِ وَذَكِّرُوهُ أَنْفُسَكُمْ. مَنْ كَانَ يُحِبُّ أَنْ يَّعْلَمَ مَنْزِلَتَهُ عِنْدَ اللهِ فَلْيَنْظُرْ كَيْفَ مَنْزِلَةُ اللهِ عِنْدَهُ، فَإِنَّ اللهَ يُنْزِلُ الْعَبْدَ مِنْهُ حَيْثُ أَنْزَلَهُ مِنْ نَفْسِهِ

The Holy Prophet ﷺ came to us and said, "O people! There are armies
of Allāh's angels who come to dhikr sessions on earth and stay there, so eat
wholeheartedly from the gardens of Paradise!" The Companions said,
"Where are the Gardens of Paradise?" He replied, "Dhikr sessions,
so remember Allāh ﷻ morning and evening and continually remind yourselves
of Him. Whoever wants to know his own status and station in the Sight of Allāh ﷻ
should see what he deems of Allāh ﷻ, because Allāh ﷻ
ranks a person as he believes Him in his heart."[136]

Fa 'idhā marartum bi riyāḍ al-jannatu farta'ū. The Prophet ﷺ said, "If you pass by the Gardens of Paradise sit there, don't move." The Ṣaḥābah ؓ asked, "What are these Gardens of Paradise, where can we find them?" The Prophet ﷺ said, "They are the circles of *dhikr*," such as this one or in *masājid* and homes, anywhere you sit and remember Allāh ﷻ and Prophet ﷺ. The

---

[136] Abū Y'ala in his *Musnad*; al-Bayhaqī; al-Ḥākim said it is *ṣaḥīḥ*.

Prophet ﷺ said, "Anytime you pass by such gatherings, sit with them, as they are *riyāḍ al-jannah*, the Gardens of Paradise."

May Allāh give us Gardens of Paradise and make us always to be with the Prophet ﷺ in *dunyā* and *Ākhirah!*

May Allāh forgive us and may Allāh bless us.

Wa min Allāhi 't-tawfīq, bi ḥurmati 'l-ḥabīb, bi ḥurmati 'l-Fātiḥah.
And with Allāh is success. For the sake of the Beloved, for his sake we recite the opening chapter of Holy Qur'ān.

The Rights of Prayer

A'ūdhu billāhi min ash-Shayṭāni 'r-rajīm. Bismillāhi' r-Raḥmāni 'r-Raḥīm.
Nawaytu 'l-arbā'īn, nawaytu 'l-'itikāf, nawaytu 'l-khalwah, nawaytu 'l-'uzlah,
nawaytu 'r-riyāḍa, nawaytu 's-sulūk, lillāhi Ta'ala fī hādha 'l-masjid.
Atī'ūllāha wa atī'ū 'r-Rasūla wa ūli 'l-amri minkum. (4:59)

Iṭa'tullāh wājibatun 'alā kulli insān laysa 'alā kulli muslim faqad, "Obedience to
Allāh is a must on every person, not only for Muslims, but for everyone,"
and to do what He ordered us to do.

We mentioned yesterday in the previous session about *ṣalāt*, how much
the prayer is a very delicate matter, that it is not something that you don't
give any attention because you must remember. Anyone who wants to go to
pray must prepare all his ammunition to fight Shayṭān, because Shayṭān is
not going to let us pray correctly. When you pray you pray, but there are
differences between what you have done between one and another, like the
differences between Heavens and Earth there are differences. Someone
whose heart Shayṭān cannot enter is not like the one whose heart Shayṭān
enters. The one whose heart Shayṭān does not enter compared to the one
whose heart Shayṭān enters is like the difference between Heavens and
Earth. That is why prayers are so important, as we mentioned before in the
ḥadīth of Prophet ﷺ:

ما بَيْنَ الْكُفْرِ وَالْإِيمَان تَرْكُ الصَّلَاةِ

What is between disbelief and belief is the leaving of prayers.[137]

"Between *kufr* and faith, non-Believers and Believers, are those who
leave their prayers; they are unBelievers." May Allāh ﷻ protect us as there is
no protection except from Allāh ﷻ! For this reason, as soon as you say
"*Allāhu Akbar*" and begin to recite *Fātiḥah*, Shayṭān enters. Try and check
what comes to your heart: all kinds of gossips and different matters come in
the mind as if he is speaking in your ears, "Do you remember that day when
I showed you my love, I took care of you?" Yes, the Cursed One! You took
care of us, you brought us from Heavens to Earth! He enters, as Allāh lets
him to enter for some and for others stops him from entering. This does not

---

[137] Tirmidhī.

mean that He lets Shayṭān take revenge from others, no! It means Allāh does not protect the one whose heart is weak and so He lets Shayṭān enter, whereas the one who tries his best with full ammunition, making *wuḍū* and praying the prayer as it should be, will have a struggle between him and Shayṭān and he will win, because he is focusing on Allāh ﷻ!

I heard a story, an *athar*, not a *ḥadīth*, from Grandshaykh ʿAbdAllāh, may Allāh bless his soul, that one day the Prophet ﷺ was sitting with the *Ṣaḥābah* ؓ, as he always used to sit with them as a family in *ṣuḥbat*, companionship; they were *Aṣḥāb*, Companions to him. He ﷺ said, "Whoever can pray two *rakaʿats* without distraction, I will give him my *jubba*, cloak." And as I said, this is a story; sometimes stories are correct and sometimes things in them have been changed, but because it has wisdom we will mention it, no problem. So everyone was trying to pray two *rakaʿats* and none of them were successful in preventing distraction as something happened at that time and distracted them.

Then Sayyīdinā ʿAlī ؓ said, "I will pray two *rakaʿats* and I will not be distracted." He said "*Allāhu Akbar...*" and prayed with complete presence to the Prophet ﷺ and to Allāh ﷻ. When he finished his prayer and wanted to say, "*As-salāmu ʿalaykum wa raḥmatullāh,*" immediately a distraction came (when he thought), "Which cloak is the Prophet ﷺ going to give me? The red one, the black one or the green one?" Prophet ﷺ said, "It is finished, you lost."

That is a story, what we call *laṭīfa*, with humor; it is a teaching for us to know that we have to struggle, but the only thing is not to go along with the distraction. When Shayṭān tries to distract you stop him by moving your focus, because sometimes when you are distracted your focus is on the distraction and you move it quickly back to normal. Sometimes it goes away if you blink your eyes, but don't go along with the distraction as that's where it is not accepted. You have to remember that your heart is owned by Allāh ﷻ and Allāh does not like partnership, so if you listen to Shayṭān you are partnering with him, you are putting Shayṭān as the focus and Allāh ﷻ does not like that!

As you all know the story of Sayyīdinā Yʿaqūb ؑ, when his children took Sayyīdinā Yūsuf ؑ with them for a *sayd*, shooting deer, hunting with their bows and arrows. They took Yūsuf ؑ although the father didn't want that, but in any case, they took him and threw him in the well. Some scholars say it was from when he was young that some merchants took him from the well and sold him to the governor of Egypt, where he remained for thirty years. Sayyīdinā Yūsuf's ﷺ father was crying and crying, until he became blind. He never found Yūsuf ﷺ, but he felt he was there and told his sons to go and find him until finally they did. The wisdom of that is Allāh doesn't like anyone to share their heart with anyone except Him! Sayyīdinā Y'aqūb ﷺ had too much love to his son Yūsuf ﷺ; Allāh doesn't like anyone's heart, especially a prophet, to be other than a house for Allāh ﷻ, to share the heart with other than Him. So that's why when we pray, we must not share our heart with the enemy of Allāh; our hearts must be *khāliṣan li wajhillāh*, pure and sincere to Allāh ﷻ.

That is why a group of people called *al-Muḥibūn* said, *yaqulūna nuṣalli fa nastarīḥ*, "When prayers come we take *wuḍū* and run to pray quickly, because we feel relaxed in our prayer." On the contrary to us, we are lazy to pray. We feel in our self all kinds of negativity and laziness that will dress us at the time of prayer in order to keep delaying and delaying. I don't say, "You are missing it," but "delaying," and some people even miss it. That group of people who delayed it are the lazy ones, those who do not really love Allāh and love the Prophet ﷺ!

Al-Muḥibūn, the Lovers, wait for the prayer from time to time and for them the time between the two prayers is so long! They feel, "When is it going to come, when is it going to come because we feel relaxed between the Hands of Allāh ﷻ!" So, *qāla Rasūlullāhi* ﷺ, one day he said, "*Yā Bilāl, ariḥnā bi 'ṣ-ṣalāt*, relieve us with the prayers, call the *adhān*, let us pray, we want to be relieved." And the Prophet ﷺ said:

قرة عيني في الصلاة

The coolness of my eyes is in the prayers.[138]

Qurratu 'aynī fi 'ṣ-ṣalāt, "The thing most dear for my eyes is prayer, because I am there between the Hands of Allāh ﷻ." Prayers are the *mi'rāj* of *mu'min* and as it is said, only the Prophet ﷺ has *Mi'rāj* that he went to Allāh ﷻ, and not only went, but is still going in Ascension, physically and spiritually! The only *mi'rāj* for Muslims is when they pray, as they ascend spiritually depending on how much power or ammunition they have against Shayṭān. Allāh will protect them and their *ṣalāt* is like an ascension to Allāh.

---

138 Āḥmad, Nasā'ī.

The Prophet ﷺ said, "*ṣalāt* is the dearest thing to me," so how was he feeling between the two prayers? His patience was so strong, wanting for the second prayer to come as soon as possible in order that he will be relaxed another time. *Wa ammā ṣalātu 'l-mufridu 'l-mudayyi'u 'l-ḥuqūqīya hudūdiyahu, fa taqul ḍa'yak-allāhu kamā ḍa'yatanī,* "The one who doesn't care for his *ṣalāt*, who is lazy, at the end of his prayer the prayer will say to him, 'May Allāh make you lost, as you lost me.'" So it means our prayers have to be perfectly done, not like roosters (pecking) their heads up and down! One time the Prophet ﷺ saw one of the *Ṣaḥābah* ؇ praying, standing and moving quickly, and said to him, "Don't be like a rooster, picking the food quickly, raising and lowering your head. Repeat that prayer as it is not accepted."

And it is said in a *ḥadīth* of Prophet ﷺ:

ما من مؤمن يتم الوضوء إلى أمكانه ثم يقوم إلى الصلاة في وقتها فيؤديها لله عز و جل لم ينقص من وقتها وركوعها وسجودها ومعالمها شيئا إلا رفعت له إلى الله عز و جل بيضاء مسفرة يستضيء بنورها ما بين الخافقين حتى ينتهي بها إلى الرحمن عز و جل ومن قام إلى الصلاة فلم يكمل وضوءها واخرها عن وقتها واسترق ركوعها وسجودها ومعالمها رفعت عنه سوداء مظلمة ثم لا تجاوز شعر رأسه تقول : ضيعك الله كما ضيعتني ضيعك كما ضيعتني

"Anyone who perfects his *wuḍū*," and there are conditions for *wuḍū*, as well. Some people put water only part way up their arms. No, it must come up past the elbow and as much as it is high up where the water reaches, there will be *nūr* coming on the Day of Judgment from wherever that water reached. That is why you will be known from the light of *wuḍū* coming from your body parts that you are *mu'min*, from *Ummat an-Nabī* ﷺ. So when you do your face, you make sure you do your whole face; when you do your hands, when you do your feet, not just a little bit of water and finish! So, perfect the *wuḍū* up to its *amkānihā*, where it is assigned for the water to reach and even beyond, up on the arm. "Then he stands up going to pray and then, *fa yu'addīha lillāhi 'azza wa jall lam yanquṣ min waqtihā wa rukū'ihā wa sujūdihā,* "Nothing will be less, he will give it its full conditions, its full rights for the prayer." You pray slowly and give the prayer its time. "Give the prayer its *ruku'*, its *sujūd*, and at this time the prayer will be raised to Allāh ﷻ by angels, white, shining with light," *yastaḍī'u bi-nūrihā mā bayna 'l-khāfiqayn,* "With its light it will fill the universe until it reaches the Presence of Allāh ﷻ.

On the contrary, if someone went to pray and he did not perfect his *wuḍū* and delayed it from its time, and you steal from the prayer by not giving the *qiyām, rukūʿ* and *sujūd* its right; you are stealing, as if stealing something from someone, you are stealing something from your prayer and it will be raised black, darkened in darkness and does not reach up to the hair on your head," that is the maximum that it reaches. The other one goes white with a lot of light when you perfect it and it goes all the way between the Hands of Allāh ﷻ. This one will not raise above your head and will say to you, *ḍaʿyak-Allāhu kamā ḍaʿyatanī,* "May Allāh leave you as you left me! May Allāh ﷻ punish you because you didn't give me my right!"

The *ṣalāt* that is accepted by Allāh ﷻ is a *ṣalāt* that is like someone, *tulīqu li-rabbihi taʿalā,* that is fit for Allāh's ﷻ right, like you go to meet someone and you wear the best dress. Also, when you go to your prayer you must know that you are between the Hands of your Lord, so you must give the best perfection in your *ṣalāt.* What is accepted from people are two kinds of *ʿamal:* one *an yuṣalli 'l-ʿabdi yaʿmal sā'ira 'ṭ-ṭaʿāt,* "For the servant of Allāh ﷻ to pray and to do all kind of orders," to be obedient to Allāh and his heart has to be always in Divine Presence. And second, *dhākiran lillāhi ʿazza wa jalla ʿalā 'd-dawām,* "Always he must remember Allāh ﷻ, doing *dhikrullāh* non-stop." This person, this servant of Allāh ﷻ, Allāh will receive his *ʿamal* and accept it and He will protect him and bring him near to Him, as Allāh ﷻ said in the Holy Qur'ān:

أَلَا إِنَّ أَوْلِيَاء اللَّهِ لَا خَوْفٌ عَلَيْهِمْ وَلَا هُمْ يَحْزَنُونَ

Behold! Verily on the Friends of Allāh there is no fear,
nor shall they grieve; they who have attained faith
and have always been conscious of Him.[139]

So Allāh ﷻ will protect those people and open for them in every *ṣalāt* you pray in the right way, that *ṣalāt* is the key for one Paradise. That key has its own code; it will not open anyone else's Paradise, only yours. That has a code and you put the key inside and that Paradise will open specially for you. On the other hand, the one who prays with heedlessness is praying with his body, but his mind is somewhere else; you are praying, you are Muslim, but you are not reaching the level that Allāh accepts your prayer.

---

[139] Sūrah Yūnus, 10:62-63.

Why was there a fight between Cain and Abel, Qābīl *wa* Hābīl? Because Allāh ﷻ accepted from one of them his sacrifice and not from the other. When Allāh asked them to offer a sacrifice, Hābīl offered the best ram that he had and put it on the altar. At that time, the fire would come down and take the animal; that was a sign that it is accepted, that was in their time and that was the situation. So Hābīl got the best one and put it on the altar, then Qābīl came and found an animal that had no eye, no ear, deaf, the worst of them and was sick, and that one he put on the altar. Then the fire came and took Hābīl's sacrifice. So Allāh ﷻ accepted from one and did not accept from the other:

فَتُقُبِّلَ مِن أَحَدِهِمَا وَلَمْ يُتَقَبَّلْ مِنَ الآخَرِ

It was accepted from one, but not from the other.[140]

So he accepted from the one who showed more love and respect for Allāh ﷻ, and so the prayer is like the ram: you have to have the best that you can give for *ṣadaqah*, charity, or the best that you give as a gift. Just like when some people collect for the *masājid*, they put pennies in the charity box for the mosque, for what? Are you bargaining with Allāh ﷻ? Give the best you have, not pennies! When you give charity you are going to get Paradise, so put whatever you have, the best you have to give! How many pennies they count? Many.

So what will happen? In that prayer the body is praying, but the mind is not there, it will not be raised, but it will be put on the side until the Day of Judgment and then Allāh will look at it at that time if it is okay or it is not good. The one whose heart is present, Allāh will accept immediately and then give him one key for Paradise, key after key, until it becomes from *"the friends of Allāh, on them there is no fear, nor shall they grieve."* Allah supports them.

The Five Levels of Prayer

This is why from *The Principles of Prayers*, it is said that prayer is on five levels:

The first level is, *martabat aẓ-ẓālim fi 'ṣ-ṣalāti li nafsihi al-mufrid*, the Level of the Oppressor, *li nafsihi al-mufrid*, that he went so far from his prayer that

---

[140] Sūrat al-Māidah, 5:27.

he did not give it its full rights, he wasted his prayer. The one that did not complete the *wuḍū* and did not pray in time and did not respect its limits and principles, that one is called *martabat aẓ-ẓālim*, the Level of an Oppressor, "The one who oppressed himself with his prayer." And spiritually, if you want to advance you cannot oppress your prayer! Some people think they are *awliyāullāh* and their prayers are not completed as it should be; their prayer must not be like a rooster, it has to be respectfully done that Allāh ﷻ will accept.

The second level is, *man yuḥāfiẓ ʿalā mawaqītihā wa ḥudūdihā wa arkānihā aẓ-ẓāhira wa wuḍū'ihā*, "The one who has kept the limits and the principles of the prayer and perfected his *wuḍū*, but..." *wa lākin ḍaʿyyi mujāhadata nafsihi fi 'l-waswasa*, "...lost his prayer time with an absent mind by always listening to and going along deeper and deeper with the gossips, whispers and wishes of Shayṭān." Therefore, when such whispers come don't follow them, focus on your prayer. Therefore, I believe that where one school of thought says, "Don't recite after the *imām*, as the *imām* recites," that is one school of thought, but sometimes you like to recite along with the *imām*, as when you are saying nothing Shayṭān comes quickly and whispers, whereas if you are reciting along with the *imām* and focusing on what you are saying, that diminishes the power of Shayṭān. So that second one is going along with the whispers of Shayṭān and his heart is not present, although his prayers follow the principles of *wuḍū* and prayer.

The third level is the one who keeps and perfects the limits and principles of prayer and *wuḍū* and is struggling, *mujāhadah*, against himself in order to throw away the whispers of Shayṭān when they come to his ear. So he is busy with his ammunition to attack on Shayṭān in order for him not to steal his prayers. This prayer will be considered *fa hūwa aṣ-ṣalāti fi 'l-jihād*, "He is in a situation of doing prayers and struggling against himself," *Jihād an-Nafs*.

The fourth level is the one who prays on time, perfects the rights and principles of prayer and *wuḍū*, and goes deeply into *istighrāq*, fully present in Allāh's Divine Presence, and does not let Shayṭān steal anything and all his care is how to perfect his *ṣalāt*. He is the real *ʿabd* and will enter into the Level of *ʿUbūdiyya* to Allāh ﷻ.

The fifth level is the one who does all the prayer with its perfection and does not struggle with ammunition against Shayṭān, as he is now free from the whispers of Shayṭān. He in fact takes his heart from his body and puts it at the threshold of the Divine Presence! This is your door, by entering the Divine Presence. He looks through his heart, focusing on Allāh's Beautiful Names and Attributes and filling his heart with the Love and Greatness of Allāh ﷻ. Anyone who looks at him will understand that all these whispers and gossips have been taken away and Allāh has prevented it to attack him through Shayṭān, Allāh will protect that person. It is said that his ṣalāt is better than all the four previous kinds, like the difference between Heavens and Earth!

These are the five levels of ṣalāt, and inshā'Allāh we will continue later. So the first level *fi 'l-qismu āwwal mu'aqqab*, will be punished. The second group is not punished, but judged by Allāh, "Why did you do that?" he will still be okay. For the third level, Allāh will *mukaffir 'anhu*, erase his sins. The fourth level will be granted rewards and Heavens from Allāh ﷻ. The fifth level, *al-muqarrab min rabbihi li-annahu ja'ala rabbahu qurrata 'aynahu fi 'ṣ-ṣalāt*, will be brought very near to the Divine Presence, as he is following in the footsteps of Prophet ﷺ where he said, "The best of my time is when I am in prayer, because I am between the Hands of Allāh ﷻ." May Allāh forgive us and bless us. We will continue *inshā'Allāh* in the next session.

May Allāh forgive us and may Allāh bless us.

Wa min Allāhi 't-tawfīq, bi ḥurmati 'l-ḥabīb, bi ḥurmati 'l-Fātiḥah.
And with Allāh is success. For the sake of the Beloved, for his sake we recite the opening chapter of Holy Qur'ān.

Three Types of Hearts

مَّنْ يُطِعِ الرَّسُولَ فَقَدْ أَطَاعَ اللهَ

Whoever obeys the Prophet is obeying Allāh.[141]

Look at the greatness Allāh gave to the Prophet ﷺ: whoever obeys Prophet ﷺ is obeying Allāh! We ask Allāh ﷻ to give us the power to obey Him and to obey His Prophet ﷺ.

Today we will continue our previous discussion by repeating in a summarized way what we came across, that in their prayers people are of five different types:

1. The first one is the one who is oppressing his prayers, he doesn't keep its limits, he doesn't keep the perfection of its *wudū*, he doesn't keep its time, pray it on time, and he doesn't keep its *rukū'*, its *sujūd* and its *qiyām* in the right time and place, nor give these aspects their rights.

2. The second has kept the prayer's time, keeps its limits and observes its principles, but he loses his prayer because of too much Shaytān's whispering and gossiping in his ear; he follows what Shaytān whispers in his ear, who then takes him there; he forgets how many *raka'ats* he did, five or six or two or one, and is longer mindful of Allāh ﷻ; his focus is on the whisperings of Shaytān in his ear.

3. The third one keeps the prayer's time, keeps its principles, observes its limits and tries to push away the whispering of Shaytān, so there is a struggle between himself and Shaytān and he is busy in that in order that Shaytān does not steal his prayer from him, and that is also acceptable.

4. The fourth one prays on time, perfects the rights and principles of prayer and *wudū* and goes deeply into *istighrāq*, fully present in Allāh's

---

[141] Sūrat an-Nisā, 4:80.

Divine Presence, and does not let Shayṭān steal anything and all his care is how to perfect his ṣalāt.)

5. The last is the one is who, as soon as he goes into prayer, saying, "*Allāhu Akbar*," he is immediately in the Divine Presence, putting his heart at the Threshold of the Divine Presence, asking Allāh ﷻ for forgiveness and Allāh's ﷻ protection.

These are the five, so then we can say:

1. The first type of prayer we mentioned is *muʿaqqib*, punishable. Allāh will punish that one because he didn't keep its time, nor its principle, nor its *wuḍū*. He kept nothing of the rights of the prayer. So that person, who was listening to the whispers of Shayṭān, is punished.

2. The second one will be taken to account; Allāh will question and judge him, and audit him in his prayer: how he did his prayer, is he doing it in the right way? Or he is doing it in a way that *lā talīq bihi ʿazza wa jall*, doesn't befit the Rights of Allāh ﷻ on every one of us?

3. The third one is *mukaffarun ʿanhu*, the third type of prayer we mentioned, Allāh ﷻ knows that servant is running, that Shayṭān is whispering to him, but he is running to avoid him. That one Allāh will forgive, and Allāh will change his *ṣalāt* from imitational *ṣalāt*, plastic *ṣalāt*, if we can say that, to real *ṣalāt*.

4. The fourth level will be granted rewards and Heavens from Allāh ﷻ.

5. The fifth one is *muqarrib min Allāh*, is the one that Allāh brings him nearer to Himself. He opens for him His Doors; He doesn't lock His Doors for him. He says, "Welcome, *yā ʿabdī!*"

Look in *Ḥajj* time how many people wish that they can pray two *rakaʿats* inside the Kaʿbah, to enter it; before we say, 'to enter inside,' every Muslim wishes to be in the *Ḥaram al-Makkī*, at the Sacred Mosque, *Baytullāh*, to be there and observe his prayers there. And there is a higher-level person who not only wants to pray there, but to enter the Kaʿbah and pray two *rakaʿats*, because you are praying inside the House of Allāh ﷻ. That one who keeps his prayer, Allāh will grant him that, Allāh is not prohibiting. Many people might not keep prayer in their life and they get an opportunity to go inside the Kaʿbah and pray two *rakaʿats*, as they might be important people, official people. Allāh does not look at your image, He looks at the heart: if your heart is to keep your prayer as much as possible clean and pure and throw Shayṭān away and put your heart at the Threshold of Allāh's Door, be sure that you are not only praying in *Kaʿbah* in *Ḥaram al-Makkī*, but Allāh ﷻ will cause you to pray in *Bayt al-Māmūr*, the House of Allāh in Heavens! Allāh gives you the manifestation, the *tajalli*, of the Fourth Paradise, which is where *Bayt al-Māmūr* is located, from that place, which is the reality of *Baytullāh*, the House of Allāh ﷻ. That is why it is said:

ما وسعني أرضي ولا سمائي ولكن وسعني قلب عبدي المؤمن

Neither My Heavens nor My Earth contain Me,
but the heart of My believing servant contains Me.[142]

It is said that, "Neither My Heavens nor My Earth contain Me, but the heart of My believer contains My Light." You cannot "contain," you cannot dare to say your heart "contains" Allāh, but "contained the Manifestation of the Light" that He will send to your heart, that Light which will shine in your heart and give it power in order that you will be always in the Presence of Allāh ﷻ.

Allāh said in Holy Qur'ān:

فَفِرُّوا إِلَى اللَّهِ

Run (away immediately) to Allāh (from harm)![143]

So our prayer is the gateway of running to Allāh ﷻ and there is no other way. How can you run to Allāh without the prayers? The prayers are, as the Prophet ﷺ said, "You are between the Hands of Allāh ﷻ, you are praying in the Presence of Allāh ﷻ, there are your prayers." So, these prayers are like polishing your heart, slowly, slowly, like you polish a stone to become a diamond, they keep polishing it, is it not? They keep polishing it, polishing it, polishing it until the diamond comes shining out of the rock. Our hearts are like rocks, they are not like diamonds, no one can convince himself that his heart is clean. People say, "My heart is clean," but your heart is clean when your prayers are clean. Your heart is clean when you become like a spotlight for people, when people run to you, then Allāh makes people run to you in order to get some power from you to guide

---

¹⁴² *Ḥadīth Qudsī, Al-Iḥyā* of Imām al-Ghazālī.

¹⁴³ Sūrat adh-Dhāriyāt, 51:50.

127

them. That power means the guidance, to guide them to perfecting their prayers and their *ṣalawāt* by perfecting your *ṣalawāt*. At that time your heart will be perfected, your heart will be clean.

قلب المو ءمن بيت الرب

The heart of the believer is the House of Allāh.

So when you say, "*Allāhu Akbar*," what are you including in your prayer? When I say, "*Allāhu Akbar*," and enter the prayer, what kinds of obligations are within the prayer? Look how much greatness Allāh ﷻ gave the prayer, so much power. As soon as you say "*Allāhu Akbar*" it means you are facing what? The *Qiblah, Ka'bah*. That means you are in a pilgrimage, a spiritual pilgrimage to *Ka'bah*, so you can imagine *Ka'bah* in front of you. Can you pray right or left or must you pray straight towards the *Ka'bah*? Straight to *Ka'bah*. So when you say, "*Allāhu Akbar*," you are in a spiritual pilgrimage. Do you think if you are in a spiritual pilgrimage, that Allāh is not going to give you support, that He is not going to welcome you? No, rather He says: "O My Servant, come! I am with you as long as you remember Me," and the prayer is to remember Allāh ﷻ. When we are remembering, we say, "*Yā Rabbī, Allāhu Akbar!*" and that is why Prophet ﷺ used to pray a lot of *nawāfil* and this is Prophet ﷺ who has been in *Qāba Qawsayni aw Adnā* already, but he was praying *nawāfil*, voluntary prayers, the *Sunnah*, in order to keep his relationship there always open with the Divine Presence, with Allāh ﷻ.

So when we say, "*Allāhu Akbar*," that door opens for us to go on a pilgrimage and in pilgrimage you face lot of good things and you will face lot of bad things. If you keep with the good thing is, you will be on a straight line to *Ka'bah* and if you deviate to exit you lose your *Ka'bah*; you are exiting where there might be a danger for you, Shayṭān is waiting, it will be a dangerous situation. But if you are keeping the straight line, the highway, your goal is the *Ka'bah*, you imagine and you are facing the *Ka'bah* in front of you, that will take you to be worshipping inside *Ka'bah* from your place:

$$\text{وَمَا ذَٰلِكَ عَلَى اللَّهِ بِعَزِيزٍ}$$

That is not at all difficult for Allāh, Who has no equal.[144]

That is not difficult for Allāh ﷻ and Allāh will give it! So let our prayer be the way to *Ḥajj*, to pilgrimage, a spiritual pilgrimage, a spiritual ascension, because when you speak about spirituality, not physicality, when you connect your heart with *Kaʿbah* through your prayer, Allāh connects you to *Bayt al-Māmūr*. He will open for you that level, Allāh is Generous, *al-Karīm* and He gives as much as you want, so take, but also do (act)!

So then what comes in your prayer? Second: you are fasting. Are you fasting in your prayer? Do you eat when you are praying? Do you drink when you are praying? Do you chew gum when you are praying? No. So what are you doing? You are fasting. And Allāh said:

$$\text{الصوم لي وانا أجزي به}$$

Fasting is for Me and I will reward it.[145]

Allāh will reward for the fasting. It is not compared to the fasting of *Ramaḍān*, *Ramaḍān* is an obligation, but we are speaking here of what the prayer includes within itself, so in these two *rakaʿats* or three *rakaʿats* or four *rakaʿats*, you are fasting. So when you are praying these *rakaʿats* you are fasting, not eating, nor drinking, not doing anything, prohibiting yourself from food for that period of time. If you eat in your prayer, your prayer is gone; you cannot take a sandwich and eat it and you are still praying. So fasting is included in the prayer.

Then *Tawḥīd*, what is the sign of *Tawḥīd*? What is the sign, the action for a non-Muslim to become Muslim? What has been asked from you first? What do you have to say? (Mawlānā raises his index finger), "*Ash-hadu an lā ilāha illa-Llāh wa Ash-hadu anna Muhammadu 'r-Rasūlullāh*," and you cannot give *salām* and leave the prayer without saying *Kalimat at-Tawḥīd* at the end. Why at the end and not at the beginning? That is to wrap it up. You are wrapping the prayer with *Tawḥīd*, so Shayṭān cannot as you wrapped it already with *Tawḥīdullāh*.

---

[144] Sūrat Ibrāhīm, 14:20.

[145] *Ḥadīth Qudsī.*

قُلْ هُوَ اللّهُ أَحَدٌ اللّهُ الصَّمَدُ لَمْ يَلِدْ وَلَمْ يُولَد وَلَمْ يَكُن لَهُ كُفُوًا أَحَد

*Say, "He is the One God, God the Eternal, the Uncaused Cause of All Being.
He begets not nor is He begotten and there is nothing that
could be compared to Him."[146]*

"Say, O Muḥammad, the Unknown One, that no one can know except through His Beautiful Names and Attributes and no one can see him." Allāh ﷻ can be seen in Paradise, at a certain level as mentioned in *ḥadīth* of the Prophet ﷺ, but Allāh cannot be seen in *dunyā*, "Say *yā* Muḥammad, He is the One who cannot be seen, is Allāh, Unique, *Āḥad*, One in Uniqueness in manifestations of His Beautiful Names and Attributes, *al-Āḥad*." *Allāhu 'ṣ-Ṣamad*, Allāh is now describing himself as: *aṣ-Ṣamad*, the One who doesn't need anything from anyone, the One who is not dependent on anyone, He is Self-Sufficient, and everyone is dependent on Him, all Humanity. *Lam yalid wa lam yūlad*, that is all *Tawḥīd*. That is why when you pray *sunnah* it is recommended to recite *Sūrat al-Ikhlāṣ*, that is *Tawḥīd*. *Lam yalid wa lam yūlad*, "He doesn't give children, have children nor is He born," that is *Tawḥīd*, believing in Allāh's Oneness. Telling people that Allāh has a wife or what they describe Him with different kinds of statues...we are not following anyone except our Prophet's ﷺ religion. So He is the one with no children and is not born, does not give children to Himself. *Wa lam yakun lahu kufūwan Āḥad*, "And He has no one with Him or like Him whatsoever." All of us are owned by Him, no one can be united with Him. We disagree with the premise of *Waḥdat al-Wujūd* as it is not Islamic, it is a mere philosophy.

So the Five Pillars of Islam are inside the prayer. You are making *Tawḥīd*, you are praying, you are fasting and you are going for *Ḥajj*. As soon as you say *"Allāhu Akbar,"* you go on a spiritual *Ḥajj* that takes you on different levels of ascension depending on the heart, and we saw (in previous sessions) the levels of hearts that exist. And the last is *ṣadaqah*, charity. How, do you give charity during prayer? Do you give money to poor people? No, but the charity is the *dunyā* work you do, so when you are capable of working and making money, you are dropping that work for Allāh's sake to pray. So that means that is a *ṣadaqah*, that prayer has a *ṣadaqah*, it contains *ṣadaqah*; you dropped what you were going to earn and

---

[146] Sūrat al-Ikhlāṣ, 112:1-4.

130

turned it into prayer to Allāh ﷻ. So the time that you would be going to work is now *ṣadaqah* of time for your *Ākhirah*.

So that is why prayer is polishing the heart as it contains the Five Pillars of Islam which make up the structure of the Building of Islam. When you build something you have to put a structure, so these Five Pillars of Islam contained inside the prayer are the structure of the building that is going to go up now, the Building of Islam. So first, that will give power to the heart.

The Three Types of Hearts

1)

قلب خال من الإيمان وجميع الخير فذلك قلب مظلم قد استراح الشيطان من إلقاء الوساوس إليه أنه قد اتخذ بيتا ووطنا وتحكم فيه بما يريد وتمكن منه غاية التمكن

Qalbun khālin min al-īmān wa jamī'i 'l-khayr, a heart that is empty of faith and does not believe in anything; such a person is always drinking, womanizing, lying, cheating and doing what Allāh ﷻ does not like and he never thinks of his prayers. During the day he is busy with *dunyā* and at night he is busy with nightclubs, and doesn't care about anything heavenly. That heart is empty of goodness, there is no goodness in it. *Fa dhālika qalbun muẓlim*, such a heart has no faith in it; this is a heart which is darkened in which there is no light, you cannot see anything. Now you are seeing with the light, but if you put the lights off you see nothing. So it is like that, the heart is in darkness, and you cannot pull it out! That heart is zero, it is dead. As when someone is in the hospital you see (on the heart monitor) electromagnetic waves and the lines are moving, but when the heart is dead it "flat lines," it shows no life in it.

So Shayṭān has no need to enter, as it is already dark, it is already useless. Why does he have to waste his time? Shayṭān's time is precious as he wants to keep something for everyone, so why does he have to spend time on someone whose heart is already dead? It is dead! So *qad istarāḥa 'sh-shayṭān min ilqā'i 'l-wasāwis ilayh*, "Shayṭān is relaxed now, not tiring to run after this person because that person already has whispering and all kinds of gossips coming to his ears," and he took that heart as a house for him and even more, a *waṭan*, country for him. He comes in and goes out, comes in and goes out and makes that person backbite everyone. Even if he is a scholar, even if he is a shaykh, if his heart is dead he will backbite, he will speak about people, he will discredit them, he will try to give them a bad reputation and spread false, bad rumors. Everything he does, he does not care. That person's heart is dead and he will never see any goodness in his life.

2)

قلب قد استنار بنور الإيمان وأوقد فيه مصباحه لكن عليه ظلمة الشهوات وعواصف الاهوية فللشيطان هنالك إقبال وإدبار ومجالات ومطامع فالحرب دول وسجال وتختلف أحوال هذا الصنف بالقلة والكثرةفمنهم من أوقات غلبته لعدوه أكثر ومنهم من أوقات غلبة عدوه له أكثر ومنهم من هو تارة وتارة

The second heart is one that has been enlightened with the Light of Faith, with the Light of *Īmān*, and like a pilot light in his heart, it is always there. As soon as he wants to do good *ʿamal* it shines, it ignites the heart, this pilot light. That little bit of faith that Allāh gives you when you are striving for good and trying hard to throw Shayṭān away, will fill your heart and Allāh puts for you a pilot light that will ignite for you immediately as a spotlight on everything to show you what you need. That is there, that pilot light is there waiting for you as you have *īmān*, and you say, "*Ash-hadu an lā ilāha illa-Llāh wa Ash-hadu anna Muḥammadu 'r-Rasūlullāh.*"

The problem is, like someone with a kerosene lamp or a flashlight, if you put a towel over it, can you see anything? It gets very dim and you can only see something vague there. If you take away the towel the light shines. So that heart that contains some faith and whose owner has put a lamp in it, and Allāh ﷻ put a pilot light for him, if his heart is covered with these "towels of gossips" and whisperings and is full of desires...he has faith, but for example he likes to go drink, making a sin, or go womanize making sin, or lie and cheat and backbite and curse; he is not humble, there is no mercy in his heart, but yet he prays. So there is light, but it is on pilot and you still have to ignite it.

So there, Shayṭān can go in and out of that heart, he is using it to whisper, "Oh! This one is bad, when you finish your prayer, go attack him, speak about him." So as soon as he says, "*As-salāmu ʿalaykum raḥmatullāh, as-salāmu ʿalaykum raḥmatullāh,*" he begins to attack or if he is giving a *ṣuḥbah* or a lecture, he is beginning to attack and backbite people, or if he is praying, he wants to finish quickly because something urgent came to his mind or to his ear that he wants to immediately act on and harm others. Such a heart is one which Shayṭān can go in and go out of.

3)

قلب محشو بالإيمان قد استنار بنور الإيمان وانقشعت عنه حجب الشهوات وأقلعت عنه تلك الظلمات فلنوره في صدره إشراق ولذلك الإشراق إيقاد لو دنا منه الوسواس احترق به فهو كالسماء التي حرست بالنجوم فلو دنا منها الشيطان يتخطاها رجم فاحترق وليست السماء بأعظم حرمة من المؤمن وحراسة الله تعالى له أتم من حراسة السماء والسماء متعبد الملائكة ومستقر الوحي وفيها أنوار الطاعات وقلب المؤمن مستقر التوحيد والمحبة والمعرفة والإيمان وفيه أنوارها فهو حقيق أن يحرس ويحفظ من كيد العدو فلا ينال منه شيئا إلا خطفه

The third one is *qalbun maḥshūwwun bi 'l-īmān wa qad istanāra bi nūru 'l-īmān*, that heart is stuffed with *īmān*, not one place is empty from *īmān*. In the third level his heart is completely full, like a perfect moon. *Wa qad istanāra bi nūru 'l-īmān*, "and *īmān* gave him so much light and that light will affect the other people's hearts who sit with him or with her!" Whatever it is, that reflection from him to others or from the others to him, it goes and comes.

That one, *inqasha'at 'anhu ḥujubu 'sh-shahawāt*, "All the curtains or veils of bad desires or good desires are lifted up from him." He doesn't any more fall into that trap of desires, even good desires are lifted! There are good desires that you can do and there are bad desires and from both desires he is clean; he doesn't want the good desires, he wants Allāh ﷻ and His Prophet ﷺ.

That heart is protected by Allāh as your prayer is, if you keep its time, keep the principles of prayer, keep its limits, make its *wuḍū*, and Allāh ﷻ protects that prayer for you.

Also, that heart will be protected by Allāh ﷻ, He takes away all darkness from his heart and keeps the power of the Light, as light emits energy and emits heat, so that heat is described as, "The heat that attacks Shayṭān and burns him when he comes to your heart." So Shayṭān cannot approach because Allāh ﷻ is protecting you. If Shayṭān approaches you, your heart is *ḥurisat bi 'n-nujūm fa law danā minhā 'sh-shayṭān yatakhaṭṭāhā rujima faḥtaraq*, "It is kept safe and protected by shooting stars." In the heart there are shooting stars and when Shayṭān approaches and your heart is protected by shooting stars it will hit on Shayṭān and burn him completely. That heart is really what Allāh ﷻ described, those who are reaching that level:

ألَا إِنَّ أَوْلِيَاء اللّهِ لَا خَوْفٌ عَلَيْهِمْ وَلَا هُمْ يَحْزَنُونَ الَّذِينَ آمَنُوا وَكَانُوا يَتَّقُونَ

Behold! Verily on the Friends of Allāh there is no fear,
nor shall they grieve; they who have attained faith
and have always been conscious of Him.[147]

"Those people who are My Saints, My Friends, My Sincere Servants, *lā khawfun ʿalayhim*, they must not fear anything." *Lā khawfun ʿalayhim* means, "no one to worry about them," *wa lā hum yaḥzanūn*, "and no one think they are sad," because Allāh is protecting their hearts, because they kept their hearts clean, they filled it with faith, with *Nūr al-Īmān*. *Al-ladhīna āmanū*, "Those who believed" with real belief, not imitational only. "Real belief" means following correctly in the footsteps of the Prophet ﷺ. *Wa kānū yattaqūn*, "And they were sincere," they were pious, they were fearing Allāh ﷻ.

So it is said the example of the three different hearts is like three homes. One, as Grandshaykh ق was describing, there is a king's house, a big palace and then there is a shack by it where they keep the hay. So the thief comes and will he go steal from hay or does he go to the house of the king to steal? He goes to the heart of the king to steal. So Shayṭān does not go to the heart of the first level, a heart that has no light as it is already dark. He runs after the treasures. So like the three houses, one house is for a king, full of jewels; the second one is a house that has some valuable goods in it, but not like the king's; and the third is completely empty. So which one will the thief steal from? The king's house. *fa in qulta min al-bayti 'l-khālī*, if you say, "From the empty house," it doesn't click in the mind for why would he go there?

قيل لابن عباس رضي الله عنهما : إن اليهود تزعم أنها لا توسوس في صلاتها فقال : وما يصنع الشيطان بالقلب الخراب ؟

That is why Sayyīdinā Ibn ʿAbbās ﷺ said, "There were a group of people, Jews, that came to the Prophet ﷺ and said, 'Yā Muḥammad ﷺ, in our prayer we don't have any whisper or gossips in our ears, we focus.' He ﷺ said, 'Shayṭān is not going to run after a heart that is already *kharāb*, destroyed, completely in ruins. Shayṭān is not going to go to ruins.'"

---

[147] Sūrah Yūnus, 10:62-63.

That means, "Your hearts are ruins, go and make your heart alive by bringing *īmān* to it." May Allāh  bring *īmān* to our hearts!

May Allāh forgive us and may Allāh bless us.

Wa min Allāhi 't-tawfīq, bi ḥurmati 'l-ḥabīb, bi ḥurmati 'l-Fātiḥah.
And with Allāh is success. For the sake of the Beloved, for his sake we recite the opening chapter of Holy Qur'ān.

Fiqh and Spirituality
are Like the Shell and the Kernel

A'ūdhu billāhi min ash-Shayṭāni 'r-rajīm. Bismillāhi' r-Raḥmāni 'r-Raḥīm.
Nawaytu 'l-arbā'īn, nawaytu 'l-'itikāf, nawaytu 'l-khalwah, nawaytu 'l-'uzlah,
nawaytu 'r-riyāḍa, nawaytu 's-sulūk, lillāhi Ta'alā fī hādha 'l-masjid.
Atī'ūllāha wa atī'ū 'r-Rasūla wa ūli 'l-amri minkum. (4:59)

مَنْ يُرِدْ اللَّهُ بِهِ خَيْرًا يُفَقِّهْهُ فِي الدِّين

The Prophet ﷺ said, "If Allāh wants good for His servant, He makes him to understand the religion," and to understand the religion is to understand *Fiqh*, which are different understandings of *ḥadīth* of the Prophet ﷺ and different verses of the Holy Qur'ān. And it has been explained that like a chestnut, there is the shell and there is the fruit inside; the shell protects the fruit and if there is no shell the fruit will disappear or go bad because there is no shell to protect it. The shell is necessary and the fruit is necessary. *Fiqh* is the shell and the fruit is the understanding of the spiritual aspect of the *ḥadīth* of the Prophet ﷺ.

If some people say, "We only want to learn *Fiqh*," which is very good, but it is not enough. You might learn *Fiqh* and become a scholar, but it is not going to change you or your characters; there might be small changes, but the Moral Excellence, if it was not important, then why did the Prophet ﷺ teach the *Ṣaḥābah* ﷺ about *Tazkīyyatu 'n-Nafs*, Purification of the Self? He would have kept it, when Jibrīl ﷺ asked about *īmān*, he would have kept it at Five Pillars, which is *Fiqh*; the Five Pillars are *Fiqh*. So the *Fiqh* is for the structure of the building, it is the foundation of the building on which you build, and *Īmān* is necessary because it is the *'Aqīdah*. *Iḥsān* is the Level of Purification, to get rid of all bad characters from us, then that jewel inside us will appear.

That light that Allāh ﷻ has put in us, as we mentioned in the previous session, there are three kinds of hearts. The best kind is the heart of a person who does not allow gossips and whispers of Shayṭān inside it; that one is the perfect heart. The others, as we mentioned, that one is already dark, there is *zhulmah* in it, there is no benefit from it and Shayṭān doesn't bother to enter it as it is already dark. The second heart is the one where one day you are on *īmān* and another day you are on the other side. That is the heart that Shayṭān can enter, and he goes in and tries to fight you. The third is the heart that Shayṭān cannot enter, as it is protected. By Whom is it protected? By Allāh ﷻ, because you have achieved the understandings from the knowledge of Islam, of Sharī'ah, of *Fiqh*, so the shell begins to get ripe and you open it to get the fruit inside it.

What is the fruit of the heart? This light that we put on, we can see with it and if you put it off, you see nothing. The heart can see, it can understand and talk, and it can relate. It can teach, because of what? From what Allāh ﷻ put in the heart of that person. And what did He put? It is mentioned by Wahb ibn Munabbih ﷺ:

عَنْ وَهْبِ بْنِ مُنَبِّهٍ أَنَّهُ قَالَ فِي بَعْضِ الْكُتُبِ : لَسْتُ أَسْكُنُ الْبُيُوتَ وَلَا تَسَعُنِي ، وَأَيُّ شَيْءٍ يَسَعُنِي وَأَيُّ بَيْتٍ يَسَعُنِي وَالسَّمَوَاتُ حَشْوُ كُرْسِيٍّ ، وَلَكِنْ أَنَا فِي قَلْبِ الْوَادِعِ التَّارِكِ لِكُلِّ شَيْءٍ سِوَايَ

I do not dwell in houses nor can they contain me; and what thing can contain Me and what house can contain Me, and the skies are the padding of My Footstool. But I am in the heart of the wādi', the one who abandons everything besides Me.

"*Lastu askunu 'l-buyūta*, I don't inhabit the houses," the houses here refers to the heart, "I don't inhabit the hearts that cannot contain Me, that cannot fit Me. *Wa ayyu baytin yasa'unī wa 's-samāwātu ḥashū kursī?* How is it possible that anything can be spacious to accept Me? As nothing can fit Me, because the Heavens and Earth are *ḥashū kursī*, like the stuffing of My Chair, *wasī'yyu kursīhu 's-samāwāti wa 'l-arḍ*, where the Chair has encompassed and contains everything in the universe." That Chair is bigger, like when you throw a ring in a desert. This whole universe, together with Heavens can be thrown in the Chair and it will disappear and Allāh's Chair is bigger than that. How then can, "The heart contain Me"? Open your eyes and open your mind! And He said, "I am in the heart of that one who left everything for Me, he left all his desires, everything he owns, he left it for Me. That is the one whose heart will fit Me."

This is the meaning of the other saying:

مَا وَسِعَتْنِي سَمَوَاتِي وَلَا أَرْضِي وَوَسِعَنِي قَلْبُ عَبْدِي الْمُؤْمِنِ

"The heart of My servant who is learning *Fiqh*, learning Sharī'ah and learning *Tazkīyyatu 'n-Nafs*, Purification of the Self, that one has a place for My Light in his heart." Allāh does not send His Light to a place that is dirty. That is why we mentioned the *hadīth* of Al-Haris in the previous session, regarding Sayyīdinā Yahyā ﷺ and the Five Orders that Allāh ﷻ gave him.

Allāh ﷻ ordered Sayyīdinā Yahyā ﷺ to mention five words, first: *an t'abud Allāh*, to worship Allāh, no *shirk*. Second *as-salat*, we explained that. Now *as-siyām*, so anyone who is doing these five obligations, *Tawhīd, ash-hadu an lā ilāha illa-Llāh wa ash-hadu anna Muhammada 'r-Rasūlullāh, wa iqāmu 's-salāti wa ītā'u 'z-zakāti wa sawmu ramadān wa Hajju 'l-bayt*, to those people Allāh ﷻ throws in their hearts because their hearts become clean. That's why He said, "In the heart comes everything, goes everything," and that's why Prophet ﷺ said:

الا وان في الجسد مضغة اذا صلحت صلح الجسد كله،
واذا فسدت فسد الجسد كله، الا وهي القلب.

In the body there is a small piece of flesh; if that piece of flesh is rectified then the whole body will be rectified and if it becomes corrupt then the whole body will become corrupt, and truly that is the heart. [149]

The heart is the main important organ in the body, and Allāh ﷻ made it so that through it the blood has to come to the heart to be cleaned, and then be pumped away. So that circulation of the blood, the pump of the blood of the body is the heart, which is pumping that blood to all of the body. So if it is correct...because it can pump anything bad, and if you are protecting the heart with *Fiqh* and *Sharī'ah* then it will be pumping in a situation that brings the Light of Allāh inside and throws Shaytān outside.

Virtues and Rewards of Fasting

And that's what we need and Prophet ﷺ has mentioned in many *ahadīth* that we will mention a little bit later, in order to make people feel that...today people say, "Oh! We are fasting and the smell of our mouth is bad." Some

---

[148] *Hadīth Qudsī, Al-Ihyā* of Imām al-Ghazālī.

[149] Bukhārī and Muslim.

people by mistake brush their teeth when they wake up, although they are fasting, which is not allowed; it is completely prohibited to brush your teeth, because you are erasing the smell of musk from your body. The Prophet ﷺ mentioned, and we will mention the *ḥadīth* later, that the smell of the mouth of a fasting person is better than the smell of this whole *dunyā* and universe. Prophet ﷺ described it as "the musk of Heavens."

Today in *dunyā* they look for the musk, which is very expensive, the real musk, and Allāh ﷻ is saying the saliva of a *mu'min* who is fasting is more important and nicer to Allāh ﷻ than that. To the saliva of the *mu'min* Allāh gives the smell of musk; that is what Allāh ﷻ is rewarding His servant with for their fasting. It means when your mouth—because through the mouth comes everything, through the tongue comes everything, all kinds of backbiting and *fitna*, confusions, fighting comes through the mouth—so when you are fasting you are preventing all this, you are cutting it and not letting Shayṭān play with you through these bad characters.

So Allāh described the person who is fasting, "His smell of the mouth is better than the smell of the musk," because in the time of the Prophet ﷺ the best perfume was musk and so Allāh is giving that as an example as the best smell of a fasting person. And that fasting musk is not the musk of *dunyā*, but the musk of *Ākhirah*. And about the musk of *Ākhirah*, it is mentioned that if Allāh allowed one *ḥūri* to open her finger and put it in *dunyā*, the smell of the musk of one fingertip will make everyone faint from that beautiful smell. That is in the mouth of a fasting person!

What did the Prophet ﷺ say? He mentioned in many places that fasting is so important to Allāh ﷻ. How it came, fasting, from the beginning?

قَالَتْ كَانَ يَوْمُ عَاشُورَاءَ تَصُومُهُ قُرَيْشٌ فِي الْجَاهِلِيَّةِ، وَكَانَ النَّبِيُّ صلى الله عليه وسلم يَصُومُهُ، فَلَمَّا قَدِمَ الْمَدِينَةَ صَامَهُ وَأَمَرَ بِصِيَامِهِ، فَلَمَّا نَزَلَ رَمَضَانُ كَانَ رَمَضَانُ الْفَرِيضَةَ، وَتُرِكَ عَاشُورَاءُ، فَكَانَ مَنْ شَاءَ صَامَهُ، وَمَنْ شَاءَ لَمْ يَصُمْهُ.

During the pre-Islamic Period of Ignorance, the Quraysh used to observe fasting on the day of ʿĀshūrā and the Prophet ﷺ himself used to observe fasting on it, too, but when he came to Madinah, he fasted on that day and ordered the Muslims to fast on it. When (the order of compulsory fasting in) Ramaḍān was revealed, fasting in

Ramaḍān became an obligation and fasting on ʿĀshūrā was given up and whoever wished to fast (on it) did so, and whoever did not wish to fast on it did not fast.[150]

The people of Quraysh in Mecca used to fast only the day of ʿĀshūrā in *Jāhiliyya*, and then Prophet ﷺ ordered the Muslims to fast the day of ʿĀshūrā. After that, when Allāh ﷻ ordered Ramaḍān, *ḥattā fūrida Ramaḍān faqāla rasūlillāh....* When Allāh ordered fasting for Ramaḍān, Prophet ﷺ said, "You are free to fast ʿĀshūrā or not to fast it, it's up to you, but you have to now fast thirty days." This was the beginning of fasting in the time of the Prophet ﷺ.

Allāh ﷻ said, *faman shahida minkumuu 'sh-shahr fal-yaṣum-hu,* "Anyone who sees the moon, let him fast for Ramaḍān," *fa rasūlillāhi annahu qāl*—and all these are *aḥadīth* Bukhārī or *muttafaqan ʿalayh.*[151]

إذا دخل رمضان فتحت أبواب الجنة وغلقت أبواب النار وسلسلت الشياطين

The Prophet ﷺ said: When Ramaḍān begins, the doors of Paradise are opened and the doors of Hell are closed and the shayāṭīn are tied with chains.[152]

"When *Ramaḍān* enters, the doors of Heavens will open and the doors of Hellfire will close." May Allāh ﷻ make all our days *Ramaḍān,* because "the one who is fasting" means the doors of *Jahannam* are closed for him and the doors of Heavens are opened for him, and the *shayāṭīn* cannot reach him even though they whisper. When you are fasting, you still get whispering in your ears when you pray. As soon as you say, *"Allāhu Akbar,"* all different things come from outside to your ears from Shayṭān, but in *Ramaḍān,* even though they come they are chained and cannot harm you and Allāh protects you from that whisper.

It is narrated by Īmām Muslim from Abi Hurayrah ؓ, that the Prophet ﷺ said that Allāh ﷻ said:

كل عمل ابن آدم يضاعف الحسنة عشرة أمثالها إلى سبعمائة ضعف. قال الله عز وجل: إلا الصوم، فإنه لي وأنا أجزي به. يدع شهوته وطعامه من أجلي. للصائم فرحتان: فرحة عند فطره، وفرحة عند لقاء ربه. ولخلوف فيه أطيب عند الله من ريح المسك. رواه مسلم

---

[150] Bukhārī.

[151] Meaning it is related by Al-Bukhari and Muslim on the authority of the Ṣaḥābi who narrated the *ḥadīth* from the Prophet ﷺ and both Al-Bukhari and Muslim agreed on the authenticity of the *ḥadīth.*

[152] Bukhārī and Muslim.

*All the deeds of the Children of Adam are multiplied so that there are ten rewards
for each good deed increasing up to 700, and Allāh said, "Except fasting, for it is
done (purely) for Me and I reward for it. He gives up his food and his drink and his
sexual desire for My Sake. There are two occasions of joy for one who fasts: a joy
when he breaks it and a joy when he meets his Lord. And the breath (of
an observer of fast) is sweeter to Allāh than the fragrance of musk."[153]*

"Every *'amal* the Children of Adam do, Allāh will increase, multiply it
by ten until 700 times," *Qāla-Llāhu ta' lā: illa 'ṣ-ṣawm,* He said, "Except
fasting. I am allowing everything, I am multiplying your *'amal* even 700
times, I reward you even 700 times more, but not fasting. Fasting is for Me,
everything else is for you. I'm giving you what you like, but *Ramaḍān*
fasting is for Me," *fa innahu lī wa anā ajzī bih,* "It is for Me and I reward for
it." There He rewards 700 times, but in *Ramaḍān* it's not limited and if you
limit it, you are making a sin. *Yada'a shahwatahu wa ta'āmahu wa sharābahu
min ajlī,* "He leaves his food and his drink for My sake," *Li 'ṣ-ṣā'im farḥatān,*
"Someone who is fasting has two happinesses: one happiness, *indā fiṭrih*
when he breaks fast." What kind of happiness? When you break fast you
will be happy? Some people might not be happy when they break fast. What
is the happiness that Allāh ﷻ is mentioning? "O *mu'mins,* Muslims, I am
giving you happiness in *Ākhirah!* I will open for you what is not opened, I
will open for you My Treasures so take what you want!"

Li 'ṣ-ṣā'im farḥatān farḥatan 'inda fiṭratihi, he has two happinesses: one
when he breaks his fast, which means, "What I will reward him as soon as
he kept his fasting until *Maghrib* and break the fast there, for that time that is
obligation for him to fast, I am going to reward him a reward that makes
him happy in *dunyā* and *Ākhirah."* *Allāhu Akbar!* And He compared the
happiness when he breaks fast like the happiness when he will meet with
Allāh ﷻ where He said, "The other happiness: *wa farḥatan 'inda liqāi rabbihi,*
when he will meet with his Lord." *Allāhu Akbar!* It means, the one who is
fasting *Ramaḍān* is going to meet with his Lord, means on every time you
break fast, Allāh gives you happiness like the happiness when you are going
to meet Him in *Ākhirah!* And all this He gave a description of what you
think to yourself that you feel bad about it and you don't like that character
and you don't like that way, but Allāh likes it. You try to perfume yourself
with all kinds of perfumes, but Allāh doesn't like that, He likes the smell of

---

[153] Muslim.

your mouth, He likes the smell of the one who is fasting. That is why He said, *wa la-khulūf fīhī aṭyabu ʿinda-Llāh min rīḥa 'l-misk*, "The smell of the mouth or the saliva of the mouth is more precious to Allāh ﷻ than the smell of heavenly musk," for that one who is fasting.

So imagine how much Allāh is giving people who are fasting! Every day that you fast, you are getting a happiness like the happiness when you meet Allāh ﷻ, and you are getting a smell that angels will run for it to carry your ʿamal to Allāh ﷻ! If you are fasting, whatever you did throughout the day the angels will come and approach you, because you have a good smell. It is like having a nice perfume and everyone says, "Put for me a little bit to smell nice." Why? To smell nice. Today they put under their arms to smell nice. So everyone now today is so concerned about their makeup, men or women. Men have a special makeup now, we never saw that before, and women have special makeup a hundred times more, in order to smell nice.

So, don't brush your teeth in the morning after *suhūr*; *suhūr* is the last moment to brush your teeth and finish. I am seeing people waking up and brushing their teeth, if something goes inside what you do, you lose your fast? In the time of the Prophet ﷺ they were using *miswāk*, but Allāh ﷻ is saying, "No, leave it, I like it, to Me it is better than the smell of musk and you will have happiness, don't do it."

The Prophet ﷺ said:

مَنْ صَامَ يَوْمًا فِي سَبِيلِ اللَّهِ بَاعَدَ اللَّهُ عَزَّ وَجَلَّ وَجْهَهُ عَنِ النَّارِ سَبْعِينَ خَرِيفًا

Whoever fasts one day in the cause of Allāh, Allāh the Mighty and Sublime will separate his face from the fire by (a distance of) seventy autumns.[154]

Anyone who fasts one day for Allāh other than *Ramaḍān*, he did it for Allāh's sake, Allāh will take his face away from punishment that day.

من صام رمضان إيمانا واحتسابا غفر له ما تقدم من ذنبه

Whoever fasts during Ramaḍān with faith and seeking his reward (from Allāh), all his past sins will be forgiven.[155]

If someone fasts *Ramaḍān* with faith and with good character, with good behavior, Allāh will forgive all the sins that were before from

---

[154] *Sunan an-Nasāʾī.*
[155] Bukhārī and Muslim.

childhood up to the present day. Like today is the tenth, then at the end of this *Ramaḍān* Allāh will forgive all your sins, as Prophet ﷺ mentioned in that *ḥadīth* that you will be forgiven every sin you committed.

الصوم لي وانا أجزي به

Fasting is for Me and I will reward it.[156]

Allāh will reward and will forgive all your sins and this is important for everyone to know. That is why people say, "Why is *Fiqh* important?" *Wa 'an 'Ayeshata* ﷻ *qālat kāna Rasūlullāh* ﷺ *yudriku 'l-fajr wa hūwa junub min āhlihi thumma yaghtasilu wa yaṣūm*, Sayyida 'Ayesha, *'alayhā riḍwān*, said, "Sometimes the Prophet ﷺ..." and this is for us, to teach us by showing us different ways, that "*Fajr* came, the *adhān* was called and he needed a shower, because he slept with his wife, so he used to take shower and then fast."

وعن عائشة رضي الله عنها قالت: كان رسول الله صلى الله عليه
وسلم يدركه الفجر وهو جنب من أهله ثم يغتسل ويصوم (متفق عليه)

'Ayesha ﷺ *reported that the Messenger of Allāh* ﷺ *woke up at Fajr time*
in a state of sexual impurity from relations with his wife, so he
took a bath before dawn and observed fasting.[157]

So it means here, that gives us an understanding that you can sleep at night with your wife and do as normal human beings and delay the *ghusl* until *Fajr*, because *Fajr* would come and Prophet ﷺ, *yudriku 'l-fajr wa hūwa junub*, would still need a shower. Some people might rush quickly when they are at the early time of sleeping to take a shower, but you are allowed to keep until *Fajr* time; however, it is better to take a shower before.

---

[156] *Ḥadīth Qudsī.*
[157] Bukhārī and Muslim.

144

Anas ibn Mālik ﷺ related that the Prophet ﷺ said:

" تَسَحَّرُوا فَإِنَّ فِي السَّحُورِ بَرَكَةً "

Eat sahoor, for in saḥūr there is blessing.[158]

Prophet ﷺ said, "Eat *saḥūr*," don't say, "I don't need it, it's okay I will drink water," no. He said, "Eat, as there is *barakah* in *saḥūr*." Allāh ﷺ will open for you what you might not know, He might open treasures for you. That means, he wants us to make *saḥūr*, as *saḥūr* is important for us. The Prophet ﷺ described the one fasting as one holding a *surrah*, a sheet or towel that he wraps and has something in it. He is describing the smell of the fasting person, the smell of his mouth is like a sheet of cloth and inside is a piece of musk. He is hiding it and doesn't open it, but a nice smell is coming out from it. It is giving vapor, but you don't see it as it is inside a piece of cloth. It is hidden, because of its high value. What do you do with anything whose value is high? You hide it.

So Allāh ﷺ wants to show His servants through the *ḥadīth* of Prophet ﷺ that the smell of the mouth of a fasting person is so dear to Allāh ﷺ that Prophet ﷺ is describing it as a piece of perfume, a musk that is put into a sheet and wrapped. Similarly, the smell of our mouth is hidden in our mouth, it doesn't come out, but people will smell that scent of musk. Allāh will turn that smell of the mouth, that saliva and all the fluid in your body into the smell of musk. Then at that time, you will be welcomed for heavenly enlightenment and since your smell is good, angels can approach you and dress you with the Dresses of Knowledge, as was the case of Sayyīdinā Khiḍr ﷺ, where Allāh ﷺ said:

وَعَلَّمْنَاهُ مِن لَّدُنَّا عِلْمًا

And We had taught him knowledge from Our Own Presence.[159]

"We taught him from a Heavenly Knowledge," because he was always in a good smell before his Lord, and this is the type of people who are fasting. It is hidden from people, because when you pray everyone can see, but if you don't tell, no one knows that you are fasting, so it is a hidden obligation that Allāh ﷺ ordered us for that hidden thing to be known.

---

[158] Bukhārī and Muslim.

[159] Sūrat al-Kahf, 18:65.

Allāh ﷻ said:

كنت كنزاً مخفياً فأحببت أن أعرف فخلقت الخلق

I was a Hidden Treasure (and) I wanted to be known, so I created Creation.[160]

"I was a Hidden Treasure and I wanted to be known, so I created Creation." Here, fasting is a hidden treasure from that divine inheritance, *tajallī* of the manifestation on us. That is why Allāh ﷻ said, *aṣ-ṣawmu lī*, "Fasting is for Me." That hidden thing is not known; Allāh alone knows if that person is fasting or not and He will reward that person. "He left his food and drink for Me and if he talks, he doesn't say anything to make people upset." *Fa ṣawmahu ṣawm al-jawāriḥ*, "Fasting is the fasting of limbs," all parts of a human body must be fasting, not only from eating and drinking, but it must be a real fasting. And he said:

رب صائم حظه من صيامه الجوع والعطش

Perhaps a person fasting will receive nothing from his fasting
except hunger and thirst.[161]

It may be that the fasting person only gets hunger and thirst, because he is not doing what Allāh ﷻ wants him to do from dealing with bad manners and listening to Shayṭān.

فوَالَّذي نَفْسُ مُحَمَّدٍ بِيَدِهِ لَخِلْفَةٌ فم الصَّائِم أطْيَبُ عِنْدَ اللَّهِ مِنْ ريح المِسْكِ

By Allāh in Whose Hand is the life of Muḥammad, the breath of the
observer of fast is sweeter to Allāh than the fragrance of musk.[162]

The Prophet ﷺ is giving an oath. *W 'alladhī nafsu Muḥammadin bi yadihi*, "The One that has the soul of Muḥammad in His Hand," *la-khilfatu fami 'ṣ-ṣāimi aṭyabu 'inda'Llāhi min rīḥa 'l-misk*, "The breath of the observer of fast is sweeter to Allāh than the fragrance of musk." Meaning to Allāh that fasting person is so important. May Allāh make us fast as much as we can and to be in good manners and moral excellence!

Allāh gives us lots of things that we don't know. He blesses with what He likes us to be. First of all, He made us Muslims. It is not because you

---

[160] *Ḥadīth Qudsī.*

[161] Ibn Mājah, Āḥmad.

[162] Muslim.

converted and became Muslim, it is Allāh's Generosity that He reminded you, "You are Muslim, come back," and there are many still coming back up to the Day of Judgment. Those who are coming as converts are better than those who are raised Muslim as their sins of whatever they did before Islam have been erased, but Muslims will be questioned for every sin they have done in their life! May Allāh  forgive us for the *barakah* and the sake of Sayyīdinā Muḥammad ﷺ.

May Allāh forgive us and may Allāh bless us.

Wa min Allāhi 't-tawfīq, bi ḥurmati 'l-ḥabīb, bi ḥurmati 'l-Fātiḥah.
And with Allāh is success. For the sake of the Beloved, for his sake we recite the opening chapter of Holy Qur'ān.

We Must Not Neglect Tafakkur (Contemplation)

A'ūdhu billāhi min ash-Shayṭāni 'r-rajīm. Bismillāhi' r-Raḥmāni 'r-Raḥīm.
Nawaytu 'l-arba'īn, nawaytu 'l-'itikāf, nawaytu 'l-khalwah, nawaytu 'l-'uzlah,
nawaytu 'r-riyāḍa, nawaytu 's-sulūk, lillāhi Ta'alā fī hādha 'l-masjid.
Atī'ullāha wa atī'ū 'r-Rasūla wa ūli 'l-amri minkum. (4:59)

Allāh said in the Holy Qur'ān:

طه مَا أَنزَلْنَا عَلَيْكَ الْقُرْآنَ لِتَشْقَى إِلَّا تَذْكِرَةً لِّمَن يَخْشَى تَنزِيلًا مِّمَّنْ خَلَقَ الْأَرْضَ وَالسَّمَاوَاتِ الْعُلَى الرَّحْمَنُ عَلَى الْعَرْشِ اسْتَوَى

We have not sent down the Qur'ān to you to be (an occasion) for your distress,
but only as an admonition to those who fear (Allāh), a revelation from Him
Who created the Earth and the Heavens on high. The Most Gracious
is firmly established on the Throne (of Authority).[163]

Allāh ﷻ is revealing to His Prophet ﷺ, and He mentioned his name
"*ṬāHā. Yā* Muḥammad! We did not reveal for you the Qur'ān in order to put
you in a difficulty, in heavy issues, in heavy stuff." Allāh ﷻ is talking to the
Prophet ﷺ through Jibrīl ﷺ, "O Muḥammad! The Qur'ān is My Words and
My Words never made anyone to be in difficulties. My Words relieve
people and everyone who is in a difficulty, the Qur'ān will relieve him."
That is why He ﷻ said, "*We have not sent down the Qur'ān to you to be (an
occasion) for your distress*". Rather, "the Holy Qur'ān is a means, a reminder
for those who want to be remembered and those who are not running away
from Me to bring them back to the Right Way, *Sirāṭ al-Mustaqīm*. The Holy
Qur'ān is coming to you, *yā* Muḥammad ﷺ" *tanzīlan mimman khalaqa 'l-arḍ
wa 's-samāwāti 'l-'ulā*, "from the One Who created Earth and the High
Heavens."

Why was this *āyah* and many other *āyāt* revealed to the Prophet ﷺ,
where it is mentioned in *Sūrat Taha*: 1,2 and in *Sūrat al-Baqarah*: 185, Allāh ﷻ
says:

يُرِيدُ اللَّهُ بِكُمُ الْيُسْرَ وَلاَ يُرِيدُ بِكُمُ الْعُسْرَ

---

[163] Sūrat ṬāHā, 20:1-5.

*Allāh wants ease and comfort for you
and He does not want difficulty for you.*[164]

Allāh ﷻ wants for you the easy way, He does not want for you difficulty. Allāh created us from His Mercy, from His Love to human beings, to His Servants. Allāh ﷻ created His Servants or else what does He need from us? Nothing. He created His Prophet ﷺ from His Light:

رواه عبد الرزاق بسنده عن جابر بن عبد الله بلفظ قلت: يا رسول الله، بأبي أنت وأمي، أخبرني عن أول شيء خلقه الله قبل الأشياء. قال: يا جابر، إن الله تعالى خلق قبل الأشياء نور نبيك من نوره،...«

*When Jābir ؓ asked, "Let my father and mother be sacrificed for you,
O Prophet of Allāh! What is the first thing that Allāh ﷻ created?"
the Prophet ﷺ said, "The first thing that Allāh ﷻ created is the
Light of your Prophet from His Light, O Jābir..."*[165]

The first thing Allāh ﷻ created is the Light of Muḥammad ﷺ from His Light, and He created Creation from that Light. If He did not create human beings, is it going to affect Allāh ﷻ? This huge Creation that is above us, which is more difficult to create, Earth and Heavens, or human beings? People say human beings are more important than Heavens and Earth, but Allāh says in Holy Qur'ān:

لَخَلْقُ السَّمَاوَاتِ وَالأرْضِ أَكْبَرُ مِنْ خَلْقِ النَّاسِ وَلَكِنَّ أَكْثَرَ النَّاسِ لَا يَعْلَمُونَ

*The creation of the Heavens and Earth is greater than the creation of Mankind, but
most of the people do not know.*[166]

Finished! The Creation of Heavens and Earth is far greater than the Creation of human beings, but too many people don't know that or don't think of that.

الَّذِينَ يَذْكُرُونَ اللَّهَ قِيَامًا وَقُعُودًا وَعَلَىٰ جُنُوبِهِمْ وَيَتَفَكَّرُونَ فِي خَلْقِ السَّمَاوَاتِ وَالأرْضِ رَبَّنَا مَا خَلَقْتَ هَذَا بَاطِلاً سُبْحَانَكَ فَقِنَا عَذَابَ النَّارِ

*There are indeed signs for men of understanding, those who remember Allāh
(always, and in prayers) standing, sitting and lying down on their sides,*

---

*and contemplating the creation of the Heavens and the Earth, (saying),
"Our Lord! You have not created (all) this without purpose! Glory to You!
Give us salvation from the torment of the Fire."*[167]

You cannot make *tafakkur* directly to Allāh ﷻ; leave that as that is a *ghaybu 'l-muṭlaq*, the Absolute Hidden. No one can know the Reality of Allāh's Essence. Allāh's Essence...you only know Allāh through His Beautiful Names and Attributes and through His Creation, that is *Maqām at-Tawḥīd*. There is *Maqām at-Tawḥīd* and there is *Maqām al-Āḥadiyya*, and there is *Maqām al-Mushāhadah*, as well as many other *maqāms*. For us, because everyone speaks about, "*Tawḥīd, Tawḥīd, Tawḥīd*," of course *Tawḥīd* is also to look at people around you. If you want to look further, first look at the people and see Allāh's Touch in everyone. Allāh's Greatness is in everyone!

We have the same name, me and Hisham (a *murīd*) have the same name, but he has a different touch, I have a different touch. Allāh ﷻ gave him different things, He gave me different things. Look at the greatness: every human being on Earth has his own unique characteristics, you cannot find two that are similar. How many software do you need for each different person? Different people, different software and different technology in everyone. You cannot see two that are the same. Even twins, when they grow up their character might be different.

So Allāh ﷻ is saying to you, *alladhīna yadhkurūnallāh...wa yatafakkarūna fī khalqi 's-samāwāti wa 'l-arḍ*, "Those who remember and understand and reflect their full focus on spiritual issues in order to move forward," and we are lacking these spiritual issues. Everyone goes to study, which is okay, correct for sure, because we have to have a strong structure, a strong base. Everyone goes to study, but they drop the most important study: *at-tafakkur*, to reflect, to concentrate and reflect on Allāh ﷻ's Greatness. How to do that? Think! *SubḥānAllāh*, this great universe...Who controls it? What is there?

Taffakur Opens Discussion and Different Opinions

Yes, we differ in issues, the Four *Madhāhib*, not only Four *Madhāhib*, but 472 different *madhāhib* according to Shaykh Muḥammad Abū Zahrā of Egypt (Azhar University), one of the greatest scholars. He counted 472 *madhāhib* in

---

[167] Sūrat Āli-'Imrān, 3:191-192.

Islam; the base is one and the branches are many, the trunk is one, but too many branches, which is good!

Al-Qāssim ibn Muḥammad ibn Sayyīdinā Abū Bakr aṣ-Ṣiddīq ﷺ said:

إِخْتِلاف أُمَّتِي رَحْمة

The difference of opinion among my nation is a mercy.

"The differences among the *ummah* is a mercy," but when they saw too many schools began to appear, *'ulamā* in that time, after Īmām Āḥmad bin Ḥanbal ق and Īmām al-ʿAwzāʿī, who was the fifth strong *madhhab* coming up, they met and said, "No, let us concentrate on four. If we go too far, then it will be difficult for people to understand, and already they are killing each other! Those who follow Īmām Mālik are not happy with Īmām Abū Ḥanīfa's students, and those students of Īmām Abū Ḥanīfa are not happy with the students of Īmām Shafiʿī, and those who were not happy with Īmām Shafiʿī are happy with Īmām Āḥmad bin Ḥanbal, all mixed up, everyone."

كُلُّ حِزْبٍ بِمَا لَدَيْهِمْ فَرِحُونَ

Each party rejoices in what is with itself (what it has).[168]

Every school of thought is happy with what they have, but we, if we are clever, we can take one and follow it. Don't create *fitna*! Take one of these *madhāhib, madhāhibu 'l-fiqhīyya*, take one and follow it; you will find safety. So do you 'want' to reflect? Allāh says you must reflect!

تفكر ساعة خير من عبادة سبعين سنة

To remember Allāh ﷻ (contemplate or meditate) for one hour
is better than seventy years of worship.

Allāhu Akbar! Or, *khayrun min ʿibādati sannah*, or in another narration in "one year." It is two narrations and it is big! Allāh ﷻ is giving you...People today go and study *Fiqh*, which is very important, yes, you have to study, and that is what we are doing in this course in *Ramaḍān*, but don't forget the other side, you have to focus on it. Now there are too many scholars around the world who do good work. They teach *Fiqh*, which is very good, but don't drop the *tafakkur, tafakkaru saʿat*. In one narration the Prophet ﷺ said,

---

[168] Sūrat al-Muʾminūn, 23:53.

"If you reflect one hour in Allāh 🕮, what He ordered, *tafakkur* in Heavens and Earth, on Allāh's Creation, thinking and focusing, meditating and contemplating, it is more than worship of one year," and in another narration, "seventy years." So Allāh 🕮 will reward you; you are getting rewards as if you worshipped seventy years!

So yes, we teach that, because this is the line we took from the beginning. There are others that took the line of *Fiqh*, but that does not mean you must not learn spirituality, *Tazkīyyatu 'n-Nafs* (the Purification of the Self). The whole criteria of the Prophet's 🕮 message and the focus of his message is *Tahdhīb al-akhlāq*, to polish and improve the characters of a human being, and characters cannot be improved without spirituality, without *rawḥānīyāt*, without this feeling of meditation, thinking about Allāh 🕮's Greatness.

The Prophet 🕮 said:

انما بعثت لاتمم مكارم الاخلاق

I have been sent to perfect the best of conduct
(your behavior and character).[169]

This is one of the Prophet's 🕮 greatest *ḥadīth*. "I have been sent to correct and polish the character of human beings," to polish. The difference between *Fiqh* and *Tazkīyyatu 'n-Nafs* is that *tazkīyyat* is inside the rock. You have a rock, you brought it from a mine from one mile or two miles down, you keep going down in the Earth to find these rocks which contain diamonds. The issue is the diamond, is it not? To get the diamond you have to cut the rock, to get to the tiny piece that is valuable. The *Fiqh* is protection for that diamond; with *Fiqh* you cut the limits and boundaries in order to get inside to the fruit, which is what we want. The Prophet 🕮 said, "I have been sent for that, to bring that *nūr* that is inside you out, into appearance!"

اللَّهُ نُورُ السَّمَاوَاتِ وَالْأَرْضِ مَثَلُ نُورِهِ كَمِشْكَاةٍ فِيهَا مِصْبَاحٌ

Allāh is the Light of the Heavens and Earth.[170]

The focus is on the light. Without the light there is darkness, as light makes everything shine. If no light, darkness appears. So the light is in

---

[169] Bazzār.

[170] Sūrat an-Nūr, 24:35.

153

meditating, in *tafakkur*, in thinking, and in order to do that you have to strengthen your belief, you have to try to do what Allāh ﷻ wants you to do. The Prophet ﷺ, out of thankfulness to Allāh ﷻ—not only by tongue by saying, "*Shukran lillāh*," but by action—was worshipping until his feet were swollen; this is by action.

Holy Qur'ān was Revealed Twice

And Allāh ﷻ said:

لَقَدْ كَانَ لَكُمْ فِي رَسُولِ اللَّهِ أُسْوَةٌ حَسَنَةٌ لِمَنْ كَانَ يَرْجُو اللَّهَ وَالْيَوْمَ الْآخِرَ وَذَكَرَ اللَّهَ كَثِيرا

Indeed in the Messenger of Allāh you have an excellent example
for anyone whose hope is in Allāh and the Last Day
and (who) remembers Allāh often.[171]

You have in the Prophet ﷺ a role model, don't follow anything else! Allāh said, "*Yā* Muḥammad ﷺ! You are the role model of the best character, I did not send down the Holy Qur'ān to you for you to be miserable." *Mā anzalnā ʿalayk al-Qur'ān li-tashqā illā tadhkiratan liman yakhshā*, "I didn't reveal the Holy Qur'ān for you to be miserable," *illā tadhkiratan liman yakhshā*, "I only sent, revealed it for them, and I revealed it to you *Yā* Muḥammad, *fī laylatin mubārakatin*, on a blessed night:

حم وَالْكِتَابِ الْمُبِينِ إِنَّا أَنزَلْنَاهُ فِي لَيْلَةٍ مُّبَارَكَةٍ إِنَّا كُنَّا مُنذِرِينَ
فِيهَا يُفْرَقُ كُلُّ أَمْرٍ حَكِيمٍ أَمْرًا مِّنْ عِندِنَا إِنَّا كُنَّا مُرْسِلِينَ

Hā. Mīm. By the Book that makes things clear, We sent it down
during a blessed night for We (ever) wish to warn (against evil).
In the (night) is made distinct every affair of wisdom by Command
from Our Presence for We (ever) send (revelations).[172]

Allāh ﷻ is saying to the Prophet ﷺ, *innā anzalnāhu fī laylatin mubārakatin*, "We have revealed the Holy Qur'ān for you, *yā* Muḥammad, on a very blessed night," *fīhā yufraqu kullu amrin ḥakīm*, "in it is every smallest thing."

وَلاَ رَطْبٍ وَلاَ يَابِسٍ إِلاَّ فِي كِتَابٍ مُّبِينٍ

---

[171] Sūrat al-Aḥzāb, 33:21.
[172] Sūrat ad-Dukhān, 44:1-5.

(There is not) anything fresh or dry (green or withered),
but is (inscribed) in a Clear Book.[173]

"Every matter, living and non-living, has been described in the Holy Qur'ān. I am giving it to you *fī laylatin mubārakatin*," on 15 *Sha'bān*, that night that Allāh has revealed the Holy Qur'ān on the Prophet ﷺ.

But Allāh ﷻ also says:

إِنَّا أَنزَلْنَاهُ فِي لَيْلَةِ القَدْرِ

We have indeed revealed this (Message) in the Night of Power.[174]

Is there any interference? It means it has been revealed in 15 *Sha'bān*, *Laylat al-Bara'ah* and also on *Laylat al-Qadr*. Does it mean one time on *Nisfu Sha'bān* and one time on *Laylat al-Qadr*? Yes. One time for the Prophet ﷺ, to tell us, "O human beings! Don't think you can understand the Holy Qur'ān. The only one to understand the Holy Qur'ān is the Prophet ﷺ." And *Sha'bān* is the month of the Prophet ﷺ, where the Prophet ﷺ said:

رجب شهر الله، وشعبان شهري، ورمضان شهر أمتي

Rajab is Allāh's month, Sha'bān is my month and
Ramaḍān is the month of my Ummah.[175]

Rajab is the month of Allāh ﷻ and *Sha'bān* is the month of Prophet ﷺ, so He sent it to him in his month according to the level of Prophet ﷺ. He revealed it to the highest one who can carry the secret with it:

وَإِنَّكَ لَعَلَى خُلُقٍ عَظِيمٍ

You are of the most exalted character.[176]

"You are on the best of manners," according to that power, according to the power of Prophet ﷺ that Allāh gave to him and according to the Light that Allāh dressed him when He created the Light of Prophet ﷺ before any creation, He revealed the Holy Qur'ān at that level of Prophet ﷺ. In *Ramaḍān* He revealed it for the *ummah*, for Allāh's Servants. They cannot understand as Prophet ﷺ understands, even if you brought all *'ulamā* together...bring

---

[173] Sūrat al-An'am, 6:59.

[174] Sūrat al-Qadr, 97:1.

[175] Abū 'l-Fatḥ ibn Abī Fawāris in his *'Amalī* from al-Ḥasan.

[176] Sūrat al-Qalam, 68:4.

them together, all of them from after the time of the *Ṣaḥābah* ﷺ up to today, bring them all together and they would not understand the Holy Qur'ān. They understand some, of course, but the meanings of Allāh's Words never end; you cannot make a limit for Allāh's Greatness in His Words, and Holy Qur'ān is Allāh's Words.

Some scholars say that the Holy Qur'ān was revealed on the night of 15 *Sha'bān* by coming out from the Hidden Treasure to the Preserved Tablets. It can be seen by the Prophet ﷺ on the Preserved Tablets, and that was on 15th of Sha'bān. It came down from the Preserved Tablets for the *Ummah* on *Laylat al-Qadr*, 27th of Ramaḍān. So that's why it is very difficult to understand the spiritual aspect and realm of Holy Qur'ān, but we can understand there is something that is hidden.

Fiqh is for getting you, as we mentioned in the previous session, the chestnut (shell) which protects the fruit inside; *Fiqh* protects the fruit, which is the spiritual realm, *Tazkīyyatu 'n-Nafs*, Purification of the Self. That is *al-akhlāq*, which is highly important. *Akhlāq an-Nabī tan'akisu 'ala 'l-makhlūqāt*, "The conduct of the Prophet ﷺ is reflected on humanity." When he said, *innamā bu'ithtu li utammimu makārim al-akhlāq*, "I have been sent to complete," he said, *li utammimu*, "to complete." It means he is completing us, he is completing our character, he is not depending on us, and to complete our characters is by how? Not only messages, not only by *aḥadīth*, but by *Fiqh*. Who is doing *Fiqh* today, who is applying it today? It's not easy.

عن عبد الله بن بسر رضي الله عنه أن رجلا قال: يا رسول الله إن شرائع الإسلام قد كثرت علي فأخبرني بشيء أتشبث به؟ قال لا يزال لسانك رطبا من ذكر الله" الترمذي.

A man came to the Prophet ﷺ and said, "O Rasūlullāh! The rules of Islam became heavy on me, so give me news of something which I can maintain." Prophet ﷺ said, "Make your tongue wet with dhikrullāh."[177]

"Really, really, I am telling you, *yā Sayyidī, yā Rasūlullāh*, that the different rules that we have to achieve in Islam I cannot, it is too hard for me." That is why if you go into *Fiqh* and you go deep, it gets harder and harder; it's not easy for everyone to learn that, especially for common people: you give them the basics, but when you go deep and deep it's not easy any more.

---

[177] Tirmidhī.

Sayyīdinā Abū Yazīd al-Bistāmī, *raḍīAllāhu ta'ala 'anhu*, and we are going from one level to another, was one of the greatest scholars in Islam who came after Prophet ﷺ by six or eight generations. He said, "*Yā Rabbī!* I am coming to You, open for me." He said, *kayfa al-wuṣūlu ilayk*, "How can I come to You? How can I reach You?" What did He tell him? What? A voice came from Heaven to his heart, *itruk nafsaka wa ta'al*, "Leave yourself and come to Me; don't come to Me with your self, as there cannot be two there. Come alone! Drop your desires completely," and he dropped. Sayyīdinā Abū Yazīd ق asked, "How can I do that?" and He said, *mazbalatan li 'ibādī*, "Be a dump for My Servants." It means, "Anyone harming you forgive him, anyone disconnects with you connect back with him, anyone that oppressed you forgive him, anyone who stole from you forgive him, and come."

It's a long story, so he made himself a dump for human beings, but when he reached that level of humble servant, he said, "*Yā Rabbī!* I am going to pray two *raka'ats* that no one has ever prayed like that," because he saw the level he is in. You cannot say, "Allāh will not open the eyes of people or their hearing to what is going around them." Without even being present they know, and that is a fact! Now when people reject this, they are rejecting the *ḥadīth* of Prophet ﷺ which is considered a Holy *Ḥadīth*, *Ḥadīth Qudsī*:

عَنْ أَبِي هُرَيْرَةَ رَضِيَ اللَّهُ عَنْهُ قَالَ : قَالَ رَسُولُ اللَّهِ صَلَّى اللَّهُ عَلَيْهِ وَسَلَّمَ : إِنَّ اللَّهَ تَعَالَى قَالَ مَنْ عَادَى لِي وَلِيًّا ، فَقَدْ آذَنْتُهُ بِالْحَرْبِ وَمَا تَقَرَّبَ إِلَيَّ عَبْدِي بِشَيْءٍ أَحَبَّ إِلَيَّ مِمَّا افْتَرَضْتُ عَلَيْهِ ، وَلَا يَزَالُ عَبْدِي يَتَقَرَّبُ إِلَيَّ بِالنَّوَافِلِ حَتَّى أُحِبَّهُ ، فَإِذَا أَحْبَبْتُهُ ، كُنْتُ سَمْعَهُ الَّذِي يَسْمَعُ بِهِ ، وَبَصَرَهُ الَّذِي يُبْصِرُ بِهِ ، وَيَدَهُ الَّتِي يَبْطِشُ بِهَا ، وَرِجْلَهُ الَّتِي يَمْشِي بِهَا ، وَلَئِنْ سَأَلَنِي لَأُعْطِيَنَّهُ ، وَلَئِنْ اسْتَعَاذَنِي لَأُعِيذَنَّهُ

Whoever comes against a saint of Mine, I declare war on him. And My servant does not approach Me with anything more beloved to Me than what I obligated him with, and My servant does not cease to approach Me through voluntary worship until I will love him. When I love him, I will become the ears with which he hears, the eyes with which he sees, the hand with which he acts, and the legs with which he walks (and other versions include, "and the tongue with which he speaks.").[178]

من تقرب إليّ شبراً تقربت منه ذراعاً، ومن تقرب مني ذراعاً تقربت منه باعاً، ومن أتاني يمشي أتيته هرولة

---

[178] *Ḥadīth Qudsī*, Bukhārī.

*If he (My Servant) draws near to Me a hand's span, I draw near
to him an arm's length. And if he draws near to Me an arm's length,
I draw near to him a fathom's length. And if he comes
to Me walking, I go to him running.*[179]

Look, He connected them, and this is a *Holy Ḥadīth*, that means it's a
revelation from Allāh to Prophet ﷺ to tell people. He connected it. He said,
"Who harmed one of My *Awliyā* I declare war on him," then immediately
He say, "If someone come to Me one hand I come to him one arm." He is
giving a chance. "Don't harm My *Awliyā*, My Saints, My Friends, because I
gave them what I did not give you, so don't deny on them." If you deny
them, you declare war on Allāh ﷻ. "What did I give them? Those who
approach Me through voluntary worship, *nawāfil*, I will love them; they are
Mine, My Lovers, I love them. I will give them hearing that I didn't give
anyone; they can hear whatever they like." Not like *jinn, istaraqa 's-samā'*.
They only reach a certain level in skies; they cannot go above the level of
samā ad-dunyā, the first level of this universe. We cannot call it Heaven, but
samā ad-dunyā, the *samā* of this world. They reach there in order to spy and
put their ears in order that they can hear, and immediately a shooting star
will come hitting on them. He ﷻ mentioned that they steal:

إلاَّ مَنِ اسْتَرَقَ السَّمْعَ فَأَتْبَعَهُ شِهَابٌ مُّبِينٌ

Except one who steals a hearing and is pursued by a clear burning flame.[180]

So they reach that level and they try to listen, but there is no
permission and the shooting star comes hitting on them. But for *awliyāullāh*,
Allāh is saying, "I gave them hearing, authority that I did not give to
anyone." It means He did not give hearing to *jinns*, means they cannot do
that, they cannot hear, which means *awliyāullāh* are higher and they can see
what is going in *samā ad-dunyā*. They can see what is going wherever Allāh
wants them to see!

So He put it together after He said, "Who comes against My *Walī*, I
declare war on him, but still there is chance to repent: if he comes to Me I
come to him, and those who come to Me worshipping through voluntary
worship," means through all kinds of worship that Prophet ﷺ has asked us

---

[179] *Ḥadīth Qudsī.*

[180] Sūrat al-Ḥijr, 15:18.

to do, "if they come to Me like that, I will open for them, I will give them hearing and vision, I will give them power to see what people cannot see."

So Sayyidinā Abū Yazīd al-Bistāmī ق reached that kind of level where people are able to see, and he said, "*Yā Rabbī!* I will pray two *raka'ats* that no one has ever prayed before," meaning in his time, not Prophet ﷺ and the Ṣaḥābah ☝, but people in his time or after his time. But wherever he reached, he said, "I am going to pray two *raka'ats* no one has ever prayed before." He said, "*Allāhu Akbar*," and he was there, seeing and hearing what no one has seen or heard before. He finished *at-Taḥiyyāt*, "As-salām 'alaykum wa raḥmatullāh..." angels, whatever he was seeing, we don't know. "As-salām 'alaykum wa raḥmatullāh," and from Allāh ﷻ, he was in that position, an angel gave him a sound in his heart, "*Yā ẓālim*, O Oppressor, your prayer is not accepted; it is the prayer of a *ẓālim* and it is thrown in your face!"

Look how much *awliyāullāh* suffered! To hear that voice from Heaven, what will that do to his feelings? The one who was saying at a moment, "I am going to pray two *raka'ats* that no one has prayed," and then at the end of the two *raka'ats*, he was kicked out, saying, "*Yā ẓālim!*" If he, in that situation (was called) "*ẓālim*," what about us? If he was able to pray according to that *ḥadīth* that there are people who can reach that level: Allāh ﷻ gave them special hearing, special vision, special talk, special power in their hands, special *nūr* and power in their feet that they walk in *Ṣirāṭ al-Mustaqīm*. Allāh ﷻ gives, He is Generous; He doesn't hide what He wants to give, He gives to everyone, but, "Come to Me."

Now this is our explanation. "O Abū Yazīd! You asked to come, and the answer came through your heart, 'Leave your desires, leave yourself and come to Me.' 'How should I come to you?' 'Make yourself a dump,' and you did that. So why do you want to make yourself, why were you claiming something, to make two *raka'ats* that no one did before? Why? Be happy with what you have. Why did you claim something there?" There it is sensitive. That is why in your countries, other than Mecca and Madinah, if you think of doing something wrong, and you planned it, but didn't yet do it, it is not written as something against you, because it is not yet materialized. But, if in Mecca and Madinah you think of something wrong, it is written immediately against you, because *Ka'bah* is in Mecca and in the Fourth Heaven there is *Bayt al-Ma'mūr*, and the angels are always in *ṭawāf* in the Fourth Paradise. So Abū Yazīd al-Bistāmī ق was in a sacred place, in a place that we don't know where it was, through his heart. Allāh opened to his heart and he was able to reach that level, as the heart has Five Levels:

Qalb, Sirr, Sirr as-Sirr, Khafā, Akhfā, The Heart, the Level of Secret, the Level of Secret of Secrets, the Level for Prophet ﷺ and the fifth one, no one entered there, it is in Allāh's Hands.

So he heard it, *"Yā Ẓālim!"* It came through an angel to his heart.

Abū Yazīd ق said, *"Yā Rabbī,* O Allāh what did I do wrong?"

And then it came to his heart, an inspiration, *ilhām* came from an angel, "You claimed something that is not yours, you were proud of it, you were filled with pride when you said, 'I want to pray two *raka'ats* that no one has prayed before.' Okay, I am to judge you according to what you have claimed."

How do we pray today? *Kanakrik duyūk,* as the Prophet ﷺ said, "Is like the rooster pecking the floor." People today are like that in their prayer, especially youngsters, they don't give it it's right. That prayer will be thrown in your face, by *Fiqh* it is not complete. You stole from, you stole its *arkān,* its principles, the conditions of the prayer, and it will be thrown in your face.

"So why you claimed? Don't claim. You claimed? Okay, now there is *hisāb,* I am judging you according to that. You oppressed yourself in the prayer." He was *ẓālim* to his *nafs.*

And he was thinking to himself, "What did I do?"

And the answer came, "You were *ẓālim* to your self,"

He was thinking, "What I did to myself?"

The answer came to his heart, "You were leaning on your right leg for a longer time than the left leg. Your right leg was carrying more weight and it was objecting, complaining, 'Why you leaned on me more than the left?'"

وَوَضَعَ الْمِيزَانَ أَلَّا تَطْغَوْا فِي الْمِيزَانِ وَأَقِيمُوا الْوَزْنَ بِالْقِسْطِ وَلَا تُخْسِرُوا الْمِيزَانَ

And He has set up the Balance, that you may not transgress (due) balance,
but observe the measure with equity and do not fall short of it.[181]

"Keep everything balanced, don't make one heavier than the other. I gave you two legs, the two must be the same. You must balance, you are not sick, or can claim that you are sick, you were leaning on one and not on the other. You were *ẓālim* to the Trust I gave you, the body that I gave you. I

---

[181] Sūrat ar-Raḥmān, 55:7-9.

trusted you to keep it balanced." All of us, we are not keeping our body balanced by (committing) sins. That is why people get sick, get this and that.

So that is for someone whom Allāh ﷻ opened his eyes and ears. The Prophet ﷺ was coming to polish our good manners and bring them up. Everything in *Fiqh*, if you really go down into it, is to polish us and clean ourselves, to have good characters by imitating and following the Prophet ﷺ, as Allāh said in Holy Qur'ān:

قُلْ إِن كُنتُمْ تُحِبُّونَ اللَّهَ فَاتَّبِعُونِي يُحْبِبْكُمُ اللَّهُ وَيَغْفِرْ لَكُمْ ذُنُوبَكُمْ وَاللَّهُ غَفُورٌ رَّحِيمٌ

*Say (O Muḥammad), "If you (really) love Allāh,
then follow me! Allāh will love you."*[182]

And Allāh ﷻ said, *Taha. mā anzalnā ʿalayk al-Qurʾān li-tashqā*, "I didn't reveal the Holy Qur'ān for you to get difficulty, to be miserable." No, *illā tadhkiratan liman yakhshā*, "I am sending that for those who are not fearing Me, or those who are away from My Presence, those who lost My Love, to bring them back, to guide them, to be on right track, not running left and right."

جَاءَ ثَلَاثَةُ رَهْطٍ إِلَى بُيُوتِ أَزْوَاجِ النَّبِيِّ صلى الله عليه وسلم يَسْأَلُونَ عَنْ عِبَادَةِ النَّبِيِّ صلى الله عليه وسلم فَلَمَّا أُخْبِرُوا كَأَنَّهُمْ تَقَالُوهَا فَقَالُوا وَأَيْنَ نَحْنُ مِنَ النَّبِيِّ صلى الله عليه وسلم قَدْ غُفِرَ لَهُ مَا تَقَدَّمَ مِنْ ذَنْبِهِ وَمَا تَأَخَّرَ. قَالَ أَحَدُهُمْ أَمَّا أَنَا فَإِنِّي أُصَلِّي اللَّيْلَ أَبَدًا. وَقَالَ آخَرُ أَنَا أَصُومُ الدَّهْرَ وَلَا أُفْطِرُ. وَقَالَ آخَرُ أَنَا أَعْتَزِلُ النِّسَاءَ فَلَا أَتَزَوَّجُ أَبَدًا. فَجَاءَ رَسُولُ اللَّهِ صلى الله عليه وسلم فقَالَ " أَنْتُمُ الَّذِينَ قُلْتُمْ كَذَا وَكَذَا أَمَا وَاللَّهِ إِنِّي لأَخْشَاكُمْ لِلَّهِ وَأَتْقَاكُمْ لَهُ، لَكِنِّي أَصُومُ وَأُفْطِرُ، وَأُصَلِّي وَأَرْقُدُ وَأَتَزَوَّجُ النِّسَاءَ، فَمَنْ رَغِبَ عَنْ سُنَّتِي فَلَيْسَ مِنِّي " .

A group of three men came to the houses of the wives of the Prophet ﷺ asking how the Prophet ﷺ worshipped (Allāh), and when they were informed about that, they considered their worship insufficient and said, "Where are we from the Prophet ﷺ as his past and future sins have been forgiven." Then one of them said, "I will offer the prayer throughout the night forever." The other said, "I will fast throughout the year and will not break my fast." The third said, "I will keep away from the women and will not marry forever." Allāh's Messenger ﷺ came to them and said, "Are you the same people who said so-and-so? By Allāh, I am more submissive to Allāh and more afraid of Him than you; yet I fast and break my fast, I do sleep and I also

---

[182] Sūrat Āli-ʿImrān, 3:31.

This will shed a little light on that a little bit, and this is a *ḥadīth* by Bukhārī and Muslim. Anas ibn Mālik ﷻ related that three different groups of people came to the houses of the Wives of the Prophet ﷺ to learn from them how the Prophet ﷺ prayed at home. When we go through the different styles of *ṣalāt*, we see that the Prophet ﷺ had different styles, different ways of praying, and they all have their own secrets and their own different taste. We don't have to look at it from only one perspective of *Fiqh*, we have to look at many other issues that come with it. *Falammā ukhbirū ka'annahum taqālūhā fa qālū*, when they asked them and they mentioned to them how the Prophet ﷺ was praying, they said, *ayna naḥnu min an-Nabiyy* ﷺ, "We cannot do what he can do," because in the other ḥadīth, the Prophet ﷺ was praying until his feet were swollen:

قَالَ صَلَّى رَسُولُ اللَّهِ صلى الله عليه وسلم حَتَّى انْتَفَخَتْ قَدَمَاهُ فَقِيلَ لَهُ أَتَتَكَلَّفُ هَذَا وَقَدْ غُفِرَ لَكَ مَا تَقَدَّمَ مِنْ ذَنْبِكَ وَمَا تَأَخَّرَ قَالَ " أَفَلاَ أَكُونُ عَبْدًا شَكُورًا "

Allāh's Messenger ﷺ performed ṣalāt until his feet were swollen, so it was said to him, "You burden yourself like this, while your past and future sins have been forgiven?" He said, "Shouldn't I be a grateful worshipper?[184]

That *ḥadīth* is under *Bāb ash-Shukr, The Chapter of Thanking Allāh* ﷻ, because it is an answer for when they asked him, "Why, *yā Rasūlullāh*? Allāh has forgiven your former and latter sins." Why? Does the Prophet ﷺ have sins to forgive him? Of course everyone needs Allāh's Forgiveness, but the Prophet ﷺ is the Lover of Allāh ﷻ, what sins would he have? He is *ma'ṣūm*, infallible, he has no sins, but he was carrying the sins of his *ummah*. Allāh ﷻ wanted to please him and said to the Prophet ﷺ, "You are concerned for your community, but I have forgiven them!"

لِيَغْفِرَ لَكَ اللّٰه مَا تَقَدَّمَ مِن ذَنبِكَ وَمَا تَأَخَّرَ وَيُتِمَّ نِعْمَتَهُ عَلَيْكَ

That Allāh may forgive you your faults of the past and those to follow.[185]

---

[183] Bukhārī and Muslim.

[184] Tirmidhī.

[185] Sūrat al-Fatḥ, 48:1,2.

"We have forgiven him of whatever sins from before and from after." How? He ﷺ has no sins. How then? It means, forgiving the sins of his *ummah* from the past and in the future, until the Day of Judgment. Look at the meaning of the *ḥadīth*. That interpretation of the *ḥadīth* is not in the books of *Fiqh*. It is from our teachers, it is a spiritual aspect of religion, that the Prophet ﷺ was carrying on his shoulder a very heavy load of sins from the *ummah*, and Allāh ﷻ was saying to him, "We have relieved you from your burden, the big load on your shoulders, the load of the *ummah*."

أَلَمْ نَشْرَحْ لَكَ صَدْرَكَ وَوَضَعْنَا عَنكَ وِزْرَكَ الَّذِي أَنقَضَ ظَهْرَكَ وَرَفَعْنَا لَكَ ذِكْرَكَ

Bismillāhi 'r-Raḥmāni 'r-Raḥīm. Have We not expanded for you your breast? And We removed from you your burden that weighed so heavily on your back.[186]

So they said, *ayna naḥnu min an-nabī* ﷺ, "Yā Rasūlullāh! How can we do that?" We cannot compare ourselves to the Prophet ﷺ for Allāh has forgiven him. One of them said, *qāla Aḥaduhum fa ammā anā fa-innī uṣalli 'l-layla abadan*, "I will pray all night continuously, non-stop," and the other said, *wa qāla ākharu anā aṣūmu 'd-dahra wa lā ufṭiru*, "I will fast the whole year, never breaking the fast, except at *Maghrib* time," and the other said, *wa qāla ākharu anā a'tazilu 'n-nisā' fa lā atazawwaju abada*, "I will never approach women in my life, I will be celibate."

So the first one said, "I will pray forever," and the second said, "I will always fast," and third said, "I will never approach women." *Fa jā'a Rasūlullāh* ﷺ, the Prophet ﷺ came and said, *antum alladhīna qultum kadhā wa kadhā*, "Are you the ones who said this and this to my wives?" *Amā w 'Allāhi innī la-akhshākum lillāhi wa atqākum lahu*, "I give an oath that I am the most conscious of Allāh, most fearful of Allāh ﷻ among you."

Look how they were happy with what they were doing: one was going to pray forever, the other one fasting the whole year and the third one not approaching women, but he said, "Still, what you will do compared to what I am doing, I am the most fearful of Allāh ﷻ," and that means in the whole universe. *Wa atqākum lahu*, "and I am the most pious among you." *Lākinnī aṣūmu wa afṭir*, "But I fast and break fast," meaning, "I don't fast continuously. Allāh gave that *rukhsah* so why do I have to license it for the *ummah*?" Because if the Prophet ﷺ had agreed, then all the Muslims would be obliged to fast all year, pray all night and be away from women. That's

---

[186] Sūrat ash-Sharḥ, 94:1-2.

why he said, "No, I am the most fearful and the most pious, I fast and break my fast." *Wa uṣallī wa arqud*, "I pray and I sleep." If he ﷺ had said "yes" to him, then all of us would have been obliged to pray all night, but the Prophet ﷺ said, "No, I pray and I sleep." *Wa atazawwaju 'n-nisā'*, "And I marry. I don't say, 'I don't marry.'" *Fa man raghiba 'an sunnatī fa laysa minnī*, "Who does not like my *Sunnah* is not from me." Meaning, he is telling them, "What you are doing is not my *Sunnah*!"

I know people from when I was younger who would fast the entire year and their country, which is Iraq, was very hot. They would fast the entire year and break their fast only five days: one day of ʿĒid al-Fiṭr and four days of ʿĒid al-Adhā. They would fast for the rest of the days. So that is why *Fiqh* is important, as it will also direct you to the literal meaning of *aḥadīth* and how to live your life, but you need the other side of the *ḥadīth* so as to help you balance your life; you need the interpretational side of the *ḥadīth*, which is *Tazkīyyatu 'n-Nafs*.

So we are ordered to make *tafakkur*, contemplate, meditate and focus on everything that Allāh created in this universe and see the Greatness of Allāh ﷻ. Imagine, the heat in the core of the sun is 50 million degrees centigrade! Prophet ﷺ mentioned in the *aḥadīth* of the Last Days that are coming in front of us, "Allāh ﷻ will order the Sun to come over the heads of people by 50 meters." If we cannot take the heat of today as we need air conditioners, what then do you think about the heat of 50 million degrees centigrade? And Allāh with His *Qudrah*, Power, will bring the sun down to 50 meters, but it will not make us to die! It will not burn you, but will make you suffer and boil your brain. You will feel the pain, but still remain in your body. It is not like you will be finished and completely disintegrated, as you would in a normal fire. You will not be disintegrated, but will feel the heat of the sun. If the core right now is 50 million centigrade, Allāh knows how hot it will feel when it is at 50 meters above our head!

O Muslims, be nice and be good.

أوصى النبي صلى الله عليه وسلم أبا هريرة بوصية عظيمة فقال: يا أبا هريرة! عليك بحسن الخلق. قال أبو هريرة رضي الله عنه: وما حسن الخلق يا رسول الله؟قال: تصل مَنْ قطعك، وتعفو عمن ظلمك، وتُعطي من حرمك.

The Prophet ﷺ advised Abū Hurayrah: O Abā Hurayrah! You must have good manners. Connect with the one who cut you off,

The Prophet ﷺ said to Sayyīdinā Abū Hurayrah ؓ: "You have to observe the best of conduct." Abū Hurayrah ؓ asked, "What is the best conduct?" Prophet ﷺ said, "Connect with the one who disconnected you, forgive the one who oppressed you, and give to the one who prevented you from getting what you like, help him."

Is that not difficult? That is the best of characters. We will continue later, *inshā'Allāh*.

May Allāh forgive us and may Allāh bless us.

Wa min Allāhi 't-tawfīq, bi ḥurmati 'l-ḥabīb, bi ḥurmati 'l-Fātiḥah.
And with Allāh is success. For the sake of the Beloved, for his sake we recite the opening chapter of Holy Qur'ān.

---

[187] al-Bayhaqī.

The Importance of Ṣadaqa

A'ūdhu billāhi min ash-Shayṭāni 'r-rajīm. Bismillāhi' r-Raḥmāni 'r-Raḥīm.
Nawaytu 'l-arbā'īn, nawaytu 'l-'itikāf, nawaytu'l-khalwah, nawaytu 'l-'uzlah,
nawaytu 'r-riyāḍa, nawaytu 's-sulūk, lillāhi Ta'ala fī hādhā 'l-masjid.
Atī'ullāha wa atī'ū 'r-Rasūla wa ūli 'l-amri minkum. (4:59)

The *ḥadīth* al-Hārith al-Asha'rī ☙ mentioned by Imām Aḥmad in his *Musnad* and in the book of Tirmidhī, he mentioned, and I will summarize it quickly that Allāh ordered Sayyīdinā Yaḥyā ☙ to tell his people about five orders that Allāh ☙ ordered them to do:

Maqām at-Tawḥīd

An ta'buda'Llāh wahdahu, to worship Allāh ☙ alone. It means, to declare His Oneness, *Maqām at-Tawḥīd,* that there is no Creator except Allāh ☙ and that He is not like us, He is with Himself, by Himself, to Himself; no one can be partner and no one can associate himself with Allāh ☙. And the Prophet ☙ is His Beloved Servant and he ☙ is very happy when Allāh ☙ calls him, "My Servant," where He mentioned in *Sūrat al-Isrā'*:

سُبْحَانَ الذِي أَسْرَى بِعَبْدِهِ لَيْلاً مِّنَ الْمَسْجِدِ الْحَرَامِ إلى الْمَسْجِدِ الأَقصَى الذِي

بَارَكْنَا حَوْلَهُ لِنُرِيَهُ مِنْ آيَاتِنَا إنَّهُ هُوَ السَّمِيعُ البَصِيرُ

Glory be to He Who transported His servant by night from the Inviolable House of Worship (at Mecca) to the Remote House of Worship (at Jerusalem), the environs of which We had blessed so that We might show him some of Our symbols, for verily He Alone is All-Hearing, All-Seeing.[188]

"Praise be to Allāh that He took His Servant, Sayyīdinā Muhammad," *'abdihi,* to be called "His Servant." "Praise be to Allāh that He took His Servant, *'abdihi,*" and the *Hā* is referring to Allāh ☙, that He owns him and through him owns everyone, that He took him for *Isrā' wa 'l-Mi'rāj.* So we explained that under the *Maqām at-Tawḥīd* section, and the other Order was prayer.

---

[188] Sūrat al-'Isrā, 17:1.

Aṣ-Ṣalāt

We explained what we were able to explain at that time in previous sessions, but there are more to explain later, *inshā-Allāh*. Then *as-siyām*, fasting, he ordered his people by Allāh's Order to fast. The importance of fasting, and we mentioned that and the main one of that, but let's go a little bit to the prayers.

We mentioned about *ṣalāh* and we explained how in your *ṣalāt* all the Five Pillars are within the *ṣalāt*, you can find within the prayer *siyām*, *ṣadaqa*, charity, *zakāt*, Hajj and you can find *tawḥīd* in the prayer, and we explained that, but there is more to explain.

Siyām

Fasting, and the importance of fasting where the Prophet ﷺ said (that Allāh said):

الصوم لي وانا أجزي به

Fasting is for Me and I will reward it.[189]

"Fasting is for Me and I will reward for that." There are no angels there as intermediary, Allāh takes our fasting directly; the fast will rise up to the Presence of Allāh ﷻ, the Divine Presence and Allāh ﷻ will reward as He likes.

Aṣ-Ṣadaqa

Now the chapter, or fourth one, which is very important and has a lot of significance is *aṣ-ṣadaqa*, donation, the importance of charity in our lives. *Ṣadaqa* cannot be compared to anything, although prayers contain the Five Pillars of Islam. *Siyām* is for Allāh and *ṣadaqa* is something you are giving from yourself, from your wealth. You can pray all the time and the human being can feel that they do not want to be asked for *ṣadaqa*. You can fast all the year but, "Don't ask me for *ṣadaqa!*" That is why *ṣadaqa* is very important because you are crushing your ego and giving when the self does not like you to give to anyone. It is very difficult to put your hand in your pocket

---

[189] *Ḥadīth Qudsī.*

and give something, but to fast, you fast. If someone will ask you, "Do you prefer to fast one day or to give 1000 golden coins?" what do you say? "I prefer to fast. Don't ask me for one golden coin." [Laughter.] But your fast is worth more than a thousand golden coins as Allāh said, "Fasting is for Me, ṣalāt is for him (who prays)."

The Power of Ṣadaqa

Ṣadaqa is very difficult to give. That's why Allāh said in Holy Qur'an:

لَيْسَ عَلَيْكَ هُدَاهُمْ وَلَـكِنَّ اللَّهَ يَهْدِي مَن يَشَاء وَمَا تُنفِقُواْ مِنْ خَيْرٍ فَلأَنفُسِكُمْ وَمَا تُنفِقُونَ إِلاَّ ابْتِغَاء وَجْهِ اللَّهِ وَمَا تُنفِقُواْ مِنْ خَيْرٍ يُوَفَّ إِلَيْكُمْ وَأَنتُمْ لاَ تُظْلَمُونَ

Not upon you, (O Muhammad), is (responsibility for) their guidance,
but Allāh guides whom He wills. And whatever good you (believers) spend
is for yourselves, and you do not spend except seeking the countenance of Allāh.
And whatever you spend of good, it will be fully repaid to you,
and you will not be wronged.[190]

"Whatever you spend, you give," ṣadaqa is not only money. If you want to know Allāh accept your ṣadaqa, try to raise your ṣadaqa higher: instead of giving 100, try to say, "Okay, I want to give 300," and check what your ego says. If it doesn't say anything and is happy to give 300, say, "500," then for sure your ego will stop you giving at a number that you cannot accept, although you may have millions!

عن عمر بن الخطاب رضي الله عنه قال: أمرنا رسول الله صلى الله عليه وسلم يوما أن نتصدق، فوافق ذلك مالا عندي، فقلت: اليوم أسبق أبا بكر إن سبقته يوما، فجئت بنصف مالي، فقال رسول الله صلى الله عليه وسلم: ما أبقيت لأهلك؟ فقلت: مثله، وأتى أبو بكر بكل ما عنده، فقال يا أبا بكر: ما أبقيت لأهلك؟ فقال: أبقيت لهم الله ورسوله، فقلت: لا أسابقك إلى شيء أبدا.

Narrated ʿUmar ibn al-Khaṭṭāb, The Messenger of Allāh ﷺ commanded us
one day to give ṣadaqa. At that time, I had some property. I said, "Today I will
surpass Abū Bakr if I surpass him any day." I, therefore, brought half my property.
The Messenger of Allāh ﷺ asked, "What did you leave for your family?" I replied,
"The same amount." Abū Bakr brought all that he had with him. The Messenger of

---

[190] Sūrat al-Baqarah, 2:272.

Allāh ﷻ asked him, "What did you leave for your family?' He replied, "I left Allāh and His Apostle for them." I said, "I will never surpass you in anything."[191]

When the Prophet ﷺ asked the *Ṣaḥābah* ؆ to give to prepare for weapons for the army against those who were attacking Prophet ﷺ, the *Ṣaḥābah* ؆ brought money; Sayyīdinā Abū Bakr ؆, Sayyīdinā 'Umar ؆, Sayyīdinā 'Uthmān ؆, Sayyīdinā 'Alī ؆ and many of the *Ṣaḥābah* ؆ brought money. The Prophet ﷺ asked Sayyīdinā Abū Bakr ؆, "What have you left for your family?"

He said, "*Yā Rasūlullāh*, I brought everything I own, everything, I have nothing now, completely nothing."

And he said to Sayyīdinā 'Umar ؆, "*Yā* 'Umar, what did you leave for your family?"

He said, "I brought half and left half."

The Prophet ﷺ said, "Abū Bakr's *imān* is stronger than your *imān*," although the Prophet ﷺ had said, "If there were another prophet to come, 'Umar would be prophet after me." But look at the *imān* of Sayyīdinā Abū Bakr ؆: he gave everything! He didn't want his ego to say no, he wanted to stop it so he gave everything *fī sabīillāh*.

So *ṣadaqa* can be wealth, money, it can be a smile in the face of your brother, as the Prophet ﷺ said:

تبسمك في وجه أخيك صدقه

Even a smile in the face of your brother is ṣadaqa.[192]

To smile is a *ṣadaqa*, to smile in the face of your brother, to visit a sick person is *ṣadaqa*, to help a homeless person is *ṣadaqa*, to help an old man is *ṣadaqa*. One time Sayyīdinā 'Alī, *raḍīAllāhu ta'ala 'anhu wa arḍāhu wa karramAllāhu wajhahu wa 'alayhi 's-salām*, was walking in *Madīnatu 'l-Munawarrah* and in his mind was the *ḥadīth* of Prophet ﷺ, "To help is a *ṣadaqa*," and he saw a lady, very old, he had never seen her in *Madīnatu 'l-Munawarrah*, like a stranger walking and carrying a basket in her hand, and limping from the weight of the basket. Slowly, slowly walking. *Adab*, respect, is not to pass someone who is walking, you walk behind.

---

[191] Abū Dāwūd.
[192] Bukhārī.

How much today they pass that one, the other one, they hit that one, hit that one and especially in cars, not only walking people, pedestrians, but cars, also especially in the countries, not here, in the Middle East...I advise anyone who lives in the West not to drive in Lebanon, or Pakistan, or India, or many Middle East countries. [Laughter.] *Adab* is to walk behind elderly people, not to pass them.

So Sayyīdinā ʿAlī ﷺ was walking behind her and this old lady was moving, and he felt bad for her; he came to her and he said, "O my mother, can I help you?"

She looked at him from top to bottom at him, studying him. And she said, "O my son, if you can, if you can, I will be happy if you helped me."

He said, "Can I carry your basket to help?"

She put it on the street and said to Sayyīdinā ʿAlī ﷺ, "You carry it."

And Sayyīdinā ʿAlī ﷺ, you know he is *Asadullāh al-Ghālib*, he is the Victorious Lion of Allāh, he is the strongest person in the universe, he carried wrestlers and threw them...not to carry a basket? She left it and Sayyīdinā ʿAlī ﷺ, doing it as a *ṣadaqa*, and we didn't go through the *aḥadīth* yet, but this is *ṣadaqa*, he took the basket and carried it. He was not able to raise it more than his knees! So heavy that he was unable to raise it up to his knees. It was falling down and the old lady was carrying it and he was carrying it but only up to his knees, while that lady was carrying it and walking.

And then Prophet ﷺ explained to him later, after he arrived at the *masjid*, "That old lady is *dunyā* and it is going, moving forward and one day is finishing. What you carried is the weight of the whole world, the Earth, that was the load, the weight of that basket was equal to the whole Earth that Allāh has created. You carried that. She gave it to you to carry it; you carried up to your knees."

Allāh ﷻ gave him that power to carry, his intention was to make *ṣadaqa* and Allāh made him to carry the *dunyā* that we are on. It means he is carrying and taking responsibility in the Presence of Prophet ﷺ and the Presence of Allāh ﷻ to help the *ummah* as much as he can. That is why he is *Asadullāh al-Ghālib*, the Victorious Lion of Allāh.

So Allāh said in Holy Qu'rān:

وَمَا تُنفِقُوا مِنْ خَيْرٍ فَلأَنفُسِكُمْ وَمَا تُنفِقُونَ إِلاَّ ابْتِغَاء وَجْهِ اللهِ
وَمَا تُنفِقُوا مِنْ خَيْرٍ يُوَفَّ إِلَيْكُمْ وَأَنتُمْ لاَ تُظْلَمُونَ

Whatever of good you give benefits your own souls, and you should only do so seeking the "Face" of Allāh. Whatever good you give will be rendered back to you, and you will not Be dealt with unjustly.[193]

"What you spend in Allāh's Way is for you, not for Me, *ṣiyām* is for Me, fasting is for Me, but what you spend is for you, I don't get anything from it, and you don't spend except seeking Allāh's Love; you want Allāh to be happy with you, that is why you are giving. So *ṣadaqa* makes Allāh happy with the *'abd*, the servant.

وصدقة السر تطفيء غضب الرب

Secret charity extinguishes the Anger of Allāh.[194]

Allāh has anger? Yes, and His anger is not like our anger; it is anger against Shayṭān and his harmful traps against the *ummah*. So, Allāh ﷻ will not get anything but you will from that *ṣadaqa*: "and whatever you spend of goodness, I have to pay you back on Day of Judgment, you will be paid back. So if you spend ten you will be paid back 700 and more," because multiplication of *ḥasanāt*, *ḥasanāt* can be up to 700. You spend one and Allāh will give up to 700. "You will never be oppressed."

O Muslims! Prophet ﷺ mentioned in many *aḥadīth*:

الصدقة ترد البلاء وتزيد فى العمر

Ṣadaqa removes sickness and calamities and prolongs life.

"*Ṣadaqa* takes away and throws away all difficulties and afflictions and extends your life, increases your life," not jogging increases your life! Seeing people, men and women jogging on the streets with headphones, listening to we don't know what and running. No, *ṣadaqa* is going to save you. Prophet ﷺ said, *aṣ-ṣadaqatu tarudd al-balā wa tazīdu fi 'l-'umr*, "*Ṣadaqa* wards off afflictions and increases life." During the time of Prophet ﷺ there was one lady, a very poor lady, not like today as Allāh is giving them a lot:

لَئِن شَكَرْتُمْ لأزِيدَنَّكُمْ

If you thank Me, I will give you more.[195]

---

[193] Sūrat al-Baqara, 2:272.

[194] aṭ-Ṭabarānī.

[195] Surah Ibrāhīm, 14:7.

"You thank Me, I give you more!" Because we are in the last days of this world. We see all the signs from Prophet ﷺ been manifested: "At that time," Prophet ﷺ said, "Allāh ordered all the favors that are planted under the earth and from Heavens to be thrown on the *Ummatun Nabī* ﷺ, to be given out, not to be kept." That is why you see richness now.

So that lady in the time of Prophet ﷺ no one was helping her, she didn't have anything, what she eats every day? She bakes three round bread, small, as it is described. One she eats in the morning after *Fajr*, one she eats at noon after *Ẓuhr* and one in the evening after *Maghrib*. That was her intention, when she baked, but every day one person came to her at noon saying, "Give me what Allāh gave you." So she give him every day one bread and she left herself one in the morning and one in the evening. It went on for many, many days and months until one day, she baked three as usual and the one came at midday, he knocked and took his bread and went. Then at *Fajr* time, as soon as she want to eat someone knocked, a beggar was there asking her for food. She took the bread that she has for *Fajr* and gave to him; the noontime one is gone. Then she sat to eat at *Maghrib* and as she broke the bread, a poor person knocked at the door and said, "Give me from what Allāh gave you." She didn't say, "I don't have." She thought to herself, "This man is asking from what Allāh gave me, can I refuse what Allāh wants? I will give." So she gave him.

Prophet ﷺ mentioned that there is a tree in Paradise that has the names of all the people on Earth on each leaf. Sayyīdinā Azra'īl ﷺ, *Malak al-Mawt*, is always looking at that tree and when a leaf falls, he knows that he has to take the soul of that person. So as soon as that leaf falls, in no time the Angel of Death will be ready to take the soul. At that moment her leaf was falling down, so immediately the Angel of Death went down to take the soul, but the bread from the morning was covering her mouth and not allowing the soul to be taken. That is according to the *ḥadīth* of the Prophet ﷺ:

الصدقة ترد البلاء وتزيد في العمر

Donations ward off afflictions and increase life.

Don't jog, what you spend on jogging is better to give to the poor. You spend a lot of money: to park the car in the parking lot, to put gas, go jog, then go back and take a shower and you need to wash the clothes, as they are now sweaty. No, give that money in *ṣadaqa*!

The first bread was covering her mouth, so the Angel of Death went to the belly button to take her soul, only to find that the second piece of bread came and blocked him. Then the Angel of Death went to her feet, as sometimes they take the soul from the toe and the *Maghrib* bread was there blocking him. He said, *"Yā Rabbī,* what can I do?" Allāh said, "Come up! Didn't you hear My Beloved Prophet ﷺ say, *aṣ-ṣadaqatu tarudd al-balā wa tazīdu fi 'l-'umr, 'Ṣadaqa* increases life and takes away affliction.' Go back! There is no need to take her soul, as I am giving more time for her!"

ما نقص مال من صدقة

Prophet ﷺ said: Money never decreases from donation.[196]

"Money will never be less from giving charity, *ṣadaqa*." If you give ten, Allāh will send you 100. Don't think that you will lose.

Grandshaykh's Ṣadaqa

There have been many poor people in the previous times and in every time as well as present day, and it happened with our teacher, may Allāh bless his soul, Grandshaykh 'AbdAllāh al-Fa'iz ad-Daghestānī ق. He always kept lots of small coins in his pocket, or his bag, to give to the poor. And this happened maybe 100 years ago. So they were moving from Turkey to Istanbul and traveling by horses, which would take four to five hours, and they stopped at different stables to rest the horses as they were tired, or change them. So when they reached the stables, there too many poor people gathered to collect money from the travelers and the shaykh gave and gave to everyone as there were many poor people. Then the horses moved forward and stopped before getting to Istanbul and more poor people were there, so he gave and gave until there was no more money. Then he reached Istanbul and more poor people were waiting and he looked and he went to take out but no more money was left.

The person was asking, "From what Allāh ﷻ gave you, give me," you cannot say to Allāh, "No, I am not giving." That one is not Allāh ﷻ, but is Allāh's Servant and the Prophet ﷺ said:

---

[196] al-Bazzār.

وأوصى النبي صلى الله عليه وسلم أبا هريرة بوصية عظيمة فقال: يا أبا هريرة! عليك
بحسن الخلق. قال أبو هريرة رضي الله عنه: وما حسن الخلق يا رسول الله؟ قال: تصل
مَنْ قطعك، وتعفو عمن ظلمك، وتُعطي من حرمك
(رواه البيهقي)

The Prophet ﷺ advised Abū Hurayrah ؓ, "O Abū Hurayrah!
Keep good manners." He said, "Yā Rasūlullāh, what are the best of manners?"
the Prophet ﷺ said, "to connect with the one who severed relations with you;
to forgive the one who oppressed you and to give to the one who
prevented you receiving your rightful claim."[197]

"Connect the one who cut relations with you and give to the one who cut you off. Give to the one who tries to block you and give to him if he asks." So the Prophet's order is to give, don't say, "No."

Grandshaykh didn't have anything to give but his watch that was given to him from Sultan 'Abdul-Ḥamīd, the Ottoman Emperor who received it from the King of France. And it was an antique, from the 14th or 15th century. He looked and he had nothing left. He took that watch that is worth millions today and gave to that person in order not to send even one person back without giving. It might have been a test, but he gave.

So when you give, as the Prophet ﷺ described it, "It is like someone traveling in the desert and some group of people, *qata'īn ṭuruq*, highway robbers in the desert,"— it's like someone going on the highway and robbers stopped him, and they want to steal from him. They say, "We want to kill you, no way, today you are finished." And he says, "Can I buy myself?" And they say, "Yes." He gives all his money to buy his life. It is like that, when you give, you are buying yourself in *Ākhirah* from Allāh ﷻ, to free yourself from punishment or from judgment.

عَنْ عَائِشَةَ، عَنِ النَّبِيِّ صلى الله عليه وسلم قَالَ " مَنْ نُوقِشَ الْحِسَابَ عُذِّبَ "

As the Prophet ﷺ said to Sayyida 'Ayeshā ؓ: "Anybody whose account
(record) is questioned will surely be punished."[198]

من حوسب عذِّب

Who will be judged will be punished for sure.[199]

---

[197] Narrated by al-Bayhaqī.
[198] Bukhārī.

"Whoever is taken to account by Allāh ﷻ, for sure they cannot be saved, for sure they will be punished." So this was to tell us: pray every day that Allāh ﷻ will not Judge you, this is for the *ummah* to pray in every prayer, "*Yā Rabbī*, don't judge me, send me without any judgment to Paradise." Because if Allāh ﷻ wants to judge someone, every detail you did, everything you did in your life will appear, nothing is hidden, like a video, or a server hiding everything inside it, and you see it in front of you.

Ibn Qayyim said:

فإن للصدقة تأثيرا عجيبا في دفع أنواع البلاء ولو كانت من فاجر أو من ظالم بل من كافرفإن الله تعالى يدفع بها عنه أنواعاً من البلاء وهذا أمر معلوم عند الناس خاصتهم وعامتهم وأهل الأرض كلهم مقرون به لأنهم جربوه

Ṣadaqa has an immense interference in preventing the most difficult
afflictions, ṣadaqa will handle it and lessen your problems, your afflictions,
even if done by a fājir, corrupted one, or ẓālim, an oppressor or even a non-believer;
if he gives ṣadaqa Allāh ﷻ will accept. For verily,
Allāh wards off many problems from you when you give ṣadaqa.

It is not only for some people, but it is for everyone. For Muslims it will be multiplied with no account, but for others it will save them, it will do its work for them.

At-Tirmidhī wrote in his *Ṣaḥīḥ* from the *ḥadīth* of Anas ibn Mālik ؓ, that the Prophet ﷺ said:

إِنَّ الصَّدَقة لَتُطْفِئُ غَضَبَ الرَّبِّ وَتَدْفَعُ مِيتَةَ السُّوء

Indeed charity extinguishes the Lord's anger and it
protects against the evil death.[200]

"*Ṣadaqa* extinguishes the anger of Allāh ﷻ," it will put it down. When you know yourself that you did something wrong or bad, quickly throw a *ṣadaqa* somewhere, it will take away Allāh's Anger. *Wa tadfaʿu maytata 's-sūw'*, "and it will take away the bad death," when someone is dying, "and change it to a good death"; you cannot see that, but the deceased can see that. For *ṣadaqa* of the *mu'min*, you cannot see how much He will take away from the servant when he is dying.

---

[199] Bukhārī.

[200] Tirmidhī.

Ibn Qayyim continues:

وكما أنها تطفئ غضب الرب تبارك وتعالى فهي تطفئ الذنوب
والخطايا كما تطفئ الماء النار

*And as it extinguishes Allāh's Anger, also it will extinguish all kinds of sins and
ma'ṣiyya, as water puts out a fire, with the ṣadaqa, Allāh ﷻ will extinguish the
punishment you might take in Hellfire.*

We can go more in detail and I want to mention this *ḥadīth*, but there is
no time. I explained it before, but I will mention it without explanation now.
It is narrated by *Bukhārī*, so make sure you understand when we say,
"*Bukhārī*," because people say, "O Bukhārī is okay, and Muslim is okay, but
the other six, we have to check," what do you have to check? What is this
stupidity in your mind? Imagine the one who was with the Prophet ﷺ day
and night...The Prophet ﷺ was sitting with the Ṣaḥābah ؓ, from morning
until night and teaching them. How many *ḥadīth* came out in one day? How
many? One or two? Hundreds, from morning *Fajr* time up to 'Isha; he would
pray 'Ishā with them and then go to his house, so they stayed with him all
that time, and now they say, "Only *Bukhārī*'s 4,000 *ḥadīth*," and now they
have reduced it to 3,000 *aḥadīth*. Is that it? There are a lot more.

How many *ḥadīth* did Sayyīdinā Abū Bakr as-Siddiq ؓ mention about
the Prophet ﷺ? He was the closest Companion and migrated with him
which took many days to go from Mecca to Madina. Did not the Prophet ﷺ
tell him different *ḥadīth* every moment? What we know from Sayyīdinā Abū
Bakr as-Siddiq ؓ is only 25 or 26 *aḥadīth*, not even 30. Where are they? They
are there. So the Ṣaḥābah ؓ were listening to the Prophet ﷺ from morning to
evening.

In this *ḥadīth*, Abū Hurayrah ؓ related that the Messenger of Allāh ﷺ
said:

وعن أبي هريرة رضي الله عنه أن رسول الله صلى الله عليه وسلم قال: " قال رجل
لأتصدقن بصدقة، فخرج بصدقته، فوضعها في يد سارق، فأصبحوا يتحدثون: تصدق على
سارق! فقال: اللهم لك الحمد لأتصدقن بصدقته، فخرج بصدقته، فوضعها في يد زانية؟!
فأصبحوا يتحدثون: تصدق على زانية فقال: اللهم لك الحمد على زانية، لأتصدقن بصدقة،
فخرج بصدقته، فوضعها في يد غني, فأصبحوا يتحدثون! تصدق الليلة على غني, فقال:
اللهم لك الحمد على سارق ، وعلى زانية، وعلى غني! فأتى فقيل له: أما صدقتك على

سارق، فلعله أن يستعف عن سرقته، وأما الزانية فلعلها تستعف عن زناها، وأما الغني فلعله أن يعتبر، فينفق مما آتاه الله"[201]

This is going to flip your mind upside-down, and down-side up! It is an amazing *ḥadīth* and there are many like that. Those who want to teach *Fiqh*, let them teach such *ḥadīth* to people, give them an opening, a mercy; give them a way out of their sins! But today they only focus on very structural *aḥadīth*, which is very good, but there are *aḥadīth* that give you hope in this life so you end well in *Ākhirah*.

A man said to himself, "Today I will give a ṣadaqa, charity." He took the charity that he wanted to give and he saw someone whom he thought is poor and put ṣadaqa in his hands and it turned out that person was not poor, rather he was a thief, and he had given his charity to a thief! The people of the town began to speak about him, "He gave charity to a thief." And that man said, "Alḥamdulillāh that I gave charity, I didn't know but You let me give charity," the thief was happy, he took it and left.

Then everyday he made intention to give ṣadaqa to someone, so the next day he took the charity to give to someone in need. There was a lady passing, she looked poor and he took his money, [like doctors, they give a lot], so he took his charity and put it in the hand of that lady. That lady was a prostitute. The people began to talk about him, "Yesterday he gave to a thief and today he gave to a prostitute."

He got upset and said, "Tomorrow I am giving my charity to a right person." The next day, he went looking and saw one poor person. You may have seen a poor person not dressing well, they have lot, but are hiding themselves. So he passed by one who looked very disgusting and very poor, but was in reality very rich. He took his money and put it in the hand of this very rich man. The people began to speak saying, "He gave money to a rich man instead of giving to a poor one." He became confused what he has to do? First he gave to a thief, second to a prostitute and third to a rich man!

So he got fed up, as he didn't know what to do. "Yā Rabbī, all praise be to You. Everything goes back to you." He was fed up and didn't know what to say. "Yā Rabbī, what can I do? I have given to a thief, a prostitute and a rich person, when my intention was to give to a poor person." He was called by an angel or

---

[201] Bukhari and Muslim with another wording.

received an inspiration, 'As for the ṣadaqa you gave the thief, it might be that the ṣadaqa you gave to the thief would turn him into a pious person.'"

I will explain a little bit here: "Your intention was something, but My Will was something else. You want to give here, but I want you to give to this. It is not your decision, but My Will that I have written. It might be that the ṣadaqa you gave to the thief would turn him into a pious person, as it is ṣadaqa from a *mu'min*."

That is what Allāh is seeing, which that man does not see. Through that money, Allāh might change that man into a good person. So it means give to anyone; don't say, "This is a thief" or "this is a prostitute." If you want to give, then give!

The *ḥadīth* continues:

> *And as for the prostitute, it might be that because of that money she changes her mind and leaves off being a prostitute and becomes a good woman. And the rich man might take an example on learning to spend in Allāh's Way and become generous instead of being stingy.*[202]

So such ṣadaqa can do miracles. If it is making miracles for the thief, the prostitute and the rich, can it not make miracles for us? Of course it can! You see the importance of these *aḥadīth*, among many *ḥadīth* of ṣadaqa or *salāt*, there are some *ḥadīth* that are not only structural, but there are those which have interpretational meanings that give an idea of Allāh's Great Mercy by which everyone will be saved. They open our minds more and more, not to be very narrow and limited, in order to understand Prophet ﷺ.

May Allāh forgive us. That is what we know and if we did something wrong, we ask forgiveness from the viewers and others.

---

[202] *Ṣaḥīḥ Bukhārī.*

May Allāh forgive us and may Allāh bless us.

Wa min Allāhi 't-tawfīq, bi ḥurmati 'l-ḥabīb, bi ḥurmati 'l-Fātiḥah.
And with Allāh is success. For the sake of the Beloved, for his sake we recite
the opening chapter of Holy Qur'ān.

Ṣadaqa Extinguishes the Anger of Allah

Aʿūdhu billāhi min ash-Shayṭāni 'r-rajīm. Bismillāhi' r-Raḥmāni 'r-Raḥīm.
Nawaytu 'l-arbāʿīn, nawaytu 'l-ʿitikāf, nawaytu'l-khalwah, nawaytu 'l-ʿuzlah,
nawaytu 'r-riyāḍa, nawaytu 's-sulūk, lillāhi Taʿalā fī hādhā 'l-masjid.
Atīʿullāha wa atīʿū 'r-Rasūla wa ūlī 'l-amri minkum. (4:59)

As-salāmu ʿalaykum wa raḥmatullāhi wa barakātuh. We are, *alḥamdulillāh*, with Allāh's Grace, continuing the obligation of fasting through the whole of Ramaḍān as it is one of the Five Pillars of Islam. And in this month Allāh ﷻ loves *ṣadaqa*, for people to give charity. And we have explained in the previous sessions, about the *ḥadīth* of al-Hārith al-Ashʿarī, about the Five Orders that Allāh ordered Sayyīdinā Yaḥyā ﷺ to declare, to announce to people, and one of them was *ṣadaqa* which we explained some of it, and we continue that today.

From the *ḥadīth* of at-Tirmidhī it is mentioned from Sayyīdinā Anas ibn Mālik ؆, *min ḥadīth Anas ibni Mālik ʿani 'n-nabī ﷺ annahu qāl,* that Prophet ﷺ said:

إِنَّ الصَّدَقة لَتُطْفِئُ غَضَبَ الرَّبِّ وَتَدْفعُ مِيتَة السُّوء

Indeed, charity extinguishes the Lord's anger and
it protects against the evil death.[203]

"Charity extinguishes Allāh's anger," means Allāh will completely erase; if He was angry with that servant who did something wrong. So it means immediately run, when you think to yourself that you did something wrong, immediately give a charity. Allāh ﷻ loves that and He takes His Anger away from that servant who does charity. And charity can be in any way: in money, in a smile, as we said before, in visiting homeless people and helping them, or sick people, helping your brother and sister in Islam; Allāh ﷻ likes that.

And *ṣadaqa* is also, when you see that you did something wrong, immediately you pray two *rakaʿats*, and it is *ṣadaqa* from your life, from your time. Say, "*Istaghfirullāh,*" as it is a *ṣadaqa* on your soul. *Ṣadaqa* on the soul is remembering Allāh's Name and asking him forgiveness; it's a *ṣadaqa, ṣadaqa*

---

[203] Tirmidhī.

from your soul, by saying, "*Yā Rabb*! This is to purify and clean me, I am offering it to You by saying, '*istaghfirullāh*.'" Allāh ﷻ loves that, and Allāh ﷻ loves His Servant that remembers Him all the time.

And Prophet ﷺ continued, *wa tuṭfi'u maytata 's-sūw*, "Charity that people do in their lives takes away the badness of the day, that someone may die with;" it takes all badness and that person will be going to Paradise instead of going to be punished. That is by *ṣadaqa*! That is why it is recommended that every day before you leave your home, have a box and put a *ṣadaqa* as much as you like: 1, 100, 1,000; it is a charity from your generosity. Allāh ﷻ is very generous with everyone and He gives everyone what they like, so give from what Allāh ﷻ gave to you. Make a favor for those who don't have, Allāh ﷻ likes that. So by this way Allāh ﷻ will clear you at death from a bad ending.

The Thankful Rich One is Better than the Worshipful Poor One

There are, for example, people who give £1, but they are poor, for them £1 is so much; they might be rewarded more than someone who gives a £100; someone who is a rich, who has millions, £100 doesn't break him, but for a poor person who gives £1, it breaks him but still he is giving. So that poor one will be rewarded more than the rich one. Unless the rich one gives more, as the Prophet ﷺ said:

غني شاكر خير من فقير صابر

The rich thankful one is better than the poor, patient worshipper.

"The thankful rich man is better than the worshipful poor one," because that rich one is giving to the needy people and Allāh ﷻ likes that, whereas the poor one who doesn't have anything cannot help anyone. So that's why a thankful rich man—and there is a condition He ﷻ put for him— 'a thankful' rich man, *shākir*, means *shākir yashkurullāh 'alā ni'amihi*, "The one who thanks Allāh ﷻ for His Favors on him," Allāh ﷻ will like that, so be *ghanīyyan shākir*, a generous person who gives charity! And as we said, if you cannot give money, give a speech and make someone happy; give a smile in the face of someone. "And as it extinguishes Allāh's Anger, for sure it will extinguish all sins and *ma'aṣīyy*." All the *ma'aṣīyya* that people do, *kamā yuṭfiu al-mā' an-nār*, as water extinguishes fire.

عَنْ مُعَاذِ بْنِ جَبَلٍ، قَالَ كُنْتُ مَعَ النَّبِيِّ صلى الله عليه وسلم فِي سَفَرٍ فَأَصْبَحْتُ يَوْمًا قَرِيبًا مِنْهُ وَنَحْنُ نَسِيرُ فَقُلْتُ يَا رَسُولَ اللَّهِ أَخْبِرْنِي بِعَمَلٍ يُدْخِلُنِي الْجَنَّةَ وَيُبَاعِدُنِي مِنَ النَّارِ . قَالَ "

لَقَدْ سَأَلْتَنِي عَنْ عَظِيمٍ وَإِنَّهُ لَيَسِيرٌ عَلَى مَنْ يَسَّرَهُ اللَّهُ عَلَيْهِ تَعْبُدُ اللَّهَ وَلَا تُشْرِكُ بِهِ شَيْئًا وَتُقِيمُ الصَّلَاةَ وَتُؤْتِي الزَّكَاةَ وَتَصُومُ رَمَضَانَ وَتَحُجُّ الْبَيْتَ " . ثُمَّ قَالَ " أَلَا أَدُلُّكَ عَلَى أَبْوَابِ الْخَيْرِ الصَّوْمُ جُنَّة وَالصَّدَقَة تُطْفِئُ الْخَطِيئَة كَمَا يُطْفِئُ الْمَاءُ النَّارَ وَصَلَاةُ الرَّجُلِ مِنْ جَوْفِ اللَّيْلِ " . قَالَ ثُمَّ تَلَا: (تَتَجَافَى جُنُوبُهُمْ عَنِ الْمَضَاجِعِ) حَتَّى بَلَغَ: (يَعْمَلُونَ) ثُم...

From Mu'adh bin Jabal ﷺ said that the Prophet ﷺ said: I accompanied the Prophet ﷺ on a journey. One day I was near him while we were moving, so I said, "O Messenger of Allāh! Inform me about an action by which I will be admitted into Paradise, and which will keep me far from the Fire." He said, "'You have asked me about something great, but it is easy for whomever Allāh makes it easy. Worship Allāh and do not associate any partners with Him, establish the ṣalāt, give the zakāt, fast Ramaḍān and perform Hajj to the Sacred House."
Then he said, "Shall I not guide you to the doors of goodness?
Fasting is a shield, and charity extinguishes sins like water extinguishes fire, and a man's praying in depths of the night." He said, "Then he recited, 'Their sides forsake their beds to call upon their Lord.'" (32:16)[204]

"I was with the Prophet ﷺ," how much he is lucky, making *siyāḥa*, making a journey with Prophet ﷺ. Now if people make a journey with a leader you will be overwhelmed, you will be very happy! If you take a picture with a leader you are so happy, even one picture makes them happy. How many spiritual pictures were taken by the angels of the Ṣaḥābah ﷺ accompanying Prophet ﷺ? Everything is recorded:

وَلَا رَطْبٍ وَلَا يَابِسٍ إِلَّا فِي كِتَابٍ مُّبِينٍ

(There is not) anything fresh or dry (green or withered), but is (inscribed) in a Clear Book.[205]

"Something living and non-living, it's always there," its picture is there. Anytime an angel will take, like today they press a button and they get a picture, and the angels press a button and all these pictures will come. Everything you did in your life, they press a button and it comes. And for the Ṣaḥābah ﷺ, every journey with Prophet ﷺ will come, every moment in their lives was spent in the love of Prophet ﷺ, all their lives will appear. How much they were lucky. May Allāh ﷺ keep us at their threshold!

---

[204] Tirmidhī.
[205] Sūrat al-An'am, 6:59.

So he was with Prophet ﷺ in a journey, and he said, "One day," it must have been a long journey, fa aṣbaḥtu yawman minhu qarīban, "I woke up and I saw myself very close walking with the Prophet ﷺ," wa naḥnu nasīru, "I saw myself, as we began the journey, moving near him," and the Prophet ﷺ said, "Yā muʿadh hal adulukum ʿalā Abwābi 'l-Khayr? O Muʿadh do you want me to show you the Doors of Goodness?"

Of course, everyone likes to know the Doors of Goodness. Now if you tell people, "Do you want the Doors of Goodness?" They say, "Yeah, what?" They like *dunyā* and forgot *Ākhirah*. So Prophet ﷺ said, *"Hal adulukum ʿalā Abwābi 'l-Khayr?"* How much they were humble, and they didn't have a lot but they were happy. The Prophet ﷺ didn't have anything in his house.

وعن عائشة رضي الله عنها قالت :جاءتني مسكينة ، تحمل ابنتين لها ، فأطعمتها ثلاث تمرات ، فأعطت كل واحدة منهما تمرة ، ورفعت إلى فمها تمرة لتأكلها ، فاستطعمتها ابنتاها، فشقت التمرة التي كانت تريد أن تأكلها إلى نصفين لابنتيها ، ثم خرجت ، فلما دخل النبي صلى الله عليه وسلم أخبرته بذلك فقال : (إن الله قد أوجب لها بها الجنة ، أو أعتقها من النار) رواه الإمام مسلم .

One day a poor person, a lady, came knocking at the door of ʿAyeshā ﵂,
saying, "Give me from what Allāh ﷻ gave you." And she had two kids
on her hands and was asking for charity. She looked through the whole house
and didn't find anything, then she remembered she had put aside
three dates, that was the food for the Prophet ﷺ in 24 hours.

Can you survive 24 hours on three dates? Everyone wants a goat or lamb in front of him! Three dates!

And that poor lady had two children on her hands, so what did she have to do? She went and took the three dates and gave one to the lady, and one to each girl; she gave everything they had, she left nothing. So immediately the two girls ate their two dates, they were very hungry, and they were looking at their mother who still had to eat her date, and they were looking at her as they had already swallowed their two dates from their hunger. So she took her date and split it in half and gave it to the two girls. Sayyida ʿAyeshā ﵂ told the Prophet ﷺ what happened and Prophet ﷺ said, "That lady saved herself with one date from punishment," means all her sins were taken away because she gave the date to her two kids.

Then imagine how much Sayyida ʿAyeshā ﵂ was rewarded for what she gave, the three dates that was the Prophet's food and her food. And us today, we are not happy with what we are eating, but Allāh ﷻ is Karīm, He will forgive.

Continuing the *ḥadīth* of Muʿadh ibn Jabal narrated by Tirmidhī:

Prophet ﷺ said, "Do you want me to tell you about the Doors of Khayr, Doors of goodness and Allāh's Favors?" And of course they said, "Yes yā Sayyidī, yā Rasūlullāh." He answered him, "Fasting is Paradise and ṣadaqa will erase the sin completely, from its roots, there will be no sin left when they give ṣadaqa."

So people, I don't know why they don't like to give, especially on *Jumuʿah* days, when they pass the basket or whatever to collect charity, people will be throwing coins. Don't throw coins, it is not a situation here of...it is a *masjid*, don't throw coins, throw paper money, or gold coins, or silver coins, not pennies, because it is ṣadaqa on Friday in a *masjid*. How much will it be multiplied? It is *barakah* for you and it will extinguish completely all the sins you have and make you clean in the *masjid*, and angels will take up the prayers clean as the ṣadaqa will purify the sins you have done; just as water extinguishes fire. *SubhānAllāh!*

What is in water that extinguishes fire? And which is stronger, fire or water? Water, because it extinguishes fire, the fire has no chance in front of water. It is said, "Don't harm *mu'min jinn* when you use water at night;" don't use water at night in the gardens or the fields, because you might harm passing *jinn*; the *jinn* will forgive if he is a *mu'min*, a believer, but if it is a devil, a non-believer *maradata 'l-jinn*, or *ʿafreet al-Jinn*, they will not forgive you, they punish you because you burnt them with water, or their child, so we have to be very careful. Water can extinguish fire, as Allāh ﷻ said:

وَجَعَلْنَا مِنَ الْمَاء كُلَّ شَيْءٍ حَيٍّ

We made every living thing from water.[206]

"We made everything alive from water," water has the power of life. So water overtakes that which destroys life, the fire. So water eats the fire, and that means that it will eat the sin in you when you give ṣadaqa. it is mentioned that most of the human body is water, so that is why when you pay ṣadaqa, that water in your body will extinguish the fire within it, and you will be cleaned from all sins.

---

[206] Sūrat al-Anbīyā, 21:30.

So the Prophet ﷺ said to him: "The favors that Allāh gave are: *aṣ-ṣawmu jannah*, fasting is Paradise," *and aṣ-ṣadaqatu tuṭfiu 'l-khatiyyāta*, "Charity will extinguish sins," *wa ṣalātu 'r-rajul min jawfi 'l-layli*, "And the prayer of a man in the depth of the night when everyone is sleeping," after midnight by one or two hours up to *Fajr*, "that prayer there is a symbol of pious and sincere servants of Allāh ﷻ." And he ﷺ recited the verse:

تَتَجَافَى جُنُوبُهُمْ عَنِ الْمَضَاجِعِ يَدْعُونَ رَبَّهُمْ خَوْفًا وَطَمَعًا وَمِمَّا رَزَقْنَاهُمْ يُنْفِقُونَ

They arise from (their) beds, they supplicate their Lord in fear and aspiration, and from what We have provided them, they spend.[207]

It means they are turning from their bed, going out from their bed in order to pray to Allāh ﷻ. *Yadʿūna rabbahum khawfan wa ṭamʿan*, "They ask Allāh ﷻ, fearing from Him, and asking more of His Mercy," *yatmaʿ min raḥmatihi*, "Seeking and wish to get more of His Mercy," *wa mimmā razaqnāhum yunfiqūn*, "and from whatever We have provided them, they are giving in charity, in Allāh's Way." So give a charity in Allāh's Way; there are a lot of people in need, especially in Ramaḍān, feeding people.

وعن علي قال : قال رسول الله ـ صلى الله عليه وسلم ـ : " بادروا بالصدقة فإن البلاء لا يتخطاها " رواه رزين

Initiate charity without delay, as calamity cannot precede/overcome charity.

وفي بعض الآثار : باكروا بالصدقة فإن البلاء لا يتخطى الصدقة

And in some stories it is said by awlīyāullāh, "make ṣadaqa early in your lifetime, (or) begin ṣadaqa in the early morning of the day, then the affliction of the day will not reach the person, as ṣadaqa will skip it."

Don't begin to do it when you are going to die only, but from the beginning. That is just like we mentioned the story of the lady giving three breads every day when poor people were coming knocking on her door. You can go back to the previous session to hear that. So it is like someone whom they want to cut his neck, he will give them money to relieve him and they relieve him. Also Allāh ﷻ will relieve you when you do something wrong, a mistake, it relieve you, by your *ṣadaqa*, from punishing you. So Allāh ﷻ will not punish someone who is giving *ṣadaqa*. You give, Allāh ﷻ gives. Keep faith in Allāh ﷻ.

---

[207] Sūrat as-Sajdah, 32:16.

Save Yourself from Hellfire Even with a Piece of a Date

Prophet ﷺ also said:

مَا نَقَصَ مَالٍ مِنْ صَدَقَة

Charity does not in any way decrease the wealth.[208]

عَنْ عَدِيِّ بْنِ حَاتِمٍ، قَالَ قَالَ رَسُولُ اللَّهِ صلى الله عليه وسلم " مَا مِنْكُمْ أَحَدٌ إِلاَّ سَيُكَلِّمُهُ رَبُّهُ، لَيْسَ بَيْنَهُ وَبَيْنَهُ تَرْجُمَانٌ، فَيَنْظُرُ أَيْمَنَ مِنْهُ فَلاَ يَرَى إِلاَّ مَا قَدَّمَ مِنْ عَمَلِهِ، وَيَنْظُرُ أَشْأَمَ مِنْهُ فَلاَ يَرَى إِلاَّ مَا قَدَّمَ، وَيَنْظُرُ بَيْنَ يَدَيْهِ فَلاَ يَرَى إِلاَّ النَّارَ تِلْقَاءَ وَجْهِهِ، فَاتَّقُوا النَّارَ وَلَوْ بِشِقِّ تَمْرَةٍ "

It is narrated by that 'Adīyy ibn Ḥātim ﷺ said that the Prophet ﷺ said:

*There will be none among you but his Lord will talk to him, and there
will be no interpreter between him and Allāh. He will look to his right
and see nothing but his deeds that he sent forward, and will look
to his left and see nothing but his deeds that he sent forward,
and will look in front of him and see nothing but the Hellfire facing him.
So save yourself from the Hellfire even with half a date (given in charity).* [209]

Laysa baynahu tarjumān, "Allāh ﷻ will speak with every one of you and
there will not be any translator between Him and you." *Fa-yanẓuru aymana
minhu falā yarā illā mā qaddama min 'amalihi,* "and He looks on the right and
doesn't see but what the servant offered of good," *Wa yanẓuru ashāma minhu
falā yarā illā mā qaddama,* "and He looks lower than that one before, and
doesn't see except what the servant gave." *Wa yanẓuru bayna yadayhi falā
yarā illa an-nāra tilqā'a wajhih,* "and that person looks in front of himself and
will not see anything except the Fire in front of him, going to punish him."

He looks right and he doesn't see except what he has made in his life;
he looks left of him and he will see what he has made a little bit on the left;
he looks straight he will see the Fire coming for him on his face. He doesn't
know where to run...he cannot run right, he cannot run left, he cannot go
back to life, his life is finished! He can only move forward and he sees Fire
coming in front of him. What he has to do? He is stuck.

So what the Prophet ﷺ said in that case? "All of us will be stuck"; don't
think you are doing a great job, or, "I am praying and fasting." No! You *have*
to pray, you *have* to fast, you *have* to make Hajj, you *have* to do charity, you

---

[208] al-Bazzār.

[209] Bukhārī and Muslim.

have to make *tawḥīd*, as it is an obligation. "Don't think you are making a favor to Allāh ﷻ," Allāh ﷻ is making favor to you!

So how to protect oneself from that, the Prophet ﷺ gave the answer: *fataqqū 'n-nār*, "Try to save yourself from Hellfire *wa law bi shaqqi tamara* even with a piece of a date," *bi shaqqi tamara* means, "half of a date". So even with a 'half of a date' that you give as charity, you are saving yourself from Hellfire. What do you think if you give £20? You can buy a box of dates. In that time, the wealthy people of Mecca and *Madīnatu 'l-Munawwarah* had date palm trees and Prophet ﷺ was saying, "Give half a date, you will save yourself from Hellfire." And if we give a box of dates, or two boxes of dates, take £100, buy five boxes of dates and give to poor people. How many times you have saved yourself from Hellfire by five boxes of dates?

روى البيهقي عن أبي ذر قال : قلت : يا رسول الله ماذا ينجي العبد من النار ؟ قال : الإيمان بالله .قلت : يا رسول الله إن مع الإيمان عملاً .قال : يرضخ مما رزقه الله [ومعنى الرضخ هو العطاء] .قلت : يا رسول الله أرأيت إن كان فقيراً لا يجد ما يرضخ به ؟ قال : يأمر بالمعروف وينهى عن المنكر .قلت : يا رسول الله ، أرأيت إن كان لا يستطيع أن يأمر بالمعروف وينهى عن المنكر؟ قال : يصنع لأخرق . [وهو الجاهل الذي لا صنعة له يكتسب منها] قلت : أرأيت إن كان أخرق لا يستطيع أن يصنع شيئاً ؟ قال : يعين مظلوماً .قلت : أرأيت إن كان ضعيفاً لا يستطيع أن يعين مظلوماً ؟ قال : ما تريد أن تترك في صاحبك من خير؟! ليمسك أذاه عن الناس .فقلت : يا رسول الله إذا فعل ذلك دخل الجنة ؟ قال : ما من مؤمن يطلب خصلة من هذه الخصال إلا أخذت بيده حتى تدخله الجنة .

Abū Dharr ﷺ said, "I said, 'O Messenger of Allāh! What will save a person from Hellfire?' He said, 'Belief in Allāh.' I said, 'O Messenger of Allāh! Are there are any deeds that should accompany that belief?' He said, 'He should give from that provision which Allāh has granted him.' I said, 'O Messenger of Allāh! What if he is poor and does not have anything to give?' He said, 'He should enjoin what is good and forbid what is evil.' I said, 'O Messenger of Allāh! What if he cannot enjoin what is good and forbid what is evil?' He said, 'He should help the one who is helpless (i.e., has no skills and cannot earn a living).' I said, 'What if he himself is helpless and cannot do anything?' He said, 'He should help one who has been wronged.' I said, 'What if he is weak and cannot help the one who has been wronged?' He said, 'You do not want to think of your companion as having any good in him? (In that case) Let him refrain from harming people.' I said, 'O Messenger of Allāh! If he does that, will he enter Paradise?' He said, 'There is no believer who does not strive to acquire one of these characteristics, but I will take him by the hand and lead him into Paradise.'"[210]

Abū Dharr ☙ said, "I asked the Prophet ﷺ, '*Yā Rasūlullāh*, what kind of thing should a person do that will save him from Hellfire?' The Prophet ﷺ said, 'To have faith in Allāh ﷻ, to believe in Allāh ﷻ as the Creator.' I said, 'With that faith, do we have to do something, some '*amal*?' The Prophet ﷺ said, 'To give, *tarḍakh*, from what Allāh ﷻ has given you, as a charity or whatever Allāh ﷻ has made it easy for you to get this *rizq*, give from that.' I said, 'What if I am poor and I cannot find anything to give?'"

Look how the *Ṣaḥābah* ☙ were clever, they kept asking to reduce and reduce, just as the Prophet ﷺ was ordered fifty prayers in *Mi'rāj* and Sayyīdinā Mūsā ﷺ said, "No, ask less!" Clever Sayyīdinā Mūsā ﷺ was telling Prophet ﷺ, "Ask less, ask less," and Prophet ﷺ asked less until it came down to five prayers. Prophets are very, very clever, especially Sayyīdinā Mūsā ﷺ. The Prophet ﷺ was very humble so didn't want to ask anything, but because Sayyīdinā Mūsā ﷺ pushed him, he asked. It is nice to be with prophets to see how they interact, it is something beyond our minds. Continuing the *ḥadīth*:

I [Abū Dharr] said, 'If he is poor how can he give, as he doesn't have anything?'
The Prophet ﷺ said, 'Let him call for the good and prevent what is bad.'
I said, 'Yā Rasūlullāh, if that person cannot call for good or prohibit bad
because he doesn't know, what should he do?' The Prophet ﷺ said, 'Let him
help the one in need of help.' I said, 'Maybe he cannot do that?' He said, 'Let him
help someone who is oppressed,' [to take him out of that situation.]
I said, 'Yā Rasūlullāh, maybe his word cannot be heard?'

He doesn't have the right business card...today you put a business card on your application you will be hired, and if no business card you will not be hired; they look at the name of the one on the card to see who is pushing you for the job, they see the right name on the business card and they give you the job although you might know nothing.

I said, 'Maybe he is a weak person he cannot help someone who is oppressed.' What is this with you?' the Prophet ﷺ said, 'You don't want to leave any goodness in anyone in his life? Let that person withhold his harm from people (keep peace with them. I said, 'O Prophet ﷺ, if he withholds from harming others, do you promise he

---

[210] Bayhaqī in his *Shu'ab al-Īmān*; *ṣaḥīḥ*.

will go to Paradise?' He ☘ said, 'Any mu'min,' (someone who says, "Ash-hadu an
lā ilāha illa-Llāh wa ash-hadu anna Muḥammadan Rasūlullāh), who will do any
one of what I mentioned to you, any one of them, I will take him by his hand on the
Day of Judgment and take him to Paradise myself!'"[211]

May Allāh forgive us and may Allāh bless us.

Wa min Allāhi 't-tawfīq, bi ḥurmati 'l-ḥabīb, bi ḥurmati 'l-Fātiḥah.
And with Allāh is success. For the sake of the Beloved, for his sake we recite
the opening chapter of Holy Qur'ān.

---

[211] Related by al-Bayhaqī in *Shu'ab al-Īmān*.

The Excessively Generous One
is the Beloved of Allah

A'ūdhu billāhi min ash-Shayṭāni 'r-rajīm. Bismillāhi' r-Raḥmāni 'r-Raḥīm.
Nawaytu 'l-arbā'īn, nawaytu 'l-'itikāf, nawaytu'l-khalwah, nawaytu 'l-'uzlah,
nawaytu 'r-riyāḍa, nawaytu 's-sulūk, lillāhi Ta'alā fī hādhā 'l-masjid.
Atī'ūllāha wa atī'ū 'r-Rasūla wa ūli 'l-amri minkum. (4:59)

Aṣ-ṣadaqa is something through which you try to show that your self is
generous when you give *ṣadaqa*, because you give *ṣadaqa* out of your wealth,
out of your money, you prevent yourself from using it and give it to
someone in need for it.

There are different levels of *ṣadaqa*. It is said that, *"As-sakhīyyu*
ḥabībullāh." As-*sakhīyy* is the same meaning as *"al-Karīm,"* and *"al-Jawād,"*
the one who gives excessive *ṣadaqa*; he doesn't try to hold back his hand
from giving *ṣadaqa* and only give traces of his wealth. The *sakhīyy* is the one
whose hand is open, who gives what Allāh ﷻ has given to him. Who is the
Absolute *Sakhīyy*? It is Allāh ﷻ! He gives without account. When you give
and you count it, that is not *sakhīyy*, as it means you still want to see in your
heart how much you are spending or how much you are giving.

تروي عنه السيدة عائشة -رضي الله عنها- أنهم ذبحوا شاة، ثم وزعوها على الفقراء؛ فسأل
النبي صلى الله عليه وسلم السيدة عائشة: (ما بقي منها؟) فقالت: ما بقي إلا كتفها؛ فقال
النبي صلى الله عليه وسلم: (بقي كلها غير كتفها) [الترمذي]

One time someone slaughtered a lamb and distributed it to the poor. some lamb.
So gave the Prophet ﷺ came in the evening and asked his wife, Sayyida ʿAyeshā ؇,
"What is left of the lamb?" Prophet ﷺ asked his wife, Sayyida ʿAyeshā ؇,
because he didn't see it, and Sayyida ʿAyeshā ؇ answered, "There is nothing
left of it, but its shoulder." That means they gave everything out, they didn't
leave anything for themselves, "nothing remains but the shoulder." The shoulder
as you know has less meat, the leg and back have a lot of meat. The Prophet ﷺ
looked at her and said, "No, all of it remained except the shoulder."
How can that be? They distributed it all and the Prophet ﷺ said,
"No, you didn't distribute it, we have all except the shoulder."[212]

---

[212] Tirmidhī.

That means that since you gave it as *ṣadaqa* in the Way of Allāh ﷺ you gave most of it. That is *sakhīyy*, to give excessively, not generously, but to be excessively generous. "We gave it all to Allāh ﷺ, which is recorded for us. If we ate it and gave the shoulder, that means the shoulder is left for us on Judgment Day as rewards, but here Allāh ﷺ is rewarding on the whole animal except the shoulder." So that is why he said to her, *baqīya kulluhā, ghayra katifuhā*, "We have it all except its shoulder."

That gives us an understanding that when you give, you should give with excessive generosity; you want to give something but you are still *bakhīl*, stingy, holding back from it. *As-sakhīyy ḥabībullāh wa 'l-bakhīl ʿadūwullāh*, Allāh ﷺ loves the one who is generous, and the stingy one is the enemy of Allāh. Who is the *sakhīyy*? It is the Prophet ﷺ who gave his whole life for his *ummah*, he didn't spend one moment of his life for himself, he spent it for his *ummah*. He is *sakhīyy*, in the Way of Allāh ﷺ.

Hūwa al-ḥabību 'Lladhī turjā shafaʿatahu.
He is the Beloved whose intercession is sought.

He gave all his life for Allāh ﷺ, as described by Muḥammad al-Buṣayrī: "He is the lover of Allāh ﷺ whose intercession is sought by all," and he is asking intercession for his *ummah*, and Allāh ﷺ gave him the power of intercession, to intercede for his *ummah*. He ﷺ is giving his life, *as-sakhīyy ḥabībullāh*, and *Hūwa al-ḥabību 'Lladhī turjā shafaʿatahu*, "He is Lover of Allāh ﷺ and everyone is in need of his Intercession." When he gives intercession, he is between the Hands of Allāh ﷺ and asking Him to forgive people and he has given all that is his away, he is standing without anything. It means he is giving excessively everything from what he has and is standing without anything.

What do you think Allāh ﷺ said? *As-sakhīyy ḥabībullāh*, "The one who is excessively generous is the lover of Allāh," and *wa 'l-bakhīl ʿadūwullāh*, "The stingy is the enemy of Allāh." May Allāh ﷺ make us not stingy and make us to give! You can give from your time, your wealth, give clothes, give a smile, as we said before all that is accepted.

يقول أحد الصحابة: كنا عند رسول الله صلى الله عليه و سلم، فجاء أناس من مصر حفاة يظهر عليهم أثر الفقر فاكفهر وجه النبي غضباً. يقول الراوي: فرأيت وجنتي النبي صلى الله عليه وسلم وقد انتفختا ووجه النبي وقد أحمر ، و قال: يا بلال أذن في الناس. فقام بلال، فجمع الناس، فصعد النبي صلى الله عليه وسلم المنبر وقال: (يا أيها الناس اتقوا ربكم الذي خلقكم من نفس واحدة وخلق منها زوجها، وبث منهما رجالاً كثيراً ونساء. واتقوا الله الذي تساءلون به والأرحام....) إلى أخر الآية...ثم قرأ النبي صلى الله عليه وسلم: (يا أيها الذين

أمنوا اتقوا الله ولتنظر نفس ما قدمت لغد واتقوا الله إن الله خبير بما تعملون). ثم قال النبي صلى الله عليه وسلم: "لينفق كل منكم من تمره، من صاعه، من ديناره، من درهمه، من ثوبه ،حتى يأكل إخوانكم". يقول: فظل النبي يرددها حتى قال: "ولو بشق تمرة، ولو بشق تمرة ". يقول: فانطلق الناس يجرون إلي بيوتهم، يقولون: وما ترك النبي المنبر حتى يعود الناس. يقولون: فجاء الناس، يأتي الرجل بالسرة، ويأتي الرجل بالثياب، ويأتي الرجل بالتمر.حتى وضع بين يدي النبي كومين.. كوم من ثياب وكوم من طعام. فتهلل وجه النبي صلى الله عليه وسلم. كأنه قطعة قمر . ثم نظر النبي صلى الله عليه وسلم إلينا وقال:"من سن سنة حسنة فله أجرها وأجر من عمل بها إلى يوم القيامة". ثم نظر إلينا وقال:"هكذا كونوا".

Jalīl ibn ʿAbdullah said, "One day during the daytime, we were with the Prophet ﷺ and there came to him a group of people wearing clothes that had stripes and an opening for the neck.

That is a wide cloth with a circle to put their head through and it covers them completely. They came to Prophet ﷺ wearing this kind of *abaya* and *mutaqalidī suyyūf*, carrying swords on their shoulders.

The Prophet's ﷺ face changed when he saw their poverty and he was not happy, and he went into his room and came out. His face was sad and he ordered Bilāl to call adhān."

At that time, whenever there was an event, they called the *adhān* to declare it, not only the five daily times, but any time.

He called adhān, made iqāmah, then prayed Ẓuhr, then he spoke.
He said, "Have fear of Allāh ﷻ that He created you from one soul…" [He wanted to tell them, "You are all equal, all from one soul], and from that soul of Sayyīdinā Ādam Allāh created his wife and created everyone."

And so the universe began with one soul, and now look how much it is huge, and Allāh is feeding all of them. Look at Allāh's Generosity, *ṣadaqa*. Allāh doesn't need anything, but He is showing generosity to people, to humanity! So Prophet ﷺ read that *āyah* and then he said:

A man will give ṣadaqa from his money, from his dīnārs, from his gold and silver, dirhams, smaller coins, from his clothes to give to people who don't have clothes, from whatever of his crops come he gives of that, from whatever he has of dates from his tree, and ṣadaqa is accepted even with half of a date. [213] *And when they heard this, one of the Anṣār, supporters of Prophet ﷺ, brought immediately a sirra, a cloth*

---

[213] And in another ḥadīth, "Save yourself from Hellfire even by donation of half a date."

basket full of dates and put it in front of the Prophet ﷺ. He could not carry it with his hands. And people began to throw food, clothes, they threw everything until they made a huge pile in front of the Prophet ﷺ. And it was said, "Until I saw the Prophet's ﷺ face shining like gold, whoever makes a sunnah,[214] who will make a good innovation in Islam, Allāh ﷻ will reward him as long as the people are doing it and following it up to Judgment Day, and whoever made bad innovation in Islam, then he will carry its wizr, sin, until Judgment Day, along with the sins of all the people who are following that."[215]

لا حسد إلا في اثنتين رجل أتاه الله مالاً فسلطه على هلكته في الحق ورجل أتاه الله الحكمة فهو يقضي بها ويعلمها.

Ibn Maʿsūd said that the Prophet ﷺ said, "You cannot have jealousy except in two things: someone whom Allāh ﷻ made very rich, ghanīyyun shākir, a rich man thankful to Allāh ﷻ, because he spent all his money for needy people,[216] and another man of whom you can get jealous is someone to whom Allāh ﷻ gave wisdom[217]."

راس الحكمة مخافة الله

The head of wisdom is to fear Allāh.

That is why when Sayyīdinā ʿAlī was teaching the Ṣaḥābah, he said, "The whole Qur'an is based on one thing." They said, "What is that, yā ʿAlī?" and he said, "Everything in the Holy Qur'an is Wisdom and the best of wisdom is fear of Allāh ﷻ."

That means when you fear Allāh ﷻ you don't want to make *shirk*, saying, "He has a child, a son," or, "He has a wife," and I don't know what else they will say about Him later; some people do all kinds of things that are outside of Islam.

ورد في الأثر أن الله عز وجل أوحى إلى إبراهيم عليه السلام أتدري لما اتخذتك خليلاً، قال لا، قال لأني رأيت العطاء أحب إليك من الأخذ.

---

[214] Meaning an innovation, as some deny innovation and this *ḥadīth* supports good innovation.

[215] Muslim.

[216] He didn't keep anything for himself of whatever Allāh ﷻ is giving him, so be jealous of that one and try to do like him.

[217] One whom Allāh ﷻ gave wisdom that he used to judge between people and to teach them about wisdom.

It means he doesn't ask for a reward out of it; it means he doesn't ask, he never takes, he is always giving, not asking anyone to take something from them, only giving. If you want to imitate Sayyīdinā Ibrāhīm ﷺ follow if you can and Allāh ﷻ will love you; Allāh ﷻ will make you a Friend. That is the story of when Allāh ﷻ said, "I am going to make a *khalīfah* on Earth."

وَإِذْ قَالَ رَبُّكَ لِلْمَلاَئِكَةِ إِنِّي جَاعِلٌ فِي الأَرْضِ خَلِيفَةً قَالُوا أَتَجْعَلُ فِيهَا مَن يُفْسِدُ فِيهَا وَيَسْفِكُ الدِّمَاء وَنَحْنُ نُسَبِّحُ بِحَمْدِكَ وَنُقَدِّسُ لَكَ قَالَ إِنِّي أَعْلَمُ مَا لاَ تَعْلَمُونَ

*And when your Lord said to the angels, "Lo! I am about to place a viceroy
in the Earth," they said, "Will You place therein one who will do harm
and will shed blood, while we only hymn Your praise and sanctify You?"
He said, "Surely I know what you know not."*[218]

Allāh Sent Jibrīl to Sayyīdina Ibrāhīm to Exemplify His Khalīfat

When Allāh ﷻ said, "I am going to make a *khalīfah* on Earth," who is Sayyīdinā Ibrāhīm ﷺ, the angels said, "How will You make a *khalīfah* when they are going to make bloodshed?" So Allāh ﷻ sent Sayyīdinā Jibrīl ﷺ to Sayyīdinā Ibrāhīm ﷺ to show him, "Why I am making a *khalīfah*, this is the kind *khalif*, My Representative on Earth."

Sayyīdinā Jibrīl ﷺ came to Sayyīdinā Ibrāhīm ﷺ, who had a huge flock of animals-sheep, cows, goats-and he veiled himself from Sayyīdinā Ibrāhīm ﷺ as an ordinary person so as not to be known.

He said to Sayyīdina Ibrāhīm ﷺ, "*Yā* Ibrāhīm, *mashā'Allāh* you have a lot. I have nothing. Allāh ﷻ gave you so much!"

Sayyīdinā Ibrāhīm ﷺ looked at him and said, "Oh! Do you want some?"

He said, "Yes, if you give me."

Sayyīdinā Ibrāhīm ﷺ said, "Of course, but I have the price for it."

"What is the price?"

---

[218] Sūrat al-Baqara, 2:30.

"Say, '*Subūḥun qudūs rabbunā wa rabbu 'l-malā'ikati wa 'r-rūḥ*,' I give you one third of what I have," only for making one *tasbīḥ*, he gave one third of his flock. Today you do one million *tasbīḥ* no one gives you anything, they don't. Then they say, "Fundraising." If you are rich, why are you doing fundraising? You don't need that, give from what you have.

That's why the definition of '*as-sakhiyy*' is two kinds: who gives from what Allāh ﷻ has given him and he gives excessively; and someone who doesn't give from what he owns, but gives from someone else. He is *sakhiyy*, but he doesn't want to put his money so he is clever; he goes and tells a story to people, fundraising from them, saying, "I am giving, sending money here and sending money there." He collects money and he is a millionaire already. Why are you collecting from poor people and you have a lot of money? But that one is called *sakhiyy* as well, because he tries to raise money to give to the poor people.

But the best of *sakhiyy* is the one who gives from what Allāh ﷻ has given him. That is why it is said, "The best of them is the first one is to give from what people have, to try to get people to give money, speak with them, whisper in their ear something and they give the one in need...this is one kind, which is the lower kind. The highest level is to give from what Allāh ﷻ has given you.

So Sayyīdinā Ibrāhīm ﷺ, Allāh ﷻ gave him this big flock and he said to Jibrīl ﷺ, who had covered himself in order not to be known. He said to him, "Say, '*Subūḥun qudūs rabbunā wa rabbu 'l-malā'ikati wa 'r-rūḥ*' and I will give you one third."

He said, "*Subūḥun qudūs rabbunā wa rabbu 'l-malā'ikati wa 'r-rūḥ*," and he gave him one third.

Then Sayyīdinā Jibrīl ﷺ said, "Oh, I am happy that you gave me one third, but still you have too much. Why don't you give more?"

And Sayyīdinā Ibrāhīm ﷺ said, "Okay, say, '*Subūḥun qudūs rabbunā wa rabbu 'l-malā'ikati wa 'r-rūḥ*,' and I will give you another half of what is left," which means one-third of the total.

He said, "*Subūḥun qudūs rabbunā wa rabbu 'l- malā'ikati wa 'r-rūḥ*," and Sayyīdinā Ibrāhīm ﷺ drew a line and said, "All of this is for you," and was going and then he looked at Jibrīl ﷺ and said, "Do you want the rest?"

He said, "Yes!"

He said, "Say, '*Subūḥun qudūs rabbunā wa rabbu 'l-malā'ikati wa 'r-rūḥ*,' I give you the rest and Allāh ﷻ will give me, Allāh is generous, will give me more. Take, take them all!" He said it, *Subūḥun qudūs rabbunā wa rabbu 'l-malā'ikati wa 'r-rūḥ*, and Jibrīl ﷺ took everything and Sayyīdinā Ibrāhīm ﷺ was going empty-handed, who can do that?

Then Jibrīl ﷺ said, "*Yā* Ibrāhīm ﷺ, I am Jibrīl!"

Sayyīdinā Ibrāhīm ﷺ said, "Jibrīl or not Jibrīl I don't know, but I gave in the Way of Allāh ﷻ, I took what I wanted, three words, three times you said, '*Subūḥun qudūs rabbunā wa rabbu 'l-malā'ikati wa 'r-rūḥ, Subūḥun qudūs rabbunā wa rabbu 'l-malā'ikati wa 'r-rūḥ, Subūḥun qudūs rabbunā wa rabbu 'l-malā'ikati wa 'r-rūḥ*' that was enough for me, I don't want more than that."

Look how much they appreciate to do *tasbīḥ*, how much they appreciate to do *dhikrullāh*. We are coming to *dhikrullāh* in the next session; that is *dhikrullāh*, "*Subūḥun qudūs rabbunā wa rabbu 'l-malā'ikati wa 'r-rūḥ*", you are remembering Allāh ﷻ you are glorifying Him and you are praising Him, Allāh ﷻ likes that.

Wa yuṭiʿmu wa lā yuṭaʿmū ʿan? "He feeds and He is not fed," *wa Hūwa Ajwadu 'l-ajwadīn wa Akramu 'l-akramīn*, "And He is the Most Generous of those who are generous and the Absolutely Generous of all who are generous, He is the Absolutely Generous," that is Allāh the Creator.

Fa innahu karīmun yuḥibbu 'l-karīm, "He is the Generous and He loves the one who is generous," *wa ʿalimun yuḥibb al-ʿulamā*, "He is the Absolute Knower and He loves scholars, ʿulamā," *wa qādiru wa yuḥibbu 'sh-shajaʿān*, "He has the power, but He loves courageous people," *wa jamīlun yuḥibbu 'l-jamāl*, "He is the Beautiful and He loves Beauty."

السخي قريب من الله قريب من الجنة قريب من الناس بعيد من النار والبخيل بعيد من الله بعيد من الجنة بعيد من الناس قريب من النار ولجاهل سخي أحب إلى الله تعالى من عابد بخيل

The Prophet ﷺ said:

> *The excessively generous one is very near to Allāh ﷻ, near to good,*
> *near to Paradise, very near to people, far from Hellfire; and the stingy one*
> *is far from Allāh ﷻ, far from all good, far from Paradise, and far from*
> *people and is near Hellfire. And the ignorant generous one is more*
> *beloved to Allāh ﷻ than the stingy worshipper.*

That is for the *bakhīl*. May Allāh ﷻ make us not *bukhalā*, stingy, but to give!

It is said that Allāh ﷻ *yuḥibu 'r-ruḥamā*, "He loves those who have compassion and He will forgive all His Servants who are compassionate," *wa hūwa satīrun man yastur 'alā 'ibādihi*, "and He is The One Who covers the faults of His Servants and loves those who cover the faults of His Creation," *wa yabghaḍ al-faẓu 'l-ghalīẓu 'l-kāsī*, "and He hates the rude one, the difficult one, the one you cannot talk to, who is always angry, always depressed," as depression is from anger. Harsh. *Wa 'afūwwan yuḥibbu man ya'fu 'anhum*, "He is The Forgiver and loves for His Servants to forgive," *wa ghafūrun yuḥibu man yaghfir lahum*, "and He is the Forgiver and loves those who forgive," *wa laṭīfun yuḥḥibu 'l-laṭīfu min 'ibādih*, "He is Kind, Subtle and loves those who are kind," *wa rafīqun yuḥibbu 'r-rafīq*, "and He is the One Who is Friendly with His Servants and He likes people to make friends with each other," *wa ḥalīmun yuḥibbu 'l-ḥulum*, "and He is the Patient One and He loves people who are patient," *wa 'adlun yuḥibbu 'l-'adl*, "and He is Just and loves those who are just," *fa man 'afā 'āfa'an*, "and who forgives, Allāh ﷻ will forgive him," *wa man ghafara ghafara lahu*, "and who forgives, He forgives that one," *wa man samāḥa samāḥahu*, "and whoever forgave, Allāh will forgive him, *samāḥa*."

Ibn Qayyim states:

فالله تعالى لعبده على ما حسب ما يكون العبد لخلقه

And Allāh ﷻ is with His Servant according to how His Servant is acting with people: if he acts good with people, Allāh ﷻ will act with him good and if that person acts bad, Allāh ﷻ will give him punishment." Wa man satara sattarahullāhu ta'alā fi 'd-dunyā wa 'l-Ākhirah, "And whoever covers the fault of a Muslim, Allāh ﷻ will cover his faults on the Day of Judgment."

What do you think about the one who exposes people's mistakes? It means they are not covering them, so Allāh ﷻ will judge them. And what about those who make false rumors, false accusations? They are going to be in the deep part of Hellfire!

And Tirmidhī related in his *Ṣaḥīḥ* that the Prophet ﷺ said:

يامعشر من آمن بلسانه ولم يدخل الإيمان إلى قلبه لا تؤذوا المسلمين ولا تتبعوا عوراتهم
فإنه من تتبع عورة أخيه يتبع الله عورته ومن يتبع الله عورته يفضحه ولو في جوف بيته
فكما تدين تدان وكن كيف شئت فإن الله تعالى لك كما تكون أنت ولعباده

O those who believed only by their tongues, but imān, faith, did not enter their hearts! Don't harm the Muslims, don't follow their mistakes, and whoever follows the mistakes of his brother, Allāh ﷻ will run to catch and punish him, even if he is

deep within his house! And as you judge you will be judged, so judge good and you will be judged good, and judge bad and on the Day of Judgment you will be judged bad. And I order you to remember Allāh ﷻ in your daily life; be someone who remembers Allāh ﷻ."

May Allāh forgive us and may Allāh bless us.

Wa min Allāhi 't-tawfīq, bi ḥurmati 'l-ḥabīb, bi ḥurmati 'l-Fātiḥah.
And with Allāh is success. For the sake of the Beloved, for his sake we recite the opening chapter of Holy Qur'ān.

Islamic Calendar and Holy Days

The Islamic calendar is lunar based, with twelve months of 29 or 30 days. A lunar year is shorter than a solar year, so Muslim holy days cycle back in the Gregorian (Western) calendar. This is how Ramaḍān is celebrated at different times of the year, as the annual Islamic calendar is ten days shorter than the Gregorian calendar.

Four Islamic months are sacred: Muḥarram, Rajab, Dhūl-Q'adah and Dhūl-Ḥijjah. Holy months include "God's Month" (Rajab), "Prophet's Month" (Sha'bān) and the "Month of the People" (Ramaḍān), in which pious acts are rewarded more generously.

Months of the Islamic Calendar

❧ Muḥarram	❧ Rajab
❧ Ṣafar	❧ Sha'bān
❧ Rabī' ul-Āwwal (Rabī' I)	❧ Ramaḍān
❧ Rabī' uth-Thāni (Rabī' II)	❧ Shawwāl
❧ Jumāda al-Āwwal (Jumādi I)	❧ Dhū'l-Q'adah
❧ Jumāda uth-Thānī (Jumādi II)	❧ Dhū'l-Ḥijjah

al-Hijrah

The 1st of Muharram marks the beginning of the Islamic New Year, chosen because it is the anniversary of Prophet Muḥammad's ﷺ historic *hijrah* (migration) from Mecca to Madinah, where he established the first, preeminent Muslim community in which he introduced unprecedented social reforms, including civil law, human and women's rights, religious tolerance, taxation to serve the community, and military ethics.

'Ashūrā

On 10th Muharram, 'Ashūrā commemorates many sacred events, such as Noah's ark coming to rest, the birth of Abraham, and the building of the Ka'bah in Mecca. 'Ashūra is a major holy day, marked with two days of fasting, on the 9th/10th or on 10th/11th based on a holy tradition (*ḥadīth*) of Sayyīdinā Muḥammad ﷺ.

Mawlid

Mawlid al-Nabī, 12th Rabīʿul-Āwwal, commemorates Prophet Muḥammad's birth in 570. Mawlid is celebrated globally throughout this month in huge communal gatherings in which a famous poem "Qasīdat al-Burdah" is recited, accompanied by drummers, illustrious poetry recitals, religious singing, eloquent sermons, gift giving, feasts, and feeding the poor. Most Muslim nations observe Mawlid as a national holiday.

Laylat al-Isrā wal-Miʿrāj

Literally, "the Night Journey and Ascension;" 27th of Rajab is when Sayyīdinā Muḥammad ﷺ physically traveled from Mecca to Jerusalem, ascended in all the levels of Heaven from a rock in the Dome of the Rock, and returned to Mecca—while his bed was still warm. In the Night Journey, Islam's five daily prayers were ordained by God. Sayyīdinā Muḥammad ﷺ also prayed with Abraham, Moses, and Jesus in Jerusalem's al-Aqṣā Mosque, signifying that Muslims, Christians, and Jews follow one god. This holy event designated Jerusalem as the third holiest site in Islam, after Mecca and Madinah.

Laylat al-Baraʿah

The "Night of Freedom from Fire" occurs on 15th Shaʿbān. On this night God's Mercy is great; hence, the night is spent reciting Holy Qurʿan and special prayers, as well as visiting the deceased.

Ramadan

Many regard Ramaḍān, the 9th month of the Islamic calendar, the holiest month of the year. Muslims observe a strict fast and participate in pious activities such as charitable giving and peace making. It is a time of intense spiritual renewal for those who observe it. Fasting is meant to instill social awareness of the needy, and to promote gratitude for God's endless favors. The fast is typically broken in a communal setting, and hence Ramaḍān is a highly social month. At night, a special Ramaḍān prayer known as "Tarawīh" is offered in congregation, in which one-thirtieth of the Holy Qurʿan is recited by the *imām* (prayer leader); thus the entire holy book of 6,000 verses is recited in this month.

ʿĒid al-Fitr

"Festival of Fast-Breaking" marks the end of Ramaḍān and is celebrated the first three days of Shawwāl. It is a time for charity and celebration with family and friends for completing a month of blessings and joy. In the Last Days of Ramaḍān, each Muslim family gives "Zakāt al-Fiṭr"(charity of fast-breaking) which consists of cash and/or food, to help the poor. On the first early morning of ʿĒid, Muslims observe a special congregational prayer, such as Christmas/Easter Mass or the High Holy Days. After ʿĒid prayer is a time to visit family and friends, and give gifts and money (especially to children). Many specialty foods and sweets are prepared solely for ʿĒid days. In most Muslim countries, the entire three days of ʿĒid is a national holiday.

Yawm al-ʿArafat

"Day of ʿArafat," the 9th Dhul-Ḥijjah, occurs just before the celebration of ʿĒid al-Adḥā. Pilgrims on *Hajj* assemble for the "standing" on the plain of ʿArafat, located outside Mecca, where they contemplate the Day of Standing (Resurrection Day). Muslims elsewhere in the world fast this day, and gather at a local mosque for prayers. Thus, those who cannot perform *Hajj* that year still honor the sacrifice of Abraham.

ʿĒid al-Adha

The "Feast of Sacrifice," celebrated from the 10th-13th Dhul-Ḥijjah, marks Prophet Abraham's willingness to sacrifice his son Ismāʿīl on God's order. To honor this event, Muslims perform *Hajj*, the pilgrimage to Mecca that is incumbent on every mature Muslim once in their life if they have the means. Celebrations begin with an animal sacrifice to commemorate Sayyīdinā Abraham's sacrifice. In Islam, he is known as *Khalīlullāh*, "God's friend." Many consider him the first Muslim and a premiere role model, for his obedience to God and willingness to sacrifice his only child without even questioning the command.

Glossary

'abd (pl. *'ibād*): lit. slave; servant.

'AbdAllāh: Lit., "servant of God"

Abū Bakr aṣ-Ṣiddīq: the closest Companion of Prophet Muḥammad; the Prophet's father-in-law, who shared the *Hijrah* with him. After the Prophet's death, he was elected the first caliph (successor); known as one of the most saintly Companions.

Abū Yazīd/Bayāzīd Bistāmī: A great ninth century *walī* and a master of the Naqshbandī Golden Chain.

adab: good manners, proper etiquette.

adhān: call to prayer.

Ākhirah: the Hereafter; afterlife.

al-: Arabic definite article, "the".

'alāmīn: world; universes.

Alḥamdūlillāh: praise God.

'Alī ibn Abī Ṭālib: first cousin of Prophet Muḥammad, married to his daughter Fāṭimah; the fourth caliph.

alif: first letter of Arabic alphabet.

'Alīm, al-: the Knower, a divine attribute

Allāh: proper name for God in Arabic.

Allāhu Akbar: God is Greater.

'amal: good deed (pl. *'amāl*).

amīr (pl., *umarā*): chief, leader, head of a nation or people.

anā: first person singular pronoun

anbiyā: prophets (sing. *nabī*).

'aql: intellect, reason; from the root *'aqila*: lit., "to fetter."

'Arafah, 'Arafat: a plain near Mecca where pilgrims gather for the principal rite of *Hajj*.

'arif: knower, Gnostic; one who has reached spiritual knowledge of his Lord.

'Ārif bi 'Llāh: knowers of God.

Ar-Raḥīm: The Mercy-Giving, Merciful, Munificent, one of Allāh's ninety-nine Holy Names.

Ar-Raḥmān: The Most Merciful, Compassionate, Beneficent; the most repeated of Allāh's Holy Names.

'arsh, al-: the Divine Throne.

aṣl: root, origin, basis.

astāghfirullāh: lit. "I seek Allāh's forgiveness."

Awliyāullāh: saints of Allāh (sing. *walī*).

āyah (pl. *ayāt*): a verse of the Holy Qur'an.

Āyat al-Kursī: "Verse of the Throne," a well-known supplication from the Qur'an (2:255).

'Azra'īl: the Archangel of Death.

Badī' al-: The Innovator; a divine name.

Banī Ādam: Children of Adam; humanity.

Bayt al-Maqdis: the Sacred Mosque in Jerusalem, built at the site where Solomon's Temple was later erected.

Bayt al-Mā'mūr: much-frequented house; this refers to the Ka'bah of the Heavens, which is the prototype of the Ka'bah on Earth, circumambulated by the angels.

baya': pledge; in the context of this book, the pledge of initiation of a disciple (*murīd*) to a Shaykh.

Bismillāhi 'r-Raḥmāni 'r-Raḥīm: "In the name of the All-Merciful, the All-Compassionate"; introductory verse to all chapters of the Qur'an, except the ninth.

Dajjāl: the False Messiah (Anti-Christ) will appear at the end-time of this world, to deceive Mankind with false divinity.

dalālah: evidence.

dhāt: self / selfhood.

dhawq (pl. *adhwāq*): tasting; technical term referring to the experiential aspect of gnosis.

dhikr: remembrance, mention of God in His Holy Names or phrases of glorification.

ḍīyā: light.

Diwān al-Awlīyā: the nightly gathering of saints with Prophet Muḥammad in the spiritual realm.

du'ā: supplication.

dunyā: world; worldly life.

'Ēid: festival; the two major celebrations of Islam are *'Ēid al-Fiṭr*, after Ramaḍān; and *'Ēid al-Adḥā*, the Festival of Sacrifice during the time of *Ḥajj*, which commemorates the sacrifice of Prophet Abraham.

farḍ: obligatory worship.

Fātiḥah: Sūratu 'l-Fātiḥah; the opening chapter of the Qur'an.

Ghafūr, al-: The Forgiver; one of the Holy Names of God.

ghawth: lit. "Helper"; the highest rank of all saints.

ghaybu 'l-muṭlaq, al-: the Absolute Unknown; known only to God.

ghusl: full shower/bath obligated by a state of ritual impurity, performed before worship.

Grandshaykh: generally, a *walī* of great stature. In this text, refers to Mawlānā 'AbdAllāh ad-Dāghestānī (d. 1973), Mawlānā Shaykh Nazim's master.

Hā: the Arabic letter ه

Ḥadīth Nabawi (pl., *aḥadīth*): prophetic *ḥadīth* whose meaning and linguistic expression are those of Prophet Muḥammad.

Ḥadīth Qudsī: divine saying whose meaning directly reflects the meaning God intended but whose linguistic expression is not divine speech as in the Qur'an.

ḥaḍr: present

Hajj: the sacred pilgrimage of Islam obligatory on every mature Muslim once in their life.

ḥalāl: permitted, lawful according to Islamic *Sharī'ah*.

ḥaqīqah, al-: reality of existence; ultimate truth.

ḥaqq: truth

Ḥaqq, al-: the Divine Reality, one of the 99 Divine Names.

ḥarām: forbidden, unlawful.

ḥasanāt: good deeds.

hāshā: God forbid.

harf: (pl. *ḥurūf*) letter; Arabic root "edge."

Ḥawā: Eve.

ḥaywān: animal.

Hijrah: emigration.

ḥikmah: wisdom.

ḥujjah: proof.

hūwa: the pronoun "he", made up of the Arabic letters *Hā'* and *Wāw*.

'ibādu 'l-Lāh: servants of God.

'ifrīt: a type of Jinn, huge and powerful.

iḥsān: doing good, "It is to worship God as though you see Him; for if you are not seeing Him, He sees you."

ikhlāṣ, al-: sincere devotion.

ilāh: (pl. *āliha*): idols or gods.

ilāhīyya: divinity.

ilhām: divine inspiration sent to *awlīyāullāh*.

206

'ilm: knowledge, science.

'ilmu 'l-awrāq: knowledge of papers.

'ilmu 'l-adhwāq: knowledge of taste.

'ilmu 'l-ḥurūf: science of letters.

'ilmu 'l-kalām: scholastic theology.

'ilmun ladunnī: divinely inspired knowledge.

imān: faith, belief.

imām: leader of congregational prayer; an advanced scholar followed by a large community.

insān: humanity; pupil of the eye.

Insānu 'l-kāmil, al-: the Perfect Man, *i.e.*, Prophet Muḥammad.

irādatullāh: the Will of God.

irshād: spiritual guidance.

ism: name.

isma-Llāh: name of God.

isrā': night journey; used here in reference to the night journey of Prophet Muḥammad.

Isrā'fīl: Archangel Rafael, in charge of blowing the Final Trumpet.

jalāl: majesty.

jamāl: beauty.

jama'ah: group, congregation.

Jannah: Paradise.

jihād: to struggle in God's Path.

Jibrīl: Gabriel, Archangel of revelation.

Jinn: a species of living beings created from fire, invisible to most humans. Jinn can be Muslims or non-Muslims.

Jumu'ah: Friday congregational prayer, held in a large mosque.

Ka'bah: the first House of God, located in Mecca, Saudi Arabia to which pilgrimage is made and to which Muslims face in prayer.

kāfir: unbeliever.

Kalāmullāh al-Qadīm: lit., Allāh's Ancient Words, *viz.* the Holy Qur'an.

kalīmat at-tawḥīd: lā ilāha illa-Llāh: "There is no god but Al-Lah (the God)."

karāmat: miracles.

khalīfah: deputy.

Khāliq, al-: the Creator, one of 99 Divine Names.

khalq: Creation.

khāniqah: designated smaller place for worship other than a mosque; *zāwiyah*.

khuluq: conduct, manners.

Kirāmun Kātabīn: honored Scribe angels.

lā: no; not; not existent; the particle of negation.

lā ilāha illa-Llāh Muḥammadun Rasūlullāh: There is no deity except Allāh, Muḥammad is the Messenger of Allāh.

lām: Arabic letter ل

al-Lawḥ al-Maḥfūẓ: the Preserved Tablets.

Laylat al-Isrā' wa'l-Mi'rāj: the Night Journey and Ascension of Prophet Muḥammad to Jerusalem and to the Seven Heavens.

Madīnātu 'l-Munawwarah: the Illuminated city; city of Prophet Muḥammad; Madinah.

mahr: dowry, given by the groom to the bride.

malakūt: divine kingdom.

Malik, al-: the Sovereign, a divine name.

Mālik: Archangel of Hell.

maqām: spiritual station; tomb of a prophet, messenger or saint.

ma'rifah: gnosis.

Māshā' Allāh: as Allāh Wills.

Mawlānā: lit. "Our master" or "our patron," referring to an esteemed person.

maẓhar: place of disclosure.

miḥrāb: prayer niche.

Mikā'īl: Michael, Archangel of rain.

mīzān: the scale that weighs our deeds on Judgment Day.

mīm: Arabic letter م.

minbar: pulpit.

Miracles: of saints, known as *karamāt*; of prophets, known as *mu'jizāt* (lit., "That which renders powerless or helpless").

mi'rāj: the ascension of Prophet Muḥammad from Jerusalem to the Seven Heavens.

Muḥammadun rasūlu 'Llāh: Muḥammad is the Messenger of God.

mulk, al-: the World of dominion.

Mu'min, al-: Guardian of Faith, one of the 99 Names of God.

mu'min: a believer.

munājāt: invocation to God in a very intimate form.

Munkir: one of the angels of the grave.

murīd: disciple, student, follower.

murshid: spiritual guide; *pir*.

mushāhadah: direct witnessing.

mushrik (pl. *mushrikūn*): idolater; polytheist.

muwwāḥid (pl. *muwāḥḥidūn*): those who affirm God's Oneness.

nabī: a prophet of God.

nāfs: lower self, ego.

Nakīr: the other angel of the grave (with Munkir).

nūr: light.

Nūḥ: the prophet Noah.

Nūr, an-: "The Source of Light"; a divine name.

Qādir, al-: "The Powerful"; a divine name.

qalam, al-: the Pen.

qiblah: direction, specifically, the direction faced by Muslims during prayer and other worship, towards the Sacred House in Mecca.

Quddūs, al-: "The Holy One"; a divine name.

qurb: nearness

quṭb (pl. *aqṭāb*): axis or pole. Among the poles are:

Quṭbu 'l-Bilād: Pole of the Lands.

Quṭbu 'l-Irshād: Pole of Guidance.

Quṭbu 'l-Aqṭāb: Pole of Poles.

Quṭbu 'l-A'ẓam: Highest Pole.

Quṭbu 'l-Mutaṣarrif: Pole of Affairs.

al-quṭbīyyatu 'l-kubrā: the highest station of poleship.

Rabb, ar-: the Lord.

Raḥīm, ar-: "The Most Compassionate"; a divine name.

Raḥmān, ar-: "The All-Merciful"; a divine name.

raḥmā: mercy.

raka'at: one full set of prescribed motions in prayer. Each prayer consists of a one or more *raka'ats*.

Ramaḍān: the ninth month of the Islamic calendar; month of fasting.

Rasūl: a messenger of God.

Rasūlullāh: the Messenger of God, Muḥammad ﷺ.

Ra'ūf, ar-: "The Most Kind"; a divine name.

Razzāq, ar-: "The Provider"; a divine name.

rawḥānīyyah: spirituality; spiritual essence of something.

Riḍwān: Archangel of Paradise.

rizq: provision; sustenance.

rūḥ: spirit. *Ar-Rūḥ* is the name of a great angel.

rukū': bowing posture of the prayer.

ṣadaqah: voluntary charity.

Ṣaḥābah (sing., *ṣaḥābī*): Companions of the Prophet; the first Muslims.

ṣaḥīḥ: authentic; term certifying validity of a *ḥadīth* of the Prophet.

ṣāim: fasting person (pl. *ṣāimūn*)

sajda (pl. *sujūd*): prostration.

ṣalāt: ritual prayer, one of the five obligatory pillars of Islam. Also, to invoke blessing on the Prophet.

Ṣalāt an-Najāt: prayer of salvation, offered in the late hours of night.

ṣalawāt (sing. *ṣalāt*): invoking blessings and peace upon the Prophet.

salām: peace.

Salām, as-: "The Peaceful"; a divine name. *As-salāmu 'alaykum*: "Peace be upon you," the Islamic greeting.

Ṣamad, aṣ-: Self-Sufficient, upon whom creatures depend.

ṣawm, ṣiyām: fasting.

sayyi'āt: bad deeds; sins.

sayyid: leader; also, a descendant of Prophet Muḥammad.

Sayyīdinā : our master (fem.

sayyīdunā; sayyīdatunā: our mistress).

shahādah: lit. testimony; the testimony of Islamic faith: *lā ilāha illa 'l-Lāh wa Muḥammadun rasūlu 'l-Lāh*, "There is no god but Allāh, the One God, and Muḥammad is the Messenger of God."

Shāh Naqshband: Shāh Muḥammad Bahāuddin Naqshband, a great eighth century *walī*, and the founder of the Naqshbandī Ṭarīqah.

shaykh: lit. "old Man," a religious guide, teacher; master of spiritual discipline.

shifā': cure.

shirk: polytheism, idolatry, ascribing partners to God

ṣiffāt: attributes; term referring to Divine Attributes.

Silsilat adh-dhahabīyya: "Golden Chain"of spiritual authority in Islam

sohbet (Arabic, *suḥbah*): association: the assembly or discourse of a Shaykh.

subḥānAllāh: glory be to God.

sulṭān/sulṭānah: ruler, monarch.

Sulṭān al-Awlīyā: lit., "King of the awlīyā; the highest-ranking saint.

Sūnnah: Practices of Prophet Muḥammad in actions and words; what he did, said, recommended, or approved of in his Companions.

sūrah: a chapter of the Qur'an; picture, image.

Sūratu 'l-Ikhlāṣ: Chapter 114 of Holy Qur'an; the Chapter of Sincerity.

ṭabīb: doctor.

tābi'īn: the Successors, one generation after the Prophet's Companions.

tafsīr: to explain, expound, explicate, or interpret; technical term for commentary or exegesis of the Holy Qur'an.

tajallī (pl. *tajallīyāt*): theophanies, God's self-disclosures, Divine Self-manifestation.

takbīr: "*Allāhu Akbar*," lit. God is Great.

tarawīḥ: the special nightly prayers of Ramaḍān.

ṭarīqat/ṭarīqah: lit., way, road or path. An Islamic order or path of discipline and devotion under a guide or shaykh; Sufism.

taṣbīḥ: recitation glorifying or praising God.

tawāḍaʿ: humbleness.

ṭawāf: the rite of circumambulating the Kaʿbah while glorifying God during *Ḥajj* and ʿUmra.

tawḥīd: unity; universal or primordial Islam, submission to God, as the sole Master of destiny and ultimate Reality.

Tawrāt: Torah

tayammum: Alternate ritual ablution performed in the absence of water.

ʿubūdiyyah: state of worshipfulness. Servanthood

ʿulamā (sing. *ʿālim*): scholars.

ʿulūmu ʾl-awwalīna wa ʾl-ākhirīn: knowledge of the "Firsts" and the "Lasts" refers to the knowledge God poured into the heart of Prophet Muḥammad during his ascension to the Divine Presence.

ʿulūm al-Islāmī: Islamic religious sciences.

Ummah: faith community, nation.

ʿUmar ibn al-Khaṭṭāb: an eminent Companion of Prophet Muḥammad and second caliph of Islam.

ʿumrah: the minor pilgrimage to Mecca, performed at any time of the year.

ʿUthmān ibn ʿAffān: eminent Companion of the Prophet; his son-in-law and third caliph of Islam, renowned for compiling the Qurʾan.

walad: a child.

waladī: my child.

wilāyah: proximity or closeness; sainthood.

walī (pl. *awliyā*): saint, or "he who assists"; guardian; protector.

wasīlah: a means; holy station of Prophet Muḥammad as God's intermediary to grant supplications.

wāw: Arabic letter و

wujūd, al-: existence; "to find," "the act of finding," and "being found."

Yʿaqūb: Jacob; the prophet.

yamīn: the right hand; previously meant "oath."

Yawm al-ʿahdi wa ʾl-mīthāq: Day of Oath and Covenant, a heavenly event before this Life, when all souls of humanity were present to God, and He took from each the promise to accept His Sovereignty as Lord.

Yawm al-Qiyāmah: Day of Judgment.

Yūsuf: Joseph; the prophet.

zāwiyah: designated smaller place for worship other than a mosque; also *khāniqah*.

zīyāra: visitation to the grave of a prophet, a prophet's companion or a saint.

Other Publications (available at www.isn1.net)

Shaykh Muhammad Nazim Adil al-Haqqani

- New Day, New Provision (2014)
- We Have Honored the Children of Adam (2013)
- Heavenly Counsel: from Darkness into Light (2013)
- In the Mystic Footsteps of Saints (eBooks) (2 volumes) (2013)
- Heavenly Showers (2012)
- The Sufilive Series (2010-12))
- Breaths from Beyond the Curtain
- In the Eye of the Needle
- Eternity: Inspirations from Heavenly Sources
- The Healing Power of Sufi Meditation
- In the Mystic Footsteps of Saints (2 volumes)
- Liberating the Soul (6 volumes)

Shaykh Muhammad Hisham Kabbani

- Benefits of *Bismillāhi 'r-Raḥmāni 'r-Rahīm & Sūrat al-Faṭihah* (2013)
- The Importance of Prophet Muhammad in Our Daily Life
- The Hierarchy of Saints (2013)
- The Heavenly Power of Divine Obedience and Gratitude (2013)
- Salawat of Tremendous Blessings (also Turkish/ Spanish)
- The Dome of Provisions (2012)
- The Prohibition of Domestic Violence in Islam (2011/*Fatwa*)
- The Sufilive Series (6 vol. 2010-12)
- Jihad: Principles of Leadership in War and Peace
- Cyprus Summer Series (2 vol.)
- The Nine-fold Ascent
- Who Are the Guides? (2008)
- Illuminations (2007)
- A Banquet for the Soul (2006)
- Symphony of Remembrance
- The Healing Power of Sufi Meditation
- In the Shadow of Saints
- Keys to the Divine Kingdom
- The Sufi Science of Self-Realization (*also in French*)
- Universe Rising: the Approach of Armageddon?
- Pearls and Coral
- Classical Islam and the Naqshbandī Sufi Tradition
- The Naqshbandī Sufi Way
- Links of Light: The Golden Chain
- Encyclopedia of Islamic Doctrine (7 volumes)
- Angels Unveiled, a Sufi Perspective
- Encyclopedia of Muhammad's Women Companions and the Traditions They Related

Hajjah Amina Adil

⁀ Muḥammad: the Messenger of Islam (2001)
⁀ The Light of Muḥammad
⁀ Lore of Light / Links of Light
⁀ My Little Lore of Light (3 vol.)

Hajjah Naziha Adil Kabbani

⁀ Heavenly Foods (2011)
⁀ Secrets of Heavenly Food (2009)